No Poor Among Them

LARRY BARKDULL

Pillars of Zion Series Titles

Introduction: *Portrait of a Zion Person*

Book 1: *Zion—Our Origin and Our Destiny*

Book 2: *The First Pillar of Zion—The New and Everlasting Covenant*

Book 3: *The Second Pillar of Zion—The Oath and Covenant of the Priesthood*

Book 4: *The Third Pillar of Zion—The Law of Consecration*

Book 5: *The Pure in Heart*

Book 6: *No Poor among Them*

Pillars of Zion Publishing
Orem, Utah

Copyright and Permission

Copyright © 2009, 2013 Barkdull Marketing, Inc

Publishing Imprint: Pillars of Zion Publishing, a division of Barkdull Marketing, Inc. Licensed for publication and distributed by BestBooks Publishing and Distribution, Spanish Fork, Utah. Phone: 801.815.5349.

All Rights Reserved. No part of this book may be reproduced in any format or in any medium without the written permision from the publisher, BestBooks Publishing and Distribution.

Contact

Contact us at info@pillarsofzion.com
Visit our Website at www.PillarsOfZion.com

Disclaimer

This series is heavily documented with some 5,000 references and 400 works cited. Every effort has been made to achieve accuracy. This work is not an official publication of the Church of Jesus Christ of Latter-day Saints, and the views expressed within this work are the sole responsibility of the author and do not necessarily reflect the position of The Church of Jesus Christ of Latter-day Saints or any other entity.

LICENSE USE

1) If you received the free PDF version of the introduction to t he series *Portrait of a Zion Person,* you have the right to store it on your computer. You also have the right to share the PDF with as many people as you please, provided that neither they nor you use part or all of the content to disparage The Church of Jesus Christ of Latter-day Saints in any manner. Neither you nor anyone with whom you share the PDF has the right to change the content of the PDF.

2) If you purchased the printed book or a version of the book for an electronic reader, you do not have the right to share those versions of the book.

Refer all copyright and permissions issues to the contact above.

Library of Congress Cataloging Publication Data is on file at the Library of Congress.
ISBN: 978-1-937399-16-0

Dedication
To Elizabeth Barkdull
Ron and Bonnie McMillan
David and Lorelea Anderson
Paul and Sharon Meyers

Acknowledgments
My wife, Elizabeth, and I would like to acknowledge a number of people, who, in one way or another, lent their support for the creation of this project.

    Lawrence and Georgia Shaw
    Lance and Jozet Richardson
    Blaine and Kathy Yorgason
    Scot and Maurine Proctor
    Clay Gorton
    Ted Gibbons
    Grover Cardon
    Gary and Bonnie Leavitt
    Bud and Barbara Poduska
    Dee Jay Bawden
    Steve Glenn
    Gavon and Tanya Barkdull

Production Staff
Thanks to Eschler Editing for editorial and design work.

    Editors—Jay A. Parry and Michele Preisendorf
    Graphic Artist—Douglass Cole
    Typesetter—Sean Graham

Note about The Three Pillars of Zion
The complete Zion series contains seven books. The full bibliography, and index are included in each of the books for ease of referencing and navigation. Each volume includes its own table of contents except for the Introduction book, *Portrait of a Zion Person*, includes the table of contents for each volume in order to introduce the entire series.

Table of Contents

Book 6
No Poor Among Them

Introduction
The Dream of a Better World 1
   Giving Opens the Doors to Blessings   2
   Laying the Foundation   3
   Lessons from the Good Samaritan   5

Chapter 1
The Ultimate Test—God or Mammon 7
   The Test of Riches   8
   Only the Pure in Heart Can Pass This Test   9
   The Lord's Willingness to Be Tested   10
   Consecration Is All about Love   11
   A Coming Change of Orders   12
   Conclusion   12

Chapter 2
Thou Shalt Not Covet—The Last Law 15
   Covetousness—The Last Law   16
   The Higher and Lower Laws of Prosperity   17
   The More Weighty Matters   18
   Trying to Mix Mammon and Zion   19
   Warnings Against Compromise   21
   Making Mammon Holy   21
   Mormon's View of the Last Days   22

Chapter 3
The First Commandments of This Dispensation 25
   No Security in Mammon   26
   Slippery Treasures   27
   Lazarus and the Rich Man   29
   Nothing Compares to the Danger   30
   Take Heed and Beware of Covetousness   31

Chapter 4
Lessons in the Scriptures Concerning Wealth 33
- Scriptural Description of the Last Days 35
- Scriptures about Idolatry and Wealth 35
- Scriptures about Seeking Wealth and Forgetting God 36
- Scriptures about Mammon, Inequality, and Divisiveness 37
- Scriptural Evidence That the Lord Despises the Selfish Rich 38

Chapter 5
Persecuting the Poor 41
- Wo unto the Rich Who Despise the Poor 42
- They Rob the Poor 42
- Building Personal Sanctuaries 43
- Wealth-Seeking—The Sin That Hinders and Destroys the Church 44
- The Ugliness of Inequality Contrasted with the Beautiful Work of Angels 45
- Withholding from and Judging the Poor Harshly 46
- The Evil of the Age: Life for Money 47
- A Curse on the Daughters of Zion 48
- Blessings for Those Who Rescue the Poor 49
- The Poor of the Lord's People Shall Trust in Zion 52

Chapter 6
Consequences of Seeking Wealth and Persecuting the Poor 55
- Loss of the Providences of Heaven 56
- Loss of Priesthood Power and Exaltation 56
- Loss of the Spirit 56
- Loss of Revelation 56
- Loss of Happy Family Life and Spiritual Commitment 57
- Loss of the Lord's Help 58
- Loss of True Worship 58
- Failure in Our Mission 58
- Loss of Peace 59
- Loss of National Security 61

Chapter 7
Who Shall Enter? 63
- What Doth It Profit? 64
- The Voice of Seven Thunders 65
- Choosing God over Mammon 66
- Obtaining a Hope in Christ 67
- Freely Ye Have Received, Freely Give 68

Feeding the Lord's Lambs	68
Choosing God's Marvelous Work over Babylon's Charms	69
Invoking the Law of Asking to Receive	70
Conclusion	71

Chapter 8
Becoming the Pure in Heart 75

Burning Out Impurities	76
Persecution of the poor	77
Inequality	77
Charitable Service Propels Zion	79
Grace to Grace by Grace for Grace	80
Lacking for Nothing	80
If Any of You Lack	82

Chapter 9
Charity—The Lifeblood of Zion 85

Charity Defines Discipleship	86
Keeping and Feeding—The Two Tests of Charity	86
Charity—The Lifeblood of Zion	87
Charity Is Defined by Service	87
Charitable Service Saves and Exalts	88
Charitable Service Protects the Giver	88
Charitable Service Prospers the Giver	89
Charity Is an Absolute	90
Charity Is a Gift—The Greatest Gift	90

Chapter 10
Without Charity We Are Nothing 93

Charity—The Pure Love of Christ	94
Charity Emerges from Faith and Hope	95
Charity Transforms the Heart	96
Charity Promotes Equality, Unity and an Abundant Life	97
Charitable Service Saves and Exalts	99
Moroni's Prayer for Latter-day Charity	100
Patience and Charity	101
Charity and Virtue—Essential Elements of Priesthood Power	101
Charity Draws the Lord Near	102
Charity Empowers All Gospel Laws	104

Chapter 11
The Hundredfold Law 105
    The Law of Restoration 106
    Struggling with Zion and Babylon Principles 106
    New Math 107
    What Doth It Profit to Cling to Our Property? 108
    Safety and Perfection in Consecration 108
    The Hundredfold Law 109
    Freely Ye Have Received, Freely Give 110

Chapter 12
Ultimate Abundance, Safety, and Security 111
    True Safety and Security 112
    Obtaining an Abundance in All Things 112
    Telestial and Celestial Wealth 112
    Wealth-seeking is Strictly Forbidden 113
    God or Mammon—The Ultimate Test 114
    Abundance and Personal Righteousness 114
    Exceedingly Prosperous 115
    Postlude 115

Bibliography 119
Index and Concordance 129
About the Author 153

Introduction
The Dream of a Better World

Imagine a world in which there is no poverty of any kind—neither the impoverishment of financial distress, ignorance, relationship problems, nor emotional, physical, or spiritual health. Amazingly, a few civilizations achieved this ideal by applying to a higher law. Enoch's people set the standard:

> The fear of the Lord was upon all nations, so great was the glory of the Lord, which was upon his people. And the Lord blessed the land, and they were blessed upon the mountains, and upon the high places, and did flourish.
> And the Lord called his people ZION, because they were of one heart and one mind, and dwelt in righteousness; and there was no poor among them.
> And Enoch continued his preaching in righteousness unto the people of God. And it came to pass in his days, that he built a city that was called the City of Holiness, even ZION.
> And it came to pass that Enoch talked with the Lord; and he said unto the Lord: Surely Zion shall dwell in safety forever.[1]

Melchizedek's people followed suit. Like Enoch's people who built "the City of Holiness, even ZION," Melchizedek's people built Salem, meaning "city of perfection"[2] or "righteousness and peace."[3] This city became the forerunner of Jerusalem,[4] the eternal city of God.[5]

> Now this Melchizedek was a king over the land of Salem and his people had waxed strong in iniquity and abomination; yea, they had all gone astray; they were full of all manner of wickedness;

---

1 Moses, 7:17,20.
2 Galbraith, Ogden, and Skinner, *Jerusalem: The Eternal City*, 41.
3 Smith, *Teachings of the Prophet Joseph Smith*, 321.
4 McConkie, *Mormon Doctrine*, 531.
5 Ezra Taft Benson, *Come unto Christ*, 114; Hebrews 12:22.

> But Melchizedek having exercised mighty faith, and received the office of the high priesthood according to the holy order of God, did preach repentance unto his people. And behold, they did repent; and Melchizedek did establish peace in the land in his days; therefore he was called the prince of peace, for he was the king of Salem; and he did reign under his father.[6]

Melchizedek, like Enoch, was enormously successful in establishing the principles of Zion in the hearts of his people: "And his people wrought righteousness, and obtained heaven, and sought for the city of Enoch."[7]

In the meridian of time, the Nephites and Lamanites achieved a society devoid of all forms of poverty.

> And it came to pass in the thirty and sixth year, the people were all converted unto the Lord, upon all the face of the land, both Nephites and Lamanites, and there were no contentions and disputations among them, and every man did deal justly one with another.
>
> And they had all things common among them; therefore there were not rich and poor, bond and free, but they were all made free, and partakers of the heavenly gift. . . .
>
> And it came to pass that there was no contention in the land, because of the love of God which did dwell in the hearts of the people.
>
> And there were no envyings, nor strifes, nor tumults, nor whoredoms, nor lyings, nor murders, nor any manner of lasciviousness; and surely there could not be a happier people among all the people who had been created by the hand of God.
>
> There were no robbers, nor murderers, neither were there Lamanites, nor any manner of -ites; but they were in one, the children of Christ, and heirs to the kingdom of God.
>
> And how blessed were they! For the Lord did bless them in all their doings; yea, even they were blessed and prospered until an hundred and ten years had passed away; and the first generation from Christ had passed away, and there was no contention in all the land.[8]

Giving Opens the Doors to Blessings

In the latter days, do we have the faith to achieve a poverty-free world? If so, how might it happen? The answer lies in a principle that is a gospel irony, a paradigm of thought that eludes the world. Here is the principle:

> *Give your way to prosperity, freedom, safety, and security.*

---

6 Alma 13:17–18.
7 JST, Genesis 14:34.
8 4 Nephi 1:2–3, 15–18.

Introduction   *The Dream of a Better World*

This principle was widely known and practiced by ancient Zion people who managed to flourish while the world around them collapsed under the weight of selfishness, greed, and wickedness. These Zion people discovered that by living this principle, they simultaneously invoked the law of restoration,[9] or the hundredfold law.[10] That is, whatever they gave was immediately returned to them in an amount many times greater than their sacrifice. Thus, by the simple act of charitable giving they prospered and, in the process, achieved greater liberty, safety, and security.

Knowing that history is wont to repeat itself, we wonder if we who will face the prophesied judgments of the last days will choose to embrace this principle and prosper by it, or choose to suffer with the world as it spirals out of control and implodes around us. One thing is certain: The days of attempting to mix Zion and Babylon are over; the day of decision is upon us.

Laying the Foundation

At the beginning of this dispensation, Joseph Smith prophesied of the impact of the glorious latter-day work while simultaneously raising the antipoverty flag: "I intend to lay a foundation that will revolutionize the whole world." The Prophet's use of the word *revolution* was not meant to suggest conflict: "It will not be by sword or gun that this kingdom will roll on," he said. "The power of truth is such that all nations will be under the necessity of obeying the Gospel."[11] What is the Lord's mandated goal that will revolutionize the world and eradicate every form of poverty? Here are his words: "You are to be equal . . . every man according to his wants and his needs, inasmuch as his wants are just."[12]

Equality! Covenant people recognize these inspired words as central to the law of consecration, the same law that governs the celestial kingdom,[13] the law that is intended to govern the kingdom of God on the earth.

How is this to be done? The Lord gives the answer: "I, the Lord, stretched out the heavens, and built the earth, my very handiwork; and all things therein are mine." That is, to achieve equality, we must first recognize that all things belong to the Lord and that by covenant we are stewards of his (not our) property. The Lord declares that this arrangement is for our good: "It is wisdom in me." To make the leap from seeing ourselves as owners and not as stewards, we must adopt a new mindset and rethink our priorities regarding our time, talents, money, property, and our treatment of the poor; then we must agree to include the Lord in the decisions we make regarding the use of the things he has entrusted to us. Moreover, we must agree to be accountable to him for the discharge of our stewardship: "Therefore, a commandment I give unto you, that ye shall organize yourselves and appoint every man his stewardship; that every man may give an account unto me of the stewardship which is appointed unto him. For it is expedient

---

9   Alma 41:3–6, 15.
10 Genesis 26:12; 2 Samuel 24:3; Matthew 13:8–23; 19:29; Mark 10:30; Luke 8:8; D&C 98:25; 132:55.
11 Joseph Smith, *Teachings of the Prophet Joseph Smith*, selected and arranged by Joseph Fielding Smith, 366.
12 D&C 82:17.
13 D&C 105:4–5.

that I, the Lord, should make every man accountable, as a steward over earthly blessings, which I have made and prepared for my creatures."[14]

We may try to excuse ourselves from living this law by appealing to a false presumption about Church history: Wasn't the law of consecration put on hold or at least lessened because of the failings of our fathers? Absolutely not. Any attempt to locate scriptural or authoritative evidence that this law was rescinded or is waiting to one day be implemented will be vain. If we are truly a covenant people, we are a consecrated people, and, as such, we have bound ourselves to be stewards dedicated to equalizing the condition of the Lord's children by the proper use of the Lord's resources he has placed in our hands. As stewards, we agree to do the work of the Lord with his resources. That work is the bringing about of the "immortality and eternal life of man."[15] While we cannot give anyone the gift of immortality, we can, through our charitable actions, help someone achieve a more exalted level of immortality. And the highest level, of course, is called eternal life. Broadly, this is the work we covenant to assume, and to do so, we agree to consecrate all that we are and have.

A central part of the Lord's work is to "level up" the condition of his impoverished children: "And it is my purpose to provide for my saints." To accomplish this feat, he employs us, his stewards who have entered into a covenant of consecration, to do this very thing. The Lord dictates the specific way that he, through us, will care for his children: "But it must needs be done in mine own way; and behold this is the way that I, the Lord, have decreed to provide for my saints, that the poor shall be exalted, in that the rich are made low."[16] On the surface, this statement may appear like the socialistic doctrine of forced redistribution of wealth; but, as we shall see, consecration is neither an experiment in socialism nor an adaptation of an economic order. The Lord's way is founded on personal agency and the condition of the steward's heart. Implemented properly, the Lord's way prospers, enlightens, and exalts while man's way impoverishes, discourages, and damns.

In the latter days, the Lord has placed an extra burden on well-to-do Saints to care for their underprivileged brothers and sisters in impoverished nations: "For I will consecrate of the riches of those who embrace my gospel among the Gentiles unto the poor of my people who are of the house of Israel."[17] The word *Gentiles* in this context means the members of the Church who live in wealthy gentile nations; the "poor of my people who are of the house of Israel" live elsewhere, in less favorable circumstances. We who are privileged are responsible to contribute generously to the programs of the Church that level up our brothers and sisters, allowing them to share equally with us in the Lord's blessings.

The Lord assures us there are ample resources to accomplish his purposes: "For the earth is full, and there is enough and to spare." Therefore, we need only go about doing all we can to care for the Lord's children. Finally, taking care of the impoverished

---

14 D&C 104:14, 11–13.
15 Moses 1:39.
16 D&C 104:15–16.
17 D&C 42:39.

remains our choice, but how we choose will bring judgment: "I prepared all things, and have given unto the children of men to be agents unto themselves. Therefore, if any man shall take of the abundance which I have made, and impart not his portion, according to the law of my gospel, unto the poor and the needy, he shall, with the wicked, lift up his eyes in hell, being in torment."[18]

Imagine, then, a world impacted by the Lord's stewards. Such people would go about doing good works in the similitude of their Master, whose work it is. Joseph Smith said, "A man filled with the love of God, is not content with blessing his family alone, but ranges through the whole world, anxious to bless the whole human race."[19] With the resources the Lord had entrusted to his stewards, they would search out and attack misery wherever they encountered it. They would always have their antennae up, seeking to become a conduit through which the Lord could channel blessings to his needy children. To such stewards the Lord would direct a continuous flow of opportunities and resources for the purpose of blessing his children. When the stewards became aware of a need, they would receive the intelligence with the attitude that the Lord had brought the matter to their attention. The stewards would not and could not turn away; rather, they would assume that the Lord expected them to do whatever they could to address the need and continue until stability and equality were achieved.

Lessons from the Good Samaritan

The parable of the good Samaritan[20] is a case in point. Although the Samaritan did not know the abused, nameless man he encountered, he nevertheless assumed responsibility for the man's welfare. The Samaritan provided generously for the man's needs, then he offered to supply anything else that might be required until the man was made whole. Clearly, the Samaritan was the Lord's steward, and as such he was continually on the Lord's errand. When he saw the beaten and destitute man, he recognized that the Lord had caused two paths to converge for the purpose of saving an impoverished soul. The Samaritan received the honor of blessing the man as the Lord would have blessed him. No matter the inconvenience and notwithstanding the required time and resources that would be needed (these things belong to the Lord anyway), the Samaritan saw life through the eyes of a steward who was under covenant to use his Master's resources as directed. Significantly, the Samaritan needed no blinding revelation to take action; the fact that he had encountered need was revelation enough. Assumedly, the Samaritan had previously made a decision that if the Lord would take occasion to make a need known to him, the Samaritan would receive it as a revelation and an invitation to act. Jesus ends this parable with a commandment to each covenant person who would be a steward: "Go, and do thou likewise."[21]

Could a group of such people change the world? The Samaritan clearly changed the

---

18   D&C 104:16–18.
19   *History of the Church*, 4:227.
20   Luke 10:30–37.
21   Luke 10:37.

world for at least one nameless, impoverished soul. Doubtless, in his lifetime, the Samaritan changed the world for many poor individuals who needed the Lord's time, talents, and resources. Is there any way the Samaritan's generosity might have diminished him or reduced the resources in his trust? Of course not. If we knew the rest of the story, we would expect that the Samaritan was restored in each instance "an hundredfold" so that he could give again. We simply cannot extend merciful blessings to God's children and not experience a harvest of merciful blessings in return.[22] As we give what we have, replacement comes with increase.[23]

This principle, then, is part of the revolutionary foundation Joseph Smith intended to establish—a principle that would one day change the entire world. When employed, this principle prospered, secured, protected, and exalted the most successful civilizations that have ever existed. It is central to "the law of the celestial kingdom,"[24] and therefore we must become converted to living it if we ever expect to inherit that kingdom. It is the last law and obstacle that stands between us and celestial glory. For now, it has the power to transform the condition of mankind and achieve the unimaginable: *No poor among them!*

---

22 Hinckley, "Blessed Are the Merciful," 68.
23 Packer, "The Candle of the Lord," 54–55.
24 D&C 105:4–5.

Chapter 1
The Ultimate Test—God or Mammon

Man entered his career on this planet when the earth was Zion-like. But soon the earth was infiltrated by a being who determined to wrest ownership from the Creator and reign as the god of this world. That being, of course, was Satan. From the outset, he systematically reversed every Zion doctrine with his anti-Christ philosophy, which he designed to appear so reasonable and close to the truth that he would even deceive the very elect.[25] One way he deceives the world and the elect is by blurring their attitude toward money and their treatment of the poor.

Jesus said we cannot serve God and mammon.[26] *Mammon* is "the standard Hebrew word for any kind of financial dealing."[27] Mammon is defined as riches,[28] or, better said, the love of riches. Serving both God and mammon is as impossible as simultaneously walking east and west.[29] The two are polar opposites, like love and hate. To the degree that we give our affection to one, we withhold our affection from the other: "Either [we] will hate the one, and love the other; or else [we] will hold to the one, and despise the other."[30] Neither can we choose to participate in both God's and Satan's economies: Zion and mammon. According to Hugh Nibley, "Every step in the direction of increasing one's personal holdings is a step away from Zion."[31]

The harshness and absoluteness of these statements is troubling. Of necessity, these statements spawn difficult questions. We hope sincere questioners will pursue answers

---

25 Matthew 24:24.
26 Matthew 6:24; Luke 16:13; 3 Nephi 13:24.
27 Nibley, *Approaching Zion*, 37.
28 Bible Dictionary, "Mammon," 728.
29 Hunter, Conference Report, Apr. 1964, 35.
30 Matthew 6:24.
31 Nibley, *Approaching Zion*, 37.

until they discover the principles upon which a Zion life is built. We are saddened when other questioners disbelieve the statements, rationalize their mammon-seeking, or say that present-day realities discount the practicality of avoiding mammon.

Almost all of us struggle with choosing between God and mammon. And the choice is supposed to be difficult. Ultimately, it defines loyalty, trustworthiness, character, priorities, faith, level of conversion, love of God, willingness to obey and sacrifice, and ultimately, the condition of the heart. Let us state here that there is no sin in wealth; there is only sin in setting our hearts on wealth and seeking it before seeking the kingdom of God; there is sin only in hoarding wealth rather than regarding it as a stewardship and disseminating it as the law of stewardship demands: to build up the kingdom of God for the establishment of Zion by blessing God's needy children. Significantly, when we choose to view wealth through the filter of Zion, we set ourselves up to become prosperous, for Zion is always described as a place and condition of exceeding abundance. But that prosperity comes only when we achieve the right type of heart and the right motivations.

The Test of Riches

The harsh reality is this: life is a test. At the center of that test is money. We can no more avoid this financial test than we can avoid choosing between the relentless opposing forces that try to influence our financial dealings. But choose we must. If we fool ourselves into believing that we can succeed in choosing *both* God and mammon, we are deceived. But that has not deterred many people from trying. Most of humanity has attempted to combine God and mammon, but not one person has ever succeeded—and we will not be the first. The moment we make the attempt, we have already chosen Satan and his economy. Jesus' words are perennially true: "No man can serve two masters."[32]

So what should we do? Should we go to extremes by taking a vow of poverty, shunning money altogether, and living lean, like medieval monks? Of course not. "You always do have to handle things," Hugh Nibley said.

> But in what spirit do we do it? Not . . . by renunciation, for example. . . . If you refuse to be concerned with these things at all, and say, 'I'm above all that,' that's as great a fault. The things of the world have got to be administered; they must be taken care of, they are to be considered. We have to keep things clean, and in order. That's required of us. This is a test by which we are being proven. This is the way by which we prepare, always showing that these things will never captivate our hearts, that they will never become our principal concern. That takes a bit of doing, and that is why we have the formula 'with an eye single to his glory' (Mormon 8:15). Keep first your eye on the star, then on all the other considerations of the ship. You will have all sorts of problems on the ship, but unless you steer by the star, forget the ship. Sink it. You won't go anywhere.[33]

---

32   Romney, Conference Report, Oct. 1962, 94, quoting Matthew 6:24.
33   Nibley, *Approaching Zion*, 336.

The test of wealth determines whether or not we can be trusted with God's resources—those things he has placed in our hands for safekeeping and prudent management. As accountable stewards, some pointed questions are always before us: Will we choose to remain within the guidelines of stewardship? Will we manage the stewardship according to God's desires, or will we "cheat" the Lord?[34] Will we redefine the terms of stewardship, claim ownership of the Lord's property, then enlarge and indulge ourselves with the proceeds rather than use the surplus for its intended use, which is to take care of God's children and build up the kingdom of God for the establishment of Zion?

Our answers to these questions determine our passing or failing the mortal test of money.

Only the Pure in Heart Can Pass This Test

Without divine intervention, we cannot have the power to choose God over mammon. Babylon simply has too great a hold on the hearts of men. Consequently, only the pure in heart who receive a spiritual endowment can obtain the power to make this choice and thereafter live the law of consecration. Only the pure in heart can receive adequate spiritual help to view money for what its purpose should be and prioritize it accordingly. These are the children of Zion who do not venture into Babylon and partake of its philosophies. Rather, they enter the temple and make an informed, resolute covenant to receive and manage the Lord's property in an ordered way; then they return to the world and implement that covenant as the Lord directs.

Clearly, this test is too hard for the natural man. Only those who know and love God can pass it. Hence, *God or mammon* is the ultimate test that determines the condition of the heart and lands us in or out of the celestial kingdom. Nibley wrote:

> God has always given his people the same choice of either living up to the covenants made with him or being in Satan's power; there is no middle ground (Moses 4:4). True, we spend this time of probation in a no-man's-land between the two camps of salvation and damnation, but at every moment of the day and night we must be moving toward the one or the other. Progressive testing takes place along the way in either direction; the same tests in every dispensation and generation mark the progress of the people of God.
>
> (1) Do you, first of all, agree to do things his way rather than your way—to follow the law of God? (2) If so, will you be obedient to him, no matter what he asks of you? (3) Will you, specifically, be willing to sacrifice anything he asks you for? (4) Will you at all times behave morally and soberly? (5) Finally, if God asks you to part with your worldly possessions by consecrating them all to his work, will you give his own back to him to be distributed as he sees fit, not as you think wise?
>
> That last test has been by far the hardest of all, and few indeed have chosen that strait and narrow way. The rich young man was careful and correct in observing every point of the law—up to that one; but that was too much for him, and the

---

34 Nibley, *Approaching Zion*, 426.

Savior, who refused to compromise or make a deal, could only send him off sorrowing, observing to the Apostles that passing that test was so difficult to those possessing the things of the world that only a special dispensation from God could get them by.[35]

The Lord's Willingness to Be Tested

Perhaps because this test requires so much faith, the Lord both promises and offers evidence that if we will live the law of consecration, he will take care of us and even prosper us. The law of tithing is one of his proofs: "Bring ye all the tithes into the storehouse, that there may be meat in mine house, *and prove me now herewith*, saith the Lord of hosts, if I will not open you the windows of heaven, and pour you out a blessing, that there shall not be room enough to receive it."[36]

Paying tithing is always an act of faith. The math doesn't make sense. Ten minus one is supposed to equal nine, but somehow when we pay our tithing the product is always more than ten. Clearly, celestial math is baffling in a telestial setting, and only faith can urge us on. But if we will persevere and apply the principle of tithing, then experience the pouring out of blessings, we will be prepared to employ that principle in other consecrated offerings that will require even greater faith.

Tithing provides us a way to test the Lord on the principle of consecration; tithing allows us to get to know and trust the Lord and for him to trust us. Once we discover that the Lord will not let us down and that he is willing to prosper us on this principle, we are willing to take the next step and pay offerings. Once again, we discover the Lord's care and willingness to recompense us abundantly.

As we pay our tithes and offerings, which are manifestations of consecration, we grow in our appreciation of this foundational law of Zion until we can finally live the law according to its ideal. We also discover that with every step (between initial tithing and eventual total consecration) we will have to venture into the darkness of uncertainty hoping that the light will appear. Each step will demand our giving before we receive, and every time we make another consecrated offering, it will make no mathematical sense. The laws in Babylon that govern telestial finances will scream at us to hold back: "It won't work!" Only our experience with the Lord, having tested him, and our testimony of tithes and offerings can provide us the confidence that all will be well and that the outcome will result in safety and abundance. Nibley wrote:

> In giving his children the law, God repeatedly specifies that he is placing before them two ways, the ways of life and death, light and darkness. For parallel to the one law runs another. It is part of the plan that Satan should be allowed to try us and to tempt us to see whether we would prove faithful in all things: Who does not live up to every covenant made with the Lord will be in his power (cf. Moses 4:4,

---

35 Nibley, *Approaching Zion*, 342.
36 Malachi 3:10; emphasis added.

> 5:23). So we find ourselves drawn in two directions (Moroni 7:11–13). *Thus this life becomes a special test of probation set before us in this world—it is an economic one. If the law of consecration is the supreme test of virtue—the final one—money is to be the supreme temptation to vice;* sex runs a poor second, but on both counts, this is the time and place for us to meet the challenge of the flesh. It is the weakness of the flesh in both cases to prove our spirits stronger than the pull of matter, to assert our command over the new medium of physical bodies before proceeding onward to another state of existence. As Brigham Young often repeats, "God has given us the things of this world to see what we will do with them." The test will be whether we will set our hearts on the four things that lead to destruction. Whoever seeks for (1) wealth, (2) power, (3) popularity, and (4) the pleasures of the flesh—anyone who seeks those will be destroyed, says the Book of Mormon (1 Nephi 22:23; 3 Nephi 6:15). Need we point out that those four things compose the whole substance of success in the present-day world. They are the things that money will get you.[37]

Tithing, therefore, *prepares* us to become Zion-like while offerings are our *opportunity* to become Zion-like. In each case, God is willing to be put to the test. The only question remaining is: Are we likewise willing to be put to the test? Do we really want to become Zion people or not?

Consecration Is All about Love

Certainly, the test of life centers on our attitude toward money, but in a more important way, the test of life has more to do with proving the heart. Hence, consecration is all about relationship: either we love God or we love mammon. If we give God our hearts, giving him our money is easy.

Think of a marriage. All lesser sacrifices are simple if we first have offered our spouse our heart. But if we are selfish and hold back, the marriage will be damaged and could possibly fail. We recall that Ananias and Sapphira withheld a portion of their consecration and lost their lives as a consequence of their selfishness.[38]

Our covenant relationship with Christ is like a marriage. He is the Bridegroom and we are his bride.[39] If both parties do not place their all on the altar and agree to live thereafter as *one*—meaning complete sacrifice, loyalty, and trust—the relationship will crumble. A husband who will not share his money with his wife is selfish and abusive; if he cannot give his money to his wife, he cannot give his wife his heart. The same could be said of a wife who selfishly withholds anything from her husband. Just so, when we give God our money for his purposes, we provide him and ourselves singular proof that we love him above our own interests. Consecration, then, is how we prove our love for God and his children.

---

37 Nibley, *Approaching Zion*, 434–35; emphasis added.
38 Acts 5:1–5.
39 Isaiah 61:10; 62:5; Jeremiah 7:34; 16:9; 25:10; 33:11; Joel 2:16; John 3:29; Revelation 18:23.

A Coming Change of Orders

At the outset of the Doctrine and Covenants, the great Jehovah declared that the order of Babylon, which has oppressed God's people for millennia, was all but used up. "The Lord insists that the whole history of the world is about to turn on its hinges," said Hugh Nibley. "It will change; this is not an order with which he is pleased."[40] Now a new order—Zion—is about to burst upon the stage of human history. Zion's advent will be an act of mercy for the salvation of all mankind.[41]

From the moment of the First Vision, Christ drew a line in the sand: Babylon on one side and Zion on the other. His call for the Saints to flee Babylon is the same call he has issued in past dispensations: "Come out of her, my people, that ye be not partakers of her sins, and that ye receive not of her plagues."[42] Once escaped from Babylon, we are not to turn back; rather, we are to embrace a new way of life: "Ye shall not live after the manner of the world."[43] Forevermore, mammon-seeking is strictly forbidden in Zion: "Touch not the evil gift, nor the unclean thing."[44] From the moment we make that decision, we will feel like and be viewed as "strangers"[45] in the earth. But that should not be a concern for Zion people. The world as it presently exists is not our home; someday Babylon and its citizenry will fall,[46] and we, the children of Zion, will inherit the earth.[47] Until then, we are to live among the people of Babylon with the charge to call as many of them out as possible. But in no case are we to be absorbed by them; rather, we are to be the "light of the world" as the King of Zion[48] is *the* Light of the world.[49]

Conclusion

Jesus said we cannot serve God and mammon,[50] but many people try. At the heart of the Lord's statement is the inference that life is a test with money at its center. The test of wealth determines the condition of the heart. It answers the question: Can we or can we not be trusted with God's resources now and in eternity? If eternal life is our aim, are we willing to become accountable stewards who remain within the guidelines of stewardship? Will we manage the resources God's way or our way?

This test is not easy. Without divine intervention, none of us can successfully pass the test of God over mammon. Therefore, the Lord helps us by offering to be tested first. He provides evidence that if we will live the law of consecration, he will take care of us and even prosper us. The law of tithes and offerings is a way he agrees to be tested. As

---

40 Nibley, *Approaching Zion*, 331.
41 D&C 1.
42 Revelation 18:4.
43 D&C 95:13.
44 Moroni 10:30.
45 D&C 45:13.
46 Revelation 18:2.
47 Matthew 5:5; 3 Nephi 12:5; D&C 59:2.
48 Moses 7:53.
49 Matthew 5:14; John 8:12.
50 Matthew 6:24; Luke 16:13; 3 Nephi 13:24.

we pay our tithes and offerings, he prospers and protects us so that our faith in the law of consecration increases. If we continue, we will one day have the faith to live this foundational law of Zion completely. God's being willing to be put to the test is intended to help us choose to be put to the test. At some point, we must decide whether or not we really want to become Zion people and embrace this foundational law of the celestial kingdom.

Although consecration defines our attitude toward money and our treatment of the poor, it has almost nothing to do with money. Consecration is a condition of the heart. The covenant of consecration is like a marriage: motivated by love, each partner consecrates all that he is and has to the other partner. Each does so for the defined work and glory to which the partnership is dedicated. Any holding back or selfishness will retard and possibly destroy the relationship. Only the complete giving of self can prosper a relationship and urge life to spring forth. Just so, when we give God our money for his purposes, we provide him and us singular proof that we love him above our own interests. Consecration is how we prove our love for God and his children.

In our day, we are preparing for a new order—Zion. That order will bring spiritual and temporal salvation to all mankind.[51] But that order waits for us to adapt to the Lord's way of living: "The length of time required 'to accomplish all things pertaining to Zion' is strictly up to us and how we live."[52] Therefore, the Lord commands his covenant people to choose between him and mammon once and for all: "Come out of her [Babylon], my people, that ye be not partakers of her sins, and that ye receive not of her plagues."[53] Once we have successfully escaped and discover the beauty, peace, abundance, safety, and security of Zion, we are charged to set an example and call as many people out of Babylon as possible. We become the spiritual and temporal rescuers of God's impoverished children. We are expected to wear out our lives and consecrate all that we are and have to the building up of God's kingdom on the earth for the establishment of Zion.

Such an attitude toward our money and God's children could revolutionize the world, eventually eradicate every form of poverty, and summon global peace and prosperity.

---

51 D&C 1.
52 Young, *Journal of Discourses*, 9:283.
53 Revelation 18:4.

Chapter 2
Thou Shalt Not Covet—
The Last Law

Few statements are as sweeping as Paul's denunciation of covetousness: "For the love of money is the root of all evil."[54] In one sentence he identifies the origin of all sin: *"the love of money."* The implications of this statement are huge. Lying, sexual transgression, taking God's name in vain, breaking the Sabbath day, pride—every transgression that grows on the tree of sin can be traced to its root cause: a covetous attitude toward money and possessions. Those who embrace this attitude (who would choose to pursue wealth) will find themselves caught in Satan's snare, from which there is little hope of escape: "But they that will be rich fall into temptation and a snare, and into many foolish and hurtful lusts, which drown men in destruction and perdition." Paul warns that those who persist in wealth-seeking "have erred from the faith, and pierced themselves through with many sorrows." This condition is one from which we must run: "But thou, O man of God, flee these things; and follow after righteousness, godliness, faith, love, patience, meekness." In the economy of God, Paul explains, "great gain" is defined as "godliness with contentment."[55]

The Book of Mormon prophet Jacob listed the love of money as one of the foremost offenses against God. Hugh Nibley wrote:

> It is at the climax of his great discourse on the Atonement that Jacob cries out, "But wo unto the rich, who are rich as to the things of the world. For because they are rich they despise the poor." This is a very important statement, setting down as a general principle that the rich as a matter of course despise the poor, for "their hearts are upon their treasures; wherefore, their treasure is their God. And

---
54 1 Timothy 6:10.
55 1 Timothy 6:6–11.

behold, their treasure shall perish with them also" (2 Nephi 9:30). Why does Jacob make this number one in his explicit list of offenses against God? Because it is the number-one device among the enticings of "that cunning one" (2 Nephi 9:39), who knows that riches are his most effective weapon in leading men astray. You must choose between being at one with God or with Mammon, not both; the one promises everything in this world for money, the other a place in the kingdom after you have "endured the crosses of the world, and despised the shame of it," for only so can you "inherit the kingdom of God, which was prepared for them from the foundation of the world," and where your "joy shall be full forever" (2 Nephi 9:18). Need we point out that the main reason for having money is precisely to avoid "the crosses of the world, and . . . the shame of it"?[56]

The counsel given by President Anthon H. Lund in 1903 is applicable today:

> The Lord, in one of His revelations given very early in the Church, says: "Seek not for riches, but for wisdom and, behold, the mysteries of God shall be unfolded unto you, and then shall you be made rich; behold he that hath eternal life is rich." The riches of eternal life we ought to seek, not the riches of the world. There is a raging thirst for riches in this land. The love of money is growing, even in our midst. We do not look upon wealth in itself as a curse. We believe that those who can handle means rightly can do much to bless their fellows. But he who is ruled by the love of money is tempted to commit sin. The love of money is the root of all evil. *There is hardly a commandment but is violated through this seeking for riches.*[57]

Covetousness—The Last Law

"Thou shalt not covet," Jehovah commanded Israel.[58] This was the last law given in the Ten Commandments. In our day, the Lord repeated the injunction: "I command thee that thou shalt not covet thy neighbor's wife. . . . I command thee that thou shalt not covet thine own property, but impart it freely."[59]

Joseph Smith expanded on the subject of this last law: "God cursed the children of Israel because they would not receive the last law from Moses. . . . The Israelites prayed that God would speak to Moses and not to them; in consequence of which he cursed them with a carnal law." The Prophet then went on to apparently connect the law prohibiting covetousness with obtaining the fullness of the priesthood: "Abraham gave a tenth part of all his spoils and then received a blessing under the hands of Melchizedek *even the last law or a fulness of the law or priesthood* which constituted him a king and priest after the order of Melchizedek or an endless life."[60]

---

56 Nibley, *Approaching Zion*, 592–93.
57 Lund, Conference Report, Apr. 1903, 97; emphasis added.
58 Exodus 20:17.
59 D&C 19:25–26.
60 Smith, *Words of Joseph Smith*, 245–46; emphasis added.

Whether or not the Prophet intended a dual meaning here is not known, but the noticeable connection is sobering. A review of history substantiates that the Israelites rejected the last law—*Thou shalt not covet*—and simultaneously rejected the last law "or a fulness of the law" of the priesthood, which would have made them kings and priests after the order of Melchizedek, which same order would have blessed them with eternal life:

> Now this Moses plainly taught to the children of Israel in the wilderness, and sought diligently to sanctify his people that they might behold the face of God;
>
> But they hardened their hearts and could not endure his presence; therefore, the Lord in his wrath, for his anger was kindled against them, swore that they should not enter into his rest while in the wilderness, which rest is the fulness of his glory.
>
> Therefore, he took Moses out of their midst, and the Holy Priesthood also.[61]

We simply cannot break this last law—*Thou shalt not covet*—and expect to receive the fullness of the priesthood along with its attendant blessings.

This injunction becomes even more sobering when we consider that abandoning covetousness was the last law of the lesser law and that the law of consecration is the last law of the higher law. Consecration protects us from covetousness and idolatry by redefining our property as a stewardship and prescribing an order for our stewardship's surpluses. If we obey these last laws (avoiding covetousness and living the law of consecration), we will prosper and experience abundance beyond any telestial effort that we might employ to enrich ourselves.

The Higher and Lower Laws of Prosperity

Mormon describes the two systems of prosperity. Beginning with the higher law, he said:

> And now, because of the steadiness of the church they began to be exceedingly rich, having abundance of all things whatsoever they stood in need—an abundance of flocks and herds, and fatlings of every kind, and also abundance of grain, and of gold, and of silver, and of precious things, and abundance of silk and fine-twined linen, and all manner of good homely cloth.
>
> And thus, in their prosperous circumstances, they did not send away any who were naked, or that were hungry, or that were athirst, or that were sick, or that had not been nourished; and they did not set their hearts upon riches; therefore they were liberal to all, both old and young, both bond and free, both male and female, whether out of the church or in the church, having no respect to persons as to those who stood in need.
>
> And thus they did prosper and become far more wealthy than those who did not belong to their church.

---

61   D&C 84:23–25.

For those who did not belong to their church did indulge themselves in sorceries, and in idolatry or idleness, and in babblings, and in envyings and strife; wearing costly apparel; being lifted up in the pride of their own eyes; persecuting, lying, thieving, robbing, committing whoredoms, and murdering, and all manner of wickedness.[62]

When the Lord determines to enrich us, we become rich indeed. But when we attempt to enrich ourselves, our abundance will subsist only for a season, and in the end we will be left impoverished temporally, emotionally, and spiritually.

The More Weighty Matters

The Lord's invitation to us is always the same: renounce mammon and choose God; flee Babylon and come to Zion. If we will open our ears, we will hear his voice continually crying, "Therefore, come up hither unto the land of my people, even Zion."

Our success in arriving in Zion depends upon our attitude toward money: "Let them repent of all their sins, and of all their covetous desires, before me, saith the Lord; for what is property unto me? saith the Lord." In other words, the things of the world are but a drop in the vast ocean of possible blessings—"the weighty matters"—and those weighty blessings await those who will make the effort to obtain them: "Is there not room enough on the mountains of Adam-ondi-Ahman, and on the plains of Olaha Shinehah, or the land where Adam dwelt, that you should covet that which is but the drop, and neglect the more weighty matters?"[63] Obviously, weighty blessings flow from our seeking after the weighty matters and not from coveting "the drop."

On the other hand, those who insist on remaining in Babylon or who try to keep one foot there and the other foot in Zion can expect the Lord's cursing: "Ye are cursed because of your riches, and also are your riches cursed because ye have set your hearts upon them, and have not hearkened unto the words of him who gave them unto you."[64] Setting our hearts upon riches is undeniable evidence of our breaking our oath of obedience; it is a manifestation of our disloyalty to God and the abandonment of our lawful affections. We have made promises to always remember the Lord,[65] his gifts,[66] and the poor,[67] but rather, we often remember and love our riches: "Ye do not remember the Lord your God in the things with which he hath blessed you, but ye do always remember your riches, not to thank the Lord your God for them; yea, your hearts are not drawn out unto the Lord, but they do swell with great pride, unto boasting, and unto great swelling, envyings, strifes, malice, persecutions, and murders, and all manner of iniquities."

In the condition of covetousness, we walk around blindly, often wondering why we are not receiving the Lord's favor. His answer is an indictment of our selfish behavior:

---

62   Alma 1:29–32.
63   D&C 117:4, 8.
64   Helaman 13:21.
65   D&C 20:77, 79.
66   D&C 46:10.
67   D&C 42:30; 52:40.

"For this cause hath the Lord God caused that a curse should come upon the land, and also upon your riches, and this because of your iniquities."[68] Who can blame him? Our affections are elsewhere, and we hardly give him a second thought. That is why in some texts covetousness is compared to adultery.[69]

Trying to Mix Mammon and Zion

With an eye on our day, Mormon apparently dug through Nephite history to find a parallel to describe the consequences of the latter-day epidemics of covetousness and wealth-seeking. He discovered a perfect example in the Zoramites. Nibley wrote about the Zoramites' sin of combining God and mammon:

> Alma found them [the Zoramites] to be the wickedest people in the world. He couldn't believe that people could be so evil. . . . With all their [supposed] virtues, they set their hearts upon riches (Alma 31:24–38). Alma couldn't stand it. He couldn't look at it anymore. It hurt too much. How could people be so wicked? This is what was wrong: "Behold, O my God, their costly apparel, and their ringlets, and their bracelets, and their ornaments of gold, and all their precious things which they are ornamented with; and behold, their hearts are set upon them, and yet they cry unto thee and say—We thank thee, O God, for we are a chosen people unto thee, while others shall perish" (Alma 31:28). "O, how long, O Lord, wilt thou suffer that thy servants shall dwell here below in the flesh, to behold such gross wickedness among the children of men? Behold, O God, they cry unto thee, and yet their hearts are swallowed up in their pride. Behold, O God, they cry unto thee with their mouths" (Alma 31:26–27). Remember, they went to church once a week, and they bore their testimony, and they were very strict in dress regulations, and so forth. They were brave and courageous and enterprising and prosperous and all those other things—but this was what was wrong: . . . "They cry unto thee with their mouths, while they are puffed up, even to greatness, . . . [with] their ringlets; . . . and behold, their hearts are set upon them, and yet they cry unto thee and say [at the same time], We thank thee, O God, for we are a chosen people unto thee" (Alma 31:27–28). And that was what the great crime was. *Don't try to combine the two.*[70]

The Zoramites had fallen into a snare. In order to justify coveting and enlarging their wealth, they pointed to their pretended piety, "supposing gain is godliness."[71] Of course, we are taught that true godliness is tied to the covenants and ordinances of the temple, not to money.[72] Suddenly, in this account, the two economies become clear: On the one hand, we see hypocrites, the worst of sinners according to Jesus, they who insist "on

---

68   Helaman 13:21–23.
69   2 Peter 2:14; D&C 19:25.
70   Nibley, *Approaching Zion*, 103–4; emphasis added.
71   1 Timothy 6:5.
72   D&C 84:20–21.

proper dress and grooming, their careful observance of all the rules, their precious concern for status symbols, their strict legality, their pious patriotism,"[73] they who appear to be good and blessed because they are rich,[74] all the while turning a blind eye to the poor. On the other hand, we see the penitent, meek folk, who are poor in heart, seeking the word of God, and ultimately being pronounced by the prophet as "blessed."[75] Some of the greatest teachings found in the Book of Mormon were given to these humble followers of Christ who finally received as a reward an inheritance in a land of promise,[76] symbolizing that they had achieved Zion.

In this dispensation, the early Saints' attempt to mix Zion with mammon broke Joseph Smith's heart. Speaking to the Saints in Far West, Missouri, concerning covetousness, he said:

> Brethren, we are gathering to this beautiful land to build up Zion; Zion, which is the pure in heart. But since I have been here I have perceived the spirit of selfishness. Covetousness exists in the hearts of the Saints which is not becoming to those who have received the gospel. Here are those who begin to spread out buying up all the land they are able to [get] to the exclusion of the poor ones who are not so much blessed with this world's goods, thinking to lay foundations for themselves, only looking to their own individual families and those who are to follow them. *Now I want to tell you that Zion cannot be built up in any such way.* We are called out from this world to learn God's ways, to become one, looking each to his brother's interest and his welfare, the widow, the fatherless, and poor without distinction. I see signs put out, beer signs, speculative schemes are being introduced. This is the way of the world, Babylon indeed, and I tell you in the name of the God of Israel, if there is not repentance with this people and a turning from ungodliness, covetousness, and self-will, you will be broken up and scattered from this choice land to the four winds of heaven. For the Lord will have a people who will serve him and keep his commandments humbly, each one seeking his neighbor's welfare, to preach the gospel, gather the poor, and aid them, and build up a holy city unto our God.[77]

Brigham Young also lamented the covetousness of the Saints:

> What does the Lord want of us up here in the tops of these mountains? He wishes us to build up Zion. What are the people doing? They are merchandizing, trafficking and trading . . . making [the merchants] immensely rich. We all have our pursuits, our different ways of supplying ourselves with the common necessaries of life and also its luxuries. This is right and the possession of earthly wealth is right, if we follow our varied pursuits, and amass the wealth of this life for the purpose of advancing righteousness and building up the kingdom of God on earth. But how easy it is to wander from the path of righteousness. We toil days and months to

---

73 Nibley, *Approaching Zion*, xvi.
74 Nibley, *Approaching Zion*, xxi.
75 Alma 32:2–8.
76 Alma 35:9.
77 Stevenson, *Life and History of Elder Edward Stevenson*, 40–41; emphasis added.

attain a certain degree of perfection, a certain victory over a failing or weakness, and in an unguarded moment slide back again to our former state. How quickly we become darkened in our minds when we neglect our duties to God and each other, and forget the great objects of our lives.[78]

On another occasion, he said:

[The Saints] do not know what to do with the revelations, commandments and blessings of God. Talking, for instance about everyday things, how many do we see here that know what to do with money and property when they get it? Are their eyes single to the building up of the kingdom of God? No; they are single to the building up of themselves. . . . There are few who understand the principles of the kingdom and whose eyes are single to the building of it up in all respects; but their eyes are like the fool's eye—looking to the ends of the earth. They want this and that, and they do not know what to do; they lack wisdom. By-and-by, perhaps, their wealth will depart from them, and when left poor and penniless, they will humble themselves before the Lord that they may be saved.[79]

Warnings Against Compromise

We cannot embrace Zion and mammon simultaneously. Hugh Nibley wrote: "Brigham Young and Joseph often warned the Saints about subsiding into this telestial order. Even though the Lord said that Zion could not be built up unless it is in the principle of the law (otherwise I cannot receive her unto myself), the Latter-day Saints still wanted to compromise and say, 'We will not go up unto Zion, and will keep our moneys' (D&C 105:8). But as long as that was their plan, there could be no Zion, they were told."[80]

The Lord asks rhetorically, "For shall the children of the kingdom pollute my holy land?" Then, answering his own question, "Verily, I say unto you, Nay."[81] We have a clear choice to make if we truly desire Zion over all other affections: either we cease coveting our own property, forsake the ways of the world, and come to the Lord's marriage or we languish in Babylon to tend our property and vainly peddle our merchandise; but we cannot do both.[82] Nibley concludes, "'Israel, Israel, God is calling,' we often sing, 'Babylon the great is falling,' But we have taken our stand between them; Brigham Young speaks of Latter-day Saints who want to take Babylon by one hand and Zion by the other—it won't work."[83]

Making Mammon Holy

We try to legitimize our desire for mammon by trying to find something holy about pursuing it. Brigham Young describes such people: "Elders of Israel are greedy after the

---

78 Young, *Journal of Discourses*, 12:155.
79 Young, *Journal of Discourses*, 11:325.
80 Nibley, *Approaching Zion*, 331.
81 D&C 84:59.
82 Matthew 22:2–14.
83 Nibley, *Approaching Zion*, 279.

things of this world. If you ask them if they are ready to build up the kingdom of God, their answer is prompt—'Why, to be sure we are, with our whole souls; but we want first to get so much gold, speculate and get rich, and then we can help the Church considerably. We will go to California and get gold, go and buy goods and get rich, trade with the emigrants, build a mill, make a farm, get a large herd of cattle, and then we can do a great deal for Israel.' When will you be ready to do it? 'In a few years, Brother Brigham, if you do not disturb us.'"[84]

In an attempt to continue seeking mammon while retaining our standing in Zion, we sometimes grasp for scriptural comfort. Often we point to the parable of the talents.[85] We say to ourselves, "Surely we are to increase our holdings if we are to be nominated as good stewards." But, according to the scriptures, there is a vast difference between expanding our stewardship for the kingdom's sake and expanding it for the sake of personal wealth.

Jacob gives us the key: "But before ye seek for riches, seek ye for the kingdom of God." First the kingdom, then riches! "And *after* ye have obtained a hope in Christ (notice the sequence) ye shall obtain riches, if ye seek them; and ye will seek them for the intent to do good—to clothe the naked, and to feed the hungry, and to liberate the captive, and administer relief to the sick and the afflicted."[86] Clearly, we are not justified in seeking riches *before* we seek (or even *simultaneously* seek) the kingdom of God; but *after* we obtain a hope in Christ (and not before), we may ask for riches with the intent to "level people up." Jacob says, "Think of your brethren like unto yourselves, and be familiar with all and free with your substance, that they may be rich like unto you."[87] It is this attitude toward money that brings us to a hope in Christ, and it is this attitude that places us in a position to make a request for more resources to bless more people.

We can become rich Zion's way or Babylon's way. But before we decide, we ought to at least know where the two ways end. The Zion way will land us in heaven, while the Babylon way will land us elsewhere, but not in heaven. We might try to convince ourselves otherwise, but in the end it will not make a difference. We can no more make mammon holy than we can possess it and Zion, too. We simply cannot have it both ways.

Mormon's View of the Last Days

Few condemnations of mammon are harsher than Moroni's. Understanding our day perhaps better than we do, the last Nephite prophet described a latter-day scene of unequalled depravity, one that rivaled the days of Noah.[88]

> Behold, I speak unto you as if ye were present, and yet ye are not. But behold, Jesus Christ hath shown you unto me, and I know your doing.

---

84 Young, *Journal of Discourses*, 1:164–65.
85 Matthew 25:14–30.
86 Jacob 2:18–19; emphasis added.
87 Jacob 2:17.
88 Joseph Smith–Matthew 1:41.

Chapter 2 Thou Shalt Not Covet—The Last Law

> And I know that ye do walk in the pride of your hearts; and there are none save a few only who do not lift themselves up in the pride of their hearts, unto the wearing of very fine apparel, unto envying, and strifes, and malice, and persecutions, and all manner of iniquities; and your churches, yea, even every one, have become polluted because of the pride of your hearts.
>
> For behold, ye do love money, and your substance, and your fine apparel, and the adorning of your churches, more than ye love the poor and the needy, the sick and the afflicted.[89]

We often read these verses and congratulate ourselves that we are not part of that wretched group . . . until Moroni points his finger at the hypocritical Saints who have polluted the holy Church of God:

> O ye pollutions, ye hypocrites, ye teachers, who sell yourselves for that which will canker, why have ye polluted the holy church of God? Why are ye ashamed to take upon you the name of Christ? Why do ye not think that greater is the value of an endless happiness than that misery which never dies—because of the praise of the world?
>
> Why do ye adorn yourselves with that which hath no life, and yet suffer the hungry, and the needy, and the naked, and the sick and the afflicted to pass by you, and notice them not?[90]

Moroni's question hangs answerless. We have no excuse. The prophet saw our generation as it really is. Our actions will indict us. They are and always have been open to prophetic view.

---

89 Mormon 8:35–37; emphasis added.
90 Mormon 8:38–39.

Chapter 3
The First Commandments of This Dispensation

A full year before the organization of the Church, the Lord gave Joseph Smith and Oliver Cowdery the first two commandments pertaining to his latter-day kingdom: (1) "Seek to bring forth and establish the cause of Zion;" and (2) "Seek not for riches but for wisdom." The promised blessings would eclipse anything that Babylon could offer: "And behold, the mysteries of God shall be unfolded unto you, and then shall you be made rich. Behold, he that hath eternal life is rich."[91]

One month later, upholding the law of witnesses,[92] the Lord repeated these commandments verbatim to Hyrum Smith.[93] Thus, the initial witnesses of the Restoration (Joseph and Oliver) and ultimate witnesses (Joseph and Hyrum), the latter two who would seal their testimony with blood, were given the first two commandments that would define all commandments to follow.

These first commandments stand in stark contrast to Satan's first commandment: *Everything shall have a price.* "Satan's first article of faithlessness has been repeated with creedal clarity since the beginning: One can buy anything in this world for money. It is a hellish philosophy, and those who operate in harmony with it sell that which is priceless for a paltry sum."[94] Satan issued his first commandment in the Garden of Eden. Concerning this, Hugh Nibley wrote:

> [Satan] flares up in his pride and announces what his program for the economic and political order of the new world is going to be. He will take the resources of

---
91 D&C 6:6–7.
92 Deuteronomy 19:15.
93 D&C 11:6–7.
94 McConkie and Millet, *Doctrinal Commentary on the Book of Mormon*, 1:302.

the earth, and with precious metals as a medium of exchange he will buy up military and naval might, or rather those who control it, and so will govern the earth—for he is the prince of this world. He does rule: he is king. Here at the outset is the clearest possible statement of a military-industrial complex ruling the earth with violence and ruin. But as we are told, this cannot lead to anything but war, because it has been programmed to do that. It was conceived in the mind of Satan in his determination 'to destroy the world' (Moses 4:6). The whole purpose of the program is to produce blood and horror on this earth.[95]

The central issue contained in the Lord's and Satan's first commandments concerns the definition and use of treasure. Consider the results of the two philosophies:

Zion: "Lay not up for yourselves treasures upon earth, where moth and rust doth corrupt, and where thieves break through and steal: But lay up for yourselves treasures in heaven, where neither moth nor rust doth corrupt, and where thieves do not break through nor steal: For where your treasure is, there will your heart be also."[96]

Babylon: "But wo unto the rich, who are rich as to the things of the world. For because they are rich they despise the poor, and they persecute the meek, and their hearts are upon their treasures; wherefore, their treasure is their God. And behold, their treasure shall perish with them also."[97]

It should be clear by now that our attitude toward money indicates in which camp we intend to set up residence. Our attitude toward money reflects the condition of our hearts.

No Security in Mammon

The quest for riches is a powerful opiate and Satan's most "deadly and effective" weapon.[98] Seeking security in mammon was prophesied by Nephi to be a latter-day Satanic strategy to destroy the Saints: "And others will he pacify, and lull them away into carnal security, that they will say: All is well in Zion; yea, Zion prospereth, all is well—and thus the devil cheateth their souls, and leadeth them away carefully down to hell."[99] Notice that only those who profess to be of Zion can qualify for this denunciation.

President Spencer W. Kimball drew a distinction between the economies of Babylon and Zion: "Zion can be built up only among those who are the pure in heart, not a people torn by covetousness or greed, but a pure and selfless people. Not a people who are pure in appearance, rather a people who are pure in heart. Zion is to be in the world and not of the world, not dulled by a sense of carnal security, nor paralyzed by materialism. No, Zion is not things of the lower, but of the higher order, things that exalt the mind and sanctify the heart."[100]

---

95 Nibley, *Approaching Zion*, 92.
96 Matthew 6:19–21.
97 2 Nephi 9:30.
98 Nibley, *Approaching Zion*, 39, 332.
99 2 Nephi 28:21.
100 Kimball, *The Teachings of Spencer W. Kimball*, 363.

Chapter 3   The First Commandments of This Dispensation   27

Seeking mammon and attempting to find security in it are illusions and cheap tricks of the devil. Brigham Young had much to say against worshiping mammon: "I would as soon see a man worshipping a little god made of brass or of wood as see him worship his property. . . . Does this congregation understand what idolatry is? The New Testament says that covetousness is idolatry; therefore, a covetous people is an idolatrous people."[101] President Young focused the last year of his life on preaching against the folly of idolatry: "We wish the wealth or things of the world; we think about them morning, noon and night; they are first in our minds when we awake in the morning, and the last thing before we go to sleep at night."[102] And at another time he said:

> One man has his eye on a gold mine, another is for a silver mine, another is for marketing his flour or his wheat, another for selling his cattle, another to raise cattle, another to get a farm, or building here and there, and trading and trafficking with each other, just like Babylon. . . . Babylon is here, and we are following in the footsteps of the inhabitants of the earth, who are in a perfect sea of confusion. Do you know this? You ought to, for there are none of you but what see it daily. . . . The Latter-day Saints [are] trying to take advantage of their brethren. There are Elders in this Church who would take the widow's last cow, for five dollars, and then kneel down and thank God for the fine bargain they had made.[103]

At one point the Lord allowed the Saints to prudently associate with mammon: "And now, verily I say unto you, and this is wisdom, make unto yourselves friends with the mammon of unrighteousness, and they will not destroy you."[104] So that we do not see in this scripture a ticket to depart Zion and enter Babylon, Hugh Nibley clarifies: "This was only to save their lives in an emergency."[105]

Wisdom demands that when we read this verse, we cross-reference it with Zenos's allegory of the olive tree. We recall that the tree's natural branches temporarily needed crucial nourishing from the wild trees, but only to preserve them for a season. Their destiny was always to be grafted back into their mother tree, and the destiny of the wild branches was always to be clipped and burned.[106]

Slippery Treasures

There is no security in mammon. Riches are hard to hold and manage—they are "slippery." They can collapse on the whim of financial markets, a dishonest or incompetent partner, or one bad personal decision. Riches are built on the same foundation as the great and spacious building—a foundation of air.[107] Samuel the Lamanite warned the Nephites of the folly of seeking security in mammon:

---

101   Young, *Journal of Discourses*, 6:196–97.
102   Young, *Journal of Discourses*, 18:239.
103   Young, *Journal of Discourses*, 17:41–42.
104   D&C 82:22.
105   Nibley, *Approaching Zion*, 20.
106   Jacob 5.
107   1 Nephi 8:26.

And behold, the time cometh that he curseth your riches, that they become slippery, that ye cannot hold them; and in the days of your poverty ye cannot retain them.

And in the days of your poverty ye shall cry unto the Lord; and in vain shall ye cry, for your desolation is already come upon you, and your destruction is made sure; and then shall ye weep and howl in that day, saith the Lord of Hosts. And then shall ye lament, and say:

O that I had repented, and had not killed the prophets, and stoned them, and cast them out. Yea, in that day ye shall say: O that we had remembered the Lord our God in the day that he gave us our riches, and then they would not have become slippery that we should lose them; for behold, our riches are gone from us.

Behold, we lay a tool here and on the morrow it is gone; and behold, our swords are taken from us in the day we have sought them for battle.

Yea, we have hid up our treasures and they have slipped away from us, because of the curse of the land.

O that we had repented in the day that the word of the Lord came unto us; for behold the land is cursed, and all things are become slippery, and we cannot hold them.

Behold, we are surrounded by demons, yea, we are encircled about by the angels of him who hath sought to destroy our souls. Behold, our iniquities are great. O Lord, canst thou not turn away thine anger from us? And this shall be your language in those days.

But behold, your days of probation are past; ye have procrastinated the day of your salvation until it is everlastingly too late, and your destruction is made sure; yea, for ye have sought all the days of your lives for that which ye could not obtain; and ye have sought for happiness in doing iniquity, which thing is contrary to the nature of that righteousness which is in our great and Eternal Head.

O ye people of the land, that ye would hear my words! And I pray that the anger of the Lord be turned away from you, and that ye would repent and be saved.[108]

Cursed are they who set their hearts on mammon and trust in its security; such riches are programmed to become slippery. Nevertheless, despite the Lord's warning, many people try to hoard their riches, or *hide* their riches unto themselves; but they *hide* them in vain. One day these people will awaken to emptiness, because that which they have loved so much will be gone. Then they will mourn, but to no avail. They will be faced with the stark reality that they are to blame: they chose mammon over God, and they rejected the words of the Lord's prophets while honoring flatterers as if they were prophets. Then Satan and his angels will rejoice.

On the other hand, Zion people are commanded to hide their treasures unto the Lord: "For I will, saith the Lord, that they shall hide up their treasures unto me; and cursed be

---
108 Helaman 13:31–39.

they who hide not up their treasures unto me; for none hideth up their treasures unto me save it be the righteous; and he that hideth not up his treasures unto me, cursed is he, and also the treasure, and none shall redeem it because of the curse of the land.'[109]

The only reasons to hide treasure are to safeguard it from an enemy and to preserve it for its intended purpose. Therefore, a Zion person might say that he hides or consecrates his treasure unto the Lord to keep it safe from unholy hands and to preserve it for its sacred purpose.

Lazarus and the Rich Man

The tragedy of choosing God over mammon and thus losing one's soul is powerfully stated in Jesus' parable of the rich man and Lazarus.

> There was a certain rich man, which was clothed in purple and fine linen, and fared sumptuously every day: And there was a certain beggar named Lazarus, which was laid at his gate, full of sores, and desiring to be fed with the crumbs which fell from the rich man's table: moreover the dogs came and licked his sores.
> And it came to pass, that the beggar died, and was carried by the angels into Abraham's bosom: the rich man also died, and was buried; and in hell he lift up his eyes, being in torments, and seeth Abraham afar off, and Lazarus in his bosom. And he cried and said, Father Abraham, have mercy on me, and send Lazarus, that he may dip the tip of his finger in water, and cool my tongue; for I am tormented in this flame.
> But Abraham said, Son, remember that thou in thy lifetime receivedst thy good things, and likewise Lazarus evil things: but now he is comforted, and thou art tormented. And beside all this, between us and you there is a great gulf fixed: so that they which would pass from hence to you cannot; neither can they pass to us, that would come from thence.
> Then he said, I pray thee therefore, father, that thou wouldest send him to my father's house: For I have five brethren; that he may testify unto them, lest they also come into this place of torment.
> Abraham saith unto him, They have Moses and the prophets; let them hear them.
> And he said, Nay, father Abraham: but if one went unto them from the dead, they will repent.
> And he said unto him, If they hear not Moses and the prophets, neither will they be persuaded, though one rose from the dead.[110]

The parable should give us pause. A dramatic change of status awaits the righteous poor and the selfish rich. If we believe the Lord's words, the day will come when the selfish

---
109 Helaman 13:19.
110 Luke 16:19–31.

rich will experience the buffetings of Satan. In that miserable condition, they will cry out to those who were poor for relief as the poor had once cried out for help from the rich and found none. James, the Lord's brother, expounded on this subject by saying that the poor who are faithful in this life are destined to become heirs of celestial glory.[111] On the other hand, as Jesus indicated, the selfish rich will neither enjoy the sweet association of the blessed nor be at rest; rather, they will be in torment with a great gulf dividing them from the righteous.

It is telling that the rich man in the parable was in agony. Perhaps for the first time, he thought of someone besides himself and pled to Abraham that he would send Lazarus to his brothers who were still on earth, hoping, we suppose, that there might be the tiniest chance that they could escape his fate. But Abraham knew the lure of mammon. Such people who are taken in the devil's snare, he said, would no more respond to an angel than they would to the prophets who constantly warn about such behavior. The lesson has sobering implications: If an angel can't turn the rich from his treasure, who or what can? The parable contains the answer: If a rich man will not choose to awaken to his awful state and impart liberally and cheerfully of his money the Lord's way, he is destined to lose all that he has, including his soul, and be turned over to the buffetings of Satan.

Nothing Compares to the Danger

"Wealth is a pleasant and heady narcotic that gives the addict an exhilarating sense of power accompanied by a growing deadening of feeling for anything of real value," wrote Hugh Nibley. "Wealth is a jealous mistress: she will not tolerate any competition; rulers of business are openly contemptuous of all other vocations; and all those 'how-to-get-rich' books by rich men virtuously assure us that the first and foremost prerequisite for acquiring wealth is to think of nothing else—the aspirant who is guilty even of a momentary lapse in his loyalty, they tell us, does not deserve the wealth he seeks."[112]

Mammon is a decoy, a trap, a lure, a snare; it dangles its bait to capture our attention long enough to grasp us in its jaws and devour us. Quoting Brigham Young, Hugh Nibley said, "[Material things] 'decoy . . . [our] minds' away from the real values of things." Then Nibley added: "They are irresistible. The merchants do research: they know what we'll take and what we'll not. They know what will sell, and they know the line that nobody can resist. This is the very real thing we are being tempted by. By these deceptions—through public relations, the skill of advertising, and people who devote their lives to nothing else than trying to entice—the devil tries to entice and tempt us, 'by sorceries and witchcraft that deceive the nations' (cf. Revelation 18:23)."[113]

On a number of occasions, Brigham Young expressed his fears concerning the Saints' pursuit of wealth over seeking the things of God: "I am more afraid of covetousness in our Elders than I am of the hordes of hell. . . . Those who are covetous and greedy, anxious to grasp the whole world, are all the time uneasy, and are constantly lay-

---

111 James 2:5.
112 Nibley, *Approaching Zion*, 39–40.
113 Nibley, *Approaching Zion*, 330–31.

ing their plans and contriving how to obtain this, that, and the other. . . . [But] riches of themselves cannot produce permanent happiness; only the Spirit that comes from above can do that. . . . How the Devil will play with a man who so worships gain!"[114]

Jesus was once confronted by a rich young man who asked him concerning eternal life. "Keep the commandments" was the Lord's reply. When the rich man said that he had done this, he asked the Lord what else he lacked. "Now when Jesus heard these things, he said unto him, Yet lackest thou one thing: sell all that thou hast, and distribute unto the poor, and thou shalt have treasure in heaven: and come, follow me. And when he heard this, he was very sorrowful: for he was very rich. And when Jesus saw that he was very sorrowful, he said, How hardly shall they that have riches enter into the kingdom of God!" It is *hard* for a rich man to enter into heaven: "It is easier for a camel to go through a needle's eye, than for a rich man to enter into the kingdom of God." It requires special intervention from heaven: "The things which are impossible with men are possible with God."[115]

We would have to be blind to miss the point: We cannot achieve eternal life as long as our hearts are set upon mammon. It is dangerous to think otherwise. Mammon and Zion do not mix. We cannot have them both. If we hold to one, we will despise the other. If we love one, we hate the other. The message is clear and scriptural: We must part with mammon to obtain the things of God. Joseph Smith taught the sacrifice of all things is the price of eternal life.[116] Loving mammon over God will not get us there; that is why it is so hard for a selfish rich man to achieve the celestial kingdom. Our only safety is to embrace the law of consecration.

Take Heed and Beware of Covetousness

When someone tried to lure Jesus into a debate about money, he soundly rebuked him. "Man, who made me a judge or a divider over you?"[117] The Savior's mission had nothing to do with mammon. Satan had also tried and failed to draw away Jesus by the lure of wealth.[118] Now here was another person expecting the Lord to take an interest in financial affairs: "Master, speak to my brother, that he divide the inheritance with me." It was an insult, and Jesus told him as much: "Take heed, and beware of covetousness: for a man's life consisteth not in the abundance of the things which he possesseth."[119] The parable that followed spoke plainly of the folly of building up possessions on earth only to end up destitute in the next life.

> And he spake a parable unto them, saying, The ground of a certain rich man brought forth plentifully:
> And he thought within himself, saying, What shall I do, because I have no room where to bestow my fruits?

---

114 Young, *Discourses of Brigham Young*, 306.
115 Luke 18:18–27.
116 Smith, *Lectures on Faith*, 6:7.
117 Luke 12:14.
118 JST, Luke 4:5–8.
119 Luke 12:13, 15.

And he said, This will I do: I will pull down my barns, and build greater; and there will I bestow all my fruits and my goods.

And I will say to my soul, Soul, thou hast much goods laid up for many years; take thine ease, eat, drink, and be merry.

But God said unto him, Thou fool, this night thy soul shall be required of thee: then whose shall those things be, which thou hast provided?

So is he that layeth up treasure for himself, and is not rich toward God.[120]

We are ever moving in the direction of our treasure, and we are daily investing our time, talents, resources, and our hearts in that treasure. Should we concentrate on filling our barns and building more barns to fill, we will most certainly abandon God and his children. Jesus poses two questions:

1. "For what shall it profit a man, if he shall gain the whole world, and lose his own soul?"
2. "Or what shall a man give in exchange for his soul?"[121]

How we answer determines our loyalties and our eternal inheritance.

---

[120] Luke 16:16–21.
[121] Mark 8:36–37.

Chapter 4
Lessons in the Scriptures Concerning Wealth

The mantra of Babylon might be summed up by one scripture: "Money answereth all things."[122] Nevertheless, in no uncertain terms the Lord forbids wealth-seeking: "Seek not after riches nor the vain things of this world; for behold, you cannot carry them with you."[123]

Wealth-seeking is a fleeting fancy that does not make a good eternal investment: "Riches are not forever."[124] Satan tempts us to seek for riches, knowing their inherent danger: "Now the cause of this iniquity of the people was this—Satan had great power, unto the stirring up of the people to do all manner of iniquity, and to the puffing them up with pride, tempting them to seek for power, and authority, and riches, and the vain things of the world."[125]

The scriptures contain many descriptions, cautions, and denunciations concerning our attitude toward wealth. We are clearly warned that "he that trusteth in riches shall fall."[126] How we obtain riches is even more damning: "He that oppresseth the poor to increase his riches shall surely come to want."[127]

Seeking and withholding riches blights the soul with a terminal spiritual disease: "Wo unto you rich men, that will not give your substance to the poor, for your riches will canker your souls; and this shall be your lamentation in the day of visitation, and of judgment, and of indignation: The harvest is past, the summer is ended, and my soul is not saved!"[128]

---

122 Ecclesiastes 10:19.
123 Alma 39:14.
124 Proverbs 27:24.
125 3 Nephi 6:15.
126 Proverbs 11:28.
127 Proverbs 22:16.
128 D&C 56:16.

As evidenced in the scriptures below, when people seek for wealth, the bells of Hades begin to ring; then fissures form in our spiritual foundation. Notice in each of these scriptures the downward sequence of events:

> But they grew proud, being lifted up in their hearts, because of their exceedingly great riches; therefore they grew rich in their own eyes, and would not give heed to their words, to walk uprightly before God.[129]
>
> And it came to pass that the fifty and second year ended in peace also, save it were the exceedingly great pride which had gotten into the hearts of the people; and it was because of their exceedingly great riches and their prosperity in the land; and it did grow upon them from day to day.[130]
>
> Now this great loss of the Nephites, and the great slaughter which was among them, would not have happened had it not been for their wickedness and their abomination which was among them; yea, and it was among those also who professed to belong to the church of God.
>
> And it was because of the pride of their hearts, because of their exceeding riches, yea, it was because of their oppression to the poor, withholding their food from the hungry, withholding their clothing from the naked, and smiting their humble brethren upon the cheek, making a mock of that which was sacred, denying the spirit of prophecy and of revelation, murdering, plundering, lying, stealing, committing adultery, rising up in great contentions, and deserting away into the land of Nephi, among the Lamanites—
>
> And because of this their great wickedness, and their boastings in their own strength, they were left in their own strength; therefore they did not prosper, but were afflicted and smitten, and driven before the Lamanites, until they had lost possession of almost all their lands.[131]
>
> And in the commencement of the sixty and seventh year the people began to grow exceedingly wicked again.
>
> For behold, the Lord had blessed them so long with the riches of the world that they had not been stirred up to anger, to wars, nor to bloodshed; therefore they began to set their hearts upon their riches; yea, they began to seek to get gain that they might be lifted up one above another; therefore they began to commit secret murders, and to rob and to plunder, that they might get gain.[132]

The scriptures are replete with warnings about mammon-seeking. If we delude ourselves into thinking that we are the exception and have a special dispensation to obtain mammon and dodge the consequences for such actions, we deceive ourselves and are destined to become sorely disappointed.

---

129 Alma 45:24.
130 Helaman 3:36.
131 Helaman 4:11–13.
132 Helaman 6:16–17.

Chapter 4   Lessons in the Scriptures Concerning Wealth

Scriptural Description of the Last Days

The themes of mammon-seeking, covetousness, and idolatry pepper the prophesies of the last days. Quoting Isaiah, Nephi paints a picture of latter-day idolatry that is chilling:

> Their land also is full of silver and gold, neither is there any end of their treasures; their land is also full of horses, neither is there any end of their chariots.
> Their land is also full of idols; they worship the work of their own hands, that which their own fingers have made.

Continuing, Isaiah foresaw that the resulting pride and lack of humility of these people would challenge the Lord's forgiveness and would be answered upon them with a harsh turn of events:

> And the mean man boweth not down, and the great man humbleth himself not, therefore, forgive him not.
> O ye wicked ones, enter into the rock, and hide thee in the dust, for the fear of the Lord and the glory of his majesty shall smite thee.
> And it shall come to pass that the lofty looks of man shall be humbled, and the haughtiness of men shall be bowed down, and the Lord alone shall be exalted in that day.[133]

In the latter days, the Lord prescribed an antidote for such spiritual sickness: "See that ye love one another; cease to be covetous; learn to impart one to another as the gospel requires."[134]

Scriptures about Idolatry and Wealth

The scriptures have much to say about the covetousness and idolatry that dominate the latter days. In fact, Paul taught that covetousness *is* idolatry.[135] In our day, the Lord pronounced a "wo" upon those whose "eyes are full of greediness."[136] It is through greediness and idolatry, he said, that many people break "the covenant through covetousness."[137]

Alma was faced with an idolatrous, selfish people ripening for destruction. His words to them could be just as well delivered today as a sermon at general conference:

> And also the Spirit saith unto me, yea, crieth unto me with a mighty voice, saying: Go forth and say unto this people—Repent, for except ye repent ye can in nowise inherit the kingdom of heaven.

---

133   2 Nephi 12:7–11.
134   D&C 88:123.
135   Colossians 3:5.
136   D&C 56:17.
137   D&C 104:4, 52.

And again I say unto you, the Spirit saith: Behold, the ax is laid at the root of the tree; therefore every tree that bringeth not forth good fruit shall be hewn down and cast into the fire, yea, a fire which cannot be consumed, even an unquenchable fire. Behold, and remember, the Holy One hath spoken it.

And now my beloved brethren, I say unto you, can ye withstand these sayings; yea, can ye lay aside these things, and trample the Holy One under your feet; yea, can ye be puffed up in the pride of your hearts; *yea, will ye still persist in the wearing of costly apparel and setting your hearts upon the vain things of the world, upon your riches?*

Yea, will ye persist in supposing that ye are better one than another; yea, will ye persist in the persecution of your brethren, who humble themselves and do walk after the holy order of God, wherewith they have been brought into this church, having been sanctified by the Holy Spirit, and they do bring forth works which are meet for repentance—

Yea, and will you persist in turning your backs upon the poor, and the needy, and in withholding your substance from them?

And finally, all ye that will persist in your wickedness, I say unto you that these are they who shall be hewn down and cast into the fire except they speedily repent.[138]

Scriptures about Seeking Wealth and Forgetting God

Wealth-seeking and idolatry are so very dangerous because they cause us to forget God. In the process of pursuing wealth, mammon becomes our god.

Nephi, the son of Helaman, described the downward spiral of sins that results from setting our hearts on mammon and thus forgetting God. Nephi challenged his people:

> O, how could you have forgotten your God in the very day that he has delivered you?
>
> But behold, it is to get gain, to be praised of men, yea, and that ye might get gold and silver. And ye have set your hearts upon the riches and the vain things of this world, for the which ye do murder, and plunder, and steal, and bear false witness against your neighbor, and do all manner of iniquity.
>
> And for this cause wo shall come unto you except ye shall repent.[139]

Centuries earlier, Moses struggled with his people who had forgotten the God who had preserved them. Hearing them boast in their own strength and observing them worship their riches, he soundly denounced them, promising destruction for their haughty attitude:

> Who led thee through that great and terrible wilderness, wherein were fiery serpents, and scorpions, and drought, where there was no water; who brought thee forth water out of the rock of flint;

---

138 Alma 5:51–56; emphasis added.
139 Helaman 7:20–22.

> Who fed thee in the wilderness with manna, which thy fathers knew not, that he might humble thee, and that he might prove thee, to do thee good at thy latter end;
>
> And thou say in thine heart, My power and the might of mine hand hath gotten me this wealth.
>
> *But thou shalt remember the Lord thy God: for it is he that giveth thee power to get wealth,* that he may establish his covenant which he sware unto thy fathers, as it is this day.
>
> And it shall be, if thou do at all forget the Lord thy God, and walk after other gods, and serve them, and worship them, I testify against you this day that ye shall surely perish.[140]

Clearly, if we seek mammon, we risk forgetting and offending God.

Scriptures about Mammon, Inequality, and Divisiveness

No redeeming quality comes from seeking mammon. Satan programs this process to cause widespread misery. The humble poor man experiences misery now because the rich man is unwilling to part with his goods. The selfish rich man experiences misery later when he loses his soul.

In 3 Nephi, Mormon chronicled the cycle of misery:

> And thus passed away the twenty and eighth year, and the people had continual peace.
>
> But it came to pass in the twenty and ninth year there began to be some disputings among the people; and some were lifted up unto pride and boastings because of their exceedingly great riches, yea, even unto great persecutions.
>
> For there were many merchants in the land, and also many lawyers, and many officers.
>
> And the people began to be distinguished by ranks, according to their riches and their chances for learning; yea, some were ignorant because of their poverty, and others did receive great learning because of their riches.
>
> Some were lifted up in pride, and others were exceedingly humble; some did return railing for railing, while others would receive railing and persecution and all manner of afflictions, and would not turn and revile again, but were humble and penitent before God.[141]

Take note of Mormon's description of the perils of mammon-seeking:
- Driven by pride, peace can devolve to disputations within a short period of time;
- Then wealth-seeking leads to more pride, boasting, and persecution;
- Then merchandising becomes a prominent, distinguishing element of society;
- Then riches define individual rank and opportunity.
- The resulting oppression of the poor shackles them to their low station.

---
140 Deuteronomy 8:15–19; emphasis added.
141 3 Nephi 6:9–13.

Mormon explained that these conditions lead to inequality and divisiveness, the offspring of Babylon and the antithesis of Zion. The sickness that had infected the Nephite nation, he said, quickly infiltrated the Church, and soon the Saints were crushed under the weight of mammon-seeking. Frighteningly, only a small number managed to climb to high ground and remain safe from the tsunami that was about to overwhelm the nation.

Mormon reported, "And thus there became a great inequality in all the land, insomuch that the church began to be broken up; yea, insomuch that in the thirtieth year the church was broken up in all the land save it were among a few of the Lamanites who were converted unto the true faith; and they would not depart from it, for they were firm, and steadfast, and immovable, willing with all diligence to keep the commandments of the Lord."

How had this insanity happened? Mormon answered, "Now the cause of this iniquity of the people was this—Satan had great power, unto the stirring up of the people to do all manner of iniquity, and to the puffing them up with pride, tempting them to seek for power, and authority, and riches, and the vain things of the world. And thus Satan did lead away the hearts of the people to do all manner of iniquity; therefore they had enjoyed peace but a few years."

If that news were not bad enough, the subsequent scene was even worse: "And thus, in the commencement of the thirtieth year—the people having been delivered up for the space of a long time to be carried about by the temptations of the devil whithersoever he desired to carry them, and to do whatsoever iniquity he desired they should—and thus in the commencement of this, the thirtieth year, they were in a state of awful wickedness. *Now they did not sin ignorantly, for they knew the will of God concerning them, for it had been taught unto them; therefore they did wilfully rebel against God.*"[142]

They knew better! The members of the Church had been warned against seeking wealth by every prophet, including Nephi, Moses, and all the way back to Adam, and they did it anyway. They thought they could serve both God and mammon, but in the end they ended up hating God, just as Jesus had predicted: "No man can serve two masters: for either he will hate the one, and love the other; or else he will hold to the one, and despise the other."[143] The Nephites were living proof.

Scriptural Evidence That the Lord Despises the Selfish Rich

Our ability to approach the Lord and receive his blessings is linked to our attitude toward money and the Lord's children. Jacob drew a distinction between those to whom the Lord responds and those whom he despises: "And whoso knocketh, to him will he open; and the wise, and the learned, and they that are rich, who are puffed up because of their learning, and their wisdom, and their riches—yea, they are they whom he despiseth; and save they shall cast these things away, and consider themselves fools before God, and come down in the depths of humility, *he will not open unto them.*"[144]

---

142 3 Nephi 6:9–18; emphasis added.
143 Matthew 6:24.
144 2 Nephi 9:42; emphasis added.

Chapter 4 Lessons in the Scriptures Concerning Wealth

Nephi ends his book with a scathing rebuke, pronouncing three woes upon the prideful rich: "O the wise, and the learned, and the rich, that are puffed up in the pride of their hearts, and all those who preach false doctrines, and all those who commit whoredoms, and pervert the right way of the Lord, wo, wo, wo be unto them, saith the Lord God Almighty, for they shall be thrust down to hell!"[145] The Lord adds another woe: "Wo unto you rich men, that will not give your substance to the poor."[146] And another woe is pronounced by King Benjamin, who reminds us that we can lay no legitimate claim on our wealth; if we attempt to do so, our selfishness will cement our condemnation.

> And now, if God, who has created you, on whom you are dependent for your lives and for all that ye have and are, doth grant unto you whatsoever ye ask that is right, in faith, believing that ye shall receive, O then, how ye ought to impart of the substance that ye have one to another.
>
> And if ye judge the man who putteth up his petition to you for your substance that he perish not, and condemn him, how much more just will be your condemnation for withholding your substance, which doth not belong to you but to God, to whom also your life belongeth; and yet ye put up no petition, nor repent of the thing which thou hast done.
>
> I say unto you, wo be unto that man, for his substance shall perish with him; and now, I say these things unto those who are rich as pertaining to the things of this world.[147]

Few things could cause the Lord to despise someone and pronounce a wo upon him. But seeking and hoarding wealth, assuming ownership of that which is rightfully the Lord's, and selfishly holding back when God's children are in need will most certainly summon divine anger and heavenly disgust.

Choosing mammon over God is always listed in the scriptures among the darkest of deeds. Moreover, choosing mammon over God is to abandon covenantal loyalty, shift affection, totally disregard sacred covenants, and forget the One who gave us our blessings in the first place. By choosing mammon, we are sending God a message that we despise and hate him and that we have found another love to serve and adore. Again, "No man can serve two masters: for either he will hate the one, and love the other; or else he will hold to the one, and despise the other. Ye cannot serve God and mammon."[148]

According to King Benjamin, the way that we can love and serve God and obtain eternal life is to take care of his children: "When ye are in the service of your fellow beings ye are only in the service of your God."[149]

---

145 2 Nephi 28:15.
146 D&C 56:16.
147 Mosiah 4:21–23.
148 Matthew 6:24.
149 Mosiah 2:17.

Chapter 5
Persecuting the Poor

Poverty takes many forms—temporal, emotional, spiritual—but in the end, poverty always is defined by a lack. Every prophet has looked upon the condition of the poor, who are oppressed by Babylon, and grieved. In his day, Ezekiel mourned, "The people of the land have used oppression, and exercised robbery, and have vexed the poor and needy: yea, they have oppressed the stranger wrongfully."[150] Mistreating the poor has always been indicative of the most depraved people. Sodom and Gomorrah are examples: "Behold, this was the iniquity of thy sister Sodom, pride, fulness of bread, and abundance of idleness was in her and in her daughters, *neither did she strengthen the hand of the poor and needy*."[151]

The human tendency toward meanness is beyond comprehension. A disfigured child whose condition should invite pity, is often teased, taunted, and otherwise cruelly mistreated by his peers. Likewise, the Psalmist laments of the poor, "The wicked in his pride doth persecute the poor."[152] To persecute is to "systematically subject a race or group of people to cruel or unfair treatment; to make somebody the victim of continual pestering or harassment."[153] The scriptures use extreme language when describing our turning away from impoverished souls. For instance, consider the verbs *persecute, rob, hate, pollute, despise*. Sadly, the poor often search in vain for mercy: "The poor is hated even of his own neighbor."[154]

If we turn our backs on one of God's children, he takes it personally: "Whoso mocketh the poor reproacheth his Maker."[155] Such a person cannot be classified as a follower of Christ: "And remember in all things the poor and the needy, the sick and the afflicted, for he that doeth not these things, the same is not my disciple."[156] On the other

---
150   Ezekiel 22:29.
151   Ezekiel 16:49; emphasis added.
152   Psalm 10:2.
153   *Encarta Dictionary*, s.v. "persecute."
154   Proverbs 14:20.
155   Proverbs 17:5.
156   D&C 52:40.

hand, the Lord loves and generously recompenses those who care for his disadvantaged children: "He that hath pity upon the poor lendeth unto the Lord; and that which he hath given will he pay him again."[157]

Wo unto the Rich Who Despise the Poor

Nephi, speaking prophetically, pronounced ten woes on those who enter into the new and everlasting covenant and receive the blessings of the Atonement then neglect or reject the Savior, who proffered those blessings. As we shall see, these woes eventually settle on the issue of mammon-seeking over caring for the poor.

The first of these woes condemns an attitude of disregard for and rebellion against the laws of God. A careful reading reveals the troubling fact that Nephi was speaking to members of the Church, those who have received "all the laws of God." Nephi said, "But wo unto him that has the law given, yea, that has all the commandments of God, like unto us, and that transgresseth them, and that wasteth the days of his probation, for awful is his state!" This depraved condition is inspired by Satan and embraced by individuals who are vain, foolish, and spiritually frail: "O that cunning plan of the evil one! O the vainness, and the frailties, and the foolishness of men! When they are learned they think they are wise, and they hearken not unto the counsel of God, for they set it aside, supposing they know of themselves, wherefore, their wisdom is foolishness and it profiteth them not. And they shall perish."

We might ask ourselves, What could create a situation so awful that even the covenant people would perish? Nephi answered by listing his set of woes, and, significantly, he began with mammon-seeking and its impact on the poor: "But wo unto the rich, who are rich as to the things of the world. For because they are rich they despise the poor, and they persecute the meek, and their hearts are upon their treasures; wherefore, their treasure is their God. And behold, their treasure shall perish with them also."[158]

We hear echoes of idolatry in these verses. Treasure had captured the hearts of the Saints. They worshipped their treasure adoringly, as if it were their god, and they were paying for their treasure with their souls.

They Rob the Poor

Elsewhere Nephi continues to use the imagery of worship to describe our latter-day adulation of money. In the following verse, he accuses people in the last days of robbing the poor by using the *Lord's* money for their personal luxuries and for building unto themselves "sanctuaries," that is, "shrines" or "temples" wherein their god of money might reside: "They rob the poor because of their fine sanctuaries; they rob the poor because of their fine clothing; and they persecute the meek and the poor in heart, because in their pride they are puffed up."[159]

Scriptures often have layers of meaning. While the word *sanctuaries* references actual places of worship, the word can simultaneously mean places or things that are not

---

157   Proverbs 19:17.
158   2 Nephi 9:27–28, 30.
159   2 Nephi 28:13.

of God—those places and things we worship instead of God. These "sanctuaries" become "holy" to us because they represent that which we of the latter days hold most sacred.

Such "sanctuaries" may take all sorts of forms: elegant homes, expensive cars, excessive leisure, "fine clothing," and other luxuries—anything we worship, anything that we can point to as evidence of our industry, ingenuity, and genius. When it comes to our devotion to these things, we are devout worshippers; we are completely loyal to our false *god*. We can always be found in our "sanctuaries" paying homage to the deity of mammon while the poor languish and suffer in the shadows of our sanctuaries.

Nephi's choice of phrase, "they rob the poor," links withholding assistance to the poor with thievery. A person can only be robbed of something that rightfully belongs to him. Plainly, we have no right to cling to or withhold that which does not rightfully belong to us. "The riches of the earth are mine to give," the Lord states emphatically. To whom does he want to bless with those riches? "The poor and the needy." For what purpose? To "administer to their relief that they shall not suffer."[160] As stewards of the Lord's property, we are under covenant to do with the Lord's resources as he directs. But if we claim ownership or hoard the resources of our stewardships, pamper ourselves with the Lord's goods, and withhold the Lord's resources from the poor, whom the goods could help, we are thieves.

Building Personal Sanctuaries

Moroni scolded the people of the latter-days: "Ye love money more than ye love the poor. For behold, ye do love money, and your substance, and your fine apparel, and the adorning of your churches [sanctuaries], more than ye love the poor and the needy, the sick and the afflicted." Once again, we hear the reference to money being used to pamper and adorn the steward rather than to help the Lord's impoverished children. We see the poor being robbed by the stewards of the Lord's property and suffering for it. Moroni couldn't stand it: "O ye pollutions, ye hypocrites, ye teachers, who sell yourselves for that which will canker, why have ye polluted the holy church of God? Why are ye ashamed to take upon you the name of Christ? Why do ye not think that greater is the value of an endless happiness than that misery which never dies—because of the praise of the world?" Our eternal happiness is at stake, and certain misery looms if we do not change our attitude toward the poor.

Moroni continued by asking us questions as if he were a judge:

> Why do ye adorn yourselves with that which hath no life, and yet suffer the hungry, and the needy, and the naked, and the sick and the afflicted to pass by you, and notice them not?
> Yea, why do ye build up your secret abominations to get gain, and cause that widows should mourn before the Lord, and also orphans to mourn before the Lord, and also the blood of their fathers and their husbands to cry unto the Lord from the ground, for vengeance upon your heads?

---

160   D&C 38:39, 35.

Divine retaliation is how the Lord answers stewards who personally pamper themselves with his resources while neglecting the poor and needy: "Behold, the sword of vengeance hangeth over you; and the time soon cometh that he avengeth the blood of the saints upon you, for he will not suffer their cries any longer."[161]

Wealth-Seeking—The Sin That Hinders and Destroys the Church

Alma's disgust with the plague of wealth-seeking among his people sent him on a mission of reclamation.

Alma, "seeing all their inequality, began to be very sorrowful."[162] The people whom he had loved so much were waxing "proud because of their exceeding riches, and their fine silks, and their fine-twined linen, and because of their many flocks and herds, and their gold and their silver, and all manner of precious things, which they had obtained by their industry; and in all these things were they lifted up in the pride of their eyes, for they began to wear very costly apparel."[163] The prophet knew where this condition would lead; therefore, he relinquished the judgment seat into capable hands so that "he might preach the word of God unto them, to stir them up in remembrance of their duty, and that he might pull down, by the word of God, all the pride and craftiness and all the contentions which were among the people."[164] The call of a prophet is to warn people about such behavior, cry repentance, and declare the truth.

Alma's task was daunting. The Nephites were enjoying a season of abundance, and the people had now grown prosperous. As we so often learn in the Book of Mormon, prosperity is a trial that few can handle. Now Alma and his companions "saw and beheld with great sorrow that the people of the church began to be lifted up in the pride of their eyes, and to set their hearts upon riches and upon the vain things of the world, that they began to be scornful, one towards another, and they began to persecute those that did not believe according to their own will and pleasure."

The results of this condition were serious; they included "great contentions among the people of the church; yea, there were envyings, and strife, and malice, and persecutions, and pride, even to exceed the pride of those who did not belong to the church of God." Moreover, the work of the Church had all but stopped because of the bad example of the members: "The wickedness of the church was a great stumbling-block to those who did not belong to the church; and thus the church began to fail in its progress." Alma knew that this situation could only lead to a disaster: "Alma saw the wickedness of the church, and he saw also that the example of the church began to lead those who were unbelievers on from one piece of iniquity to another, thus bringing on the destruction of the people."[165]

---

161 Mormon 8:38–41.
162 Alma 4:15.
163 Alma 4:6.
164 Alma 4:19.
165 Alma 4:8–11.

Chapter 5 Persecuting the Poor

The Ugliness of Inequality Contrasted with the Beautiful Work of Angels

The scene worsened: "Yea, [Alma] saw great inequality among the people, some lifting themselves up with their pride, despising others, turning their backs upon the needy and the naked and those who were hungry, and those who were athirst, and those who were sick and afflicted." Where there had been happiness, prosperity, and peace, there was now misery: "Now this was a great cause for lamentations among the people."

Only a few members of the Church had remained true to their covenants. Alma found these few humble, faithful souls bucking the trend and doing the right things: "abasing themselves, succoring those who stood in need of their succor, such as imparting their substance to the poor and the needy, feeding the hungry, and suffering all manner of afflictions, for Christ's sake, who should come according to the spirit of prophecy; looking forward to that day, thus retaining a remission of their sins; being filled with great joy because of the resurrection of the dead, according to the will and power and deliverance of Jesus Christ from the bands of death." Here we note with interest that these humble followers of Christ who were administering to the needs of the poor were also "retaining a remission of their sins.[166]

The Lord has never intended for inequality to exist among his children:

> And again I say unto you, let every man esteem his brother as himself
> For what man among you having twelve sons, and is no respecter of them, and they serve him obediently, and he saith unto the one: Be thou clothed in robes and sit thou here; and to the other: Be thou clothed in rags and sit thou there—and looketh upon his sons and saith I am just?
> Behold, this I have given unto you as a parable, and it is even as I am. I say unto you, be one; and if ye are not one ye are not mine.[167]

Commenting on this parable, Brigham Young said,

> Now the object is to improve the minds of the inhabitants of the earth, until we learn what we are here for, and become one before the Lord, that we may rejoice together and be equal. Not to make all poor, no. The whole world is before us. The earth is here, and the fulness thereof is here. It was made for man; and one man was not made to trample his fellow man under his feet, and enjoy all his heart desires, while the thousands suffer.[168]

What *are* we here for, if not to improve our minds and learn the ways of God? And what is God like? Is he selfish, self-centered, self-serving, and greedy, a God who gives us poor creatures scant notice when we plead with him for help? Or is he infinitely generous, kind, and merciful—never thinking of himself but always striving to utilize all that he

---

166 Alma 4:12–14.
167 D&C 38:25–27.
168 Young, *Discourses of Brigham Young*, 286.

is and has in caring for us? Is he not trying to prepare us to become like him? Is this existence not a training ground where we may learn to abandon self interest and minister to others with the blessings he entrusts to us? If we have the faith to do so, do we not become *one* with him and thus have reason to rejoice with him in the work we accomplish together? Finally, do we really believe that we can achieve eternal life if we claim ownership of the Lord's property, indulge ourselves with it, and withhold it from his impoverished children?

God created the earth to support his children equitably: "For the earth is full, and there is enough and to spare." There is enough as long as we do not hoard! "Therefore, if any man shall take of the abundance which I have made, and impart not his portion, according to the law of my gospel, unto the poor and the needy, he shall, with the wicked, lift up his eyes in hell, being in torment."[169] President Young added, "The course pursued by men of business in the world has a tendency to make a few rich, and to sink the masses of the people in poverty and degradation. Too many of the Elders of Israel take this course. No matter what comes, they are for gain—for gathering around them riches; and when they get rich how are those riches used? Spent on the lusts of the flesh, wasted as a thing of nought."[170]

On the other hand, some people take their covenants seriously and employ the totality of who they are and what they have in doing as the Lord directs. President Young said, "Take the men that can travel the earth over, preach the Gospel without purse or scrip, and then go to and lay their plans to gather the Saints. *That looks like the work of angels.*"[171]

Withholding from and Judging the Poor Harshly

Some ninety years before Alma, King Benjamin laid down constitutional laws mirroring those established by Moses. Central to King Benjamin's law was the condition of the heart, which translated into the people's treatment of their unfortunate brothers and sisters: "And also, ye yourselves will succor those that stand in need of your succor; ye will administer of your substance unto him that standeth in need; and ye will not suffer that the beggar putteth up his petition to you in vain, and turn him out to perish."[172]

If we also judge the poor harshly, the king said, we compound our sin against these people, and we put our inheritance in the celestial kingdom at risk: "Perhaps thou shalt say: The man has brought upon himself his misery; therefore I will stay my hand, and will not give unto him of my food, nor impart unto him of my substance that he may not suffer, for his punishments are just—But I say unto you, O man, whosoever doeth this the same hath great cause to repent; and except he repenteth of that which he hath done he perisheth forever, and hath no interest in the kingdom of God."[173]

---

169 D&C 104:17–18.
170 Young, *Journal of Discourses*, 11:349.
171 Young, *Journal of Discourses*, 8:353–54; emphasis added.
172 Mosiah 4:16.
173 Mosiah 4:17:18.

Chapter 5   Persecuting the Poor

A terrible condemnation awaits those who judge a poor person and withhold that which does not belong to the withholder: "And if ye judge the man who putteth up his petition to you for your substance that he perish not, and condemn him, how much more just will be your condemnation for withholding your substance, which doth not belong to you but to God, to whom also your life belongeth; and yet ye put up no petition, nor repent of the thing which thou hast done. I say unto you, wo be unto that man, for his substance shall perish with him; and now, I say these things unto those who are rich as pertaining to the things of this world."[174]

The Evil of the Age: Life for Money

A certain proverb pronounces a curse upon those who would enrich themselves at the expense of the poor or who would give their substance to the rich for unholy purposes: "He that oppresseth the poor to increase his riches, and he that giveth to the rich, shall surely come to want."[175]

Could there be any sin more disgusting than viewing human beings as property, their only value being that which they can produce for their employers? At its worst, this attitude leads to slavery. To a lesser degree, this attitude defines the common philosophy of business: profit is more important than people—profit at all costs. Is this philosophy ethical? For Babylon, yes; for Zion, no. Often, business ethics smack of the philosophy advanced by Korihor the anti-Christ: "Every man fared in this life according to the management of the creature; therefore every man prospered according to his genius, and . . . every man conquered according to his strength; and whatsoever a man did was no crime."[176] One need only consider modern-day business ethics to see this anti-Christ philosophy in action. Employees are often valued and compensated solely according to their profitability to their employer, and, by and large, that valuation will determine the employee's prosperity or his poverty.

Hugh Nibley traced oppression of the poor back to Cain. It was Satan, he said, who taught Cain "a special course to make him prosperous in all things: the Mahan technique, the great secret of converting life into property. Later Lamech graduates with the same degree—'Master Mahan, master of that great secret' (Moses 5:49). He glories in what he has done; it becomes the normal world economy. Nearly all the posterity of Adam, we are told, entered into business, and all Adam and Eve could do about it was to mourn before the Lord (Moses 5:27). Everyone went off following the Canaanites. And Cain did it all, we are told, for the sake of getting gain (Moses 5:31). He was not ashamed; he 'gloried in that which he had done.' He said, 'I am free; surely the flocks of my brother falleth into my hands' (Moses 5:33)."[177]

"Particularly reprehensible in Nibley's view is the common practice of some employers who, in the spirit of the perverse 'work ethic,' withhold from laborers the necessities

---
174   Mosiah 4:22–23.
175   Proverbs 22:16.
176   Alma 30:17.
177   Nibley, *Approaching Zion*, 93–94.

of life in exchange for services—'life in exchange for profits.' 'To make merchandise of another's necessity is an offense to human dignity.' 'The prevailing evil of the age' is 'that men withhold God's gifts from each other in a power game.'"[178] King Benjamin denounced such dealings: "And ye will not have a mind to injure one another, but to live peaceably, and to render to every man according to that which is his due.[179]

Fair is fair. "Therefore all things whatsoever ye would that men should do to you, do ye even so to them."[180] If the tables were turned, the selfish rich man would be the first to cry foul."

The author of Ecclesiastes speaks of accumulating wealth and withholding one's substance from the poor as "vanity" or the symptoms of an "evil disease" that can only result in loneliness, sorrow, and misery: "There is a sore evil which I have seen under the sun, namely riches kept for the owners thereof to their hurt. . . . All his days also he eateth in darkness, and he hath much sorrow and wrath with his sickness. . . . There is an evil which I have seen under the sun, and it is common among men: A man to whom God hath given riches, wealth, and honour, so that he wanteth nothing for his soul of all that he desireth, yet God giveth him not power to eat thereof, but a stranger eateth it: this is vanity, and it is an evil disease."[181]

Perhaps worse than the sins of ignoring, withholding from, and harshly judging the poor is the sin of using a poor man's labor to enrich one's self. This sin runs contrary to the Lord's law of fair pay: "The laborer is worthy of his hire."[182] As we have noted, this sin is commonplace and, unfortunately, defines the economic condition of the last days.

A Curse on the Daughters of Zion

Isaiah prophesied that the Lord, along with the righteous fathers, kings, and prophets, will pronounce severe judgment upon those who consume what should rightfully support of the poor: "The Lord will enter into judgment with the ancients of his people and the princes thereof; for ye have eaten up the vineyard and the spoil of the poor in your houses."[183] Under such an indictment we might cry, Certainly you cannot mean us! What have we done to deserve such a denunciation?

Then the Lord will answer, "Ye beat my people to pieces, and grind the faces of the poor." Could we be guilty of such a crime? After all, are we not the chosen ones, the children of Zion? Certainly, we would never stoop to such an abysmal level.

But, according to Isaiah, the Lord was adamant in his condemnation of the selfish, so much so that he pronounced a curse, which interestingly in this case was directed at his latter-day daughters who would proudly go about wanting this and that, and who would be consumed by fashion:

---

178 Nibley, *Approaching Zion*, xv.
179 Mosiah 4:13.
180 Matthew 7:12.
181 Ecclesiastes 5:12–17; 6:1–2.
182 Luke 10:7; D&C 31:5; 70:12; 84:79; 106:3.
183 2 Nephi 13:14.

> Because the daughters of Zion are haughty, and walk with stretched-forth necks and wanton eyes, walking and mincing as they go, and making a tinkling with their feet—
>
> Therefore the Lord will smite with a scab the crown of the head of the daughters of Zion, and the Lord will discover their secret parts.
>
> In that day the Lord will take away the bravery of their tinkling ornaments, and cauls, and round tires like the moon;
>
> The chains and the bracelets, and the mufflers;
>
> The bonnets, and the ornaments of the legs, and the headbands, and the tablets, and the ear-rings;
>
> The rings, and nose jewels;
>
> The changeable suits of apparel, and the mantles, and the wimples, and the crisping-pins;
>
> The glasses, and the fine linen, and hoods, and the veils.
>
> And it shall come to pass, instead of sweet smell there shall be stink; and instead of a girdle, a rent; and instead of well set hair, baldness; and instead of a stomacher, a girding of sackcloth; burning instead of beauty.[184]

We cannot read such prophecies without realizing that the Lord takes seriously self-indulgence and fashion-seeking over dedicating our resources to blessing the poor. This manifestation of pride is an affront to God.

Blessings for Those Who Rescue the Poor

From the beginning, the Lord has pled with us to step outside ourselves and help his impoverished children. The law of Moses actually mandated mercy and hospitality: "If there be among you a poor man of one of thy brethren within any of thy gates in thy land which the Lord thy God giveth thee, thou shalt not harden thine heart, nor shut thine hand from thy poor brother: But thou shalt open thine hand wide unto him, and shalt surely lend him sufficient for his need, in that which he wanteth."[185]

Other commandments ordering kindheartedness can be found in the law. For example, the Lord forbade charging interest on a loan to a poor man.[186] The temple priests were to be sensitive to underprivileged people who were doing their best to comply with the law of sacrifice but who could not manage the price.[187] During the harvest, land owners were not to completely clear their fields but to leave the corners and the gleanings for the poor.[188] The people's attitude toward giving was as important as their gift; they were to give because they wanted to and not begrudgingly: "Thou shalt surely give him, and thine heart shall not be grieved when thou givest unto him."[189]

---

184 2 Nephi 13:14–24.
185 Deuteronomy 15:7–8.
186 Exodus 22:25.
187 Leviticus 14:21.
188 Leviticus 19:10.
189 Deuteronomy 15:10.

The law promised the people that their efforts to rescue the poor would not only save an impoverished soul but also the generous givers themselves. The law reminded the people that the poor would ever be with them unless they chose to remedy the situation: "For this thing the Lord thy God shall bless thee in all thy works, and in all that thou puttest thine hand unto. For the poor shall never cease out of the land: therefore I command thee, saying, Thou shalt open thine hand wide unto thy brother, to thy poor, and to thy needy, in thy land."[190]

When we read these verses, we should keep in mind that the law of Moses was the lesser, or preparatory, law; as such, it required less of the covenant people than did the higher law of Zion revealed by Jesus. We are under covenant to live the higher law: "Bring the poor that are cast out to thy house."[191]

In our day, the Lord told the elders that they had a special priesthood assignment to provide for the poor: "And if any man shall give unto any of you a coat, or a suit, take the old and cast it unto the poor, and go on your way rejoicing."[192] This might cause us to rethink yard sales over donating our aged items to the Deseret Industries or other charitable organizations. Because this particular commandment is listed in the same section as the oath and covenant of the priesthood, elders might consider this mandate as part of their priesthood responsibility. Likewise, in that same section, bishops are charged to "search after the poor to administer to their wants by humbling the rich and the proud."[193] Elder Alexander B. Morrison made the following observation:

> A pamphlet relative to the Church Welfare Program, "Helping Others to Help Themselves," first published about 1945, points out the trials that come to those who have no work:
>
> A man out of work is of special moment to the Church because, deprived of his inheritance, he is on trial as Job was on trial—for his integrity. As days lengthen into weeks and months and even years of adversity, the hurt grows deeper, and he is sorely tempted to "curse God and die." Continued economic dependence breaks him, it humiliates him if he is strong, spoils him if he is weak. Sensitive or calloused, despondent or indifferent, rebellious or resigned—either way, he is threatened with spiritual ruin, for the dole is an evil and idleness a curse. He soon becomes the seedbed of discontent, wrong thinking, alien beliefs. The Church cannot hope to save a man on Sunday if during the week it is a complacent witness to the crucifixion of his soul.[194]

While this statement is directed at Church leaders, it applies to individual priesthood holders: We simply cannot expect people to participate fully in the gospel if they cannot provide for themselves. We must teach them before we feed them.

---

190 Deuteronomy 15:11.
191 Isaiah 58:7.
192 D&C 84:105.
193 D&C 84:112.
194 Morrison, *Visions of Zion*, 109–110.

Chapter 5   Persecuting the Poor

M. Catherine Thomas explains what the Lord expects of the priesthood, both collectively and individually:

> The Lord has his own economic order, which exists above earthly economic systems; the power of this order rests in the systems of tithes and offerings and in the proper utilization of resources in what the scriptures call the Lord's Storehouse. This storehouse is to be distinguished from the Bishop's Storehouse, where commodities are kept. The Lord's Storehouse is the aggregate of talents and resources existing among the members of any church unit, ward or stake, and its use is based on the Law of Consecration (see D&C 42:33–34, 55; 70:7–10; 82:17–18; 83:6). In order to organize and utilize the resources in the Lord's Storehouse, priesthood and Relief Society leaders must work together in priesthood counsels in order to administer the Lord's Storehouse and get the real powers of Zion moving among them.
>
> The Lord said, "*The redemption of Zion must needs come by power*" (D&C 103:15), implying that as the members follow the Lord's organization and work the program in these temporal-seeming affairs, He will extend miraculous power to create a Zion society. He promises priesthood counsels: "*Whatever ye shall ask in faith, being united in prayer according to my command, ye shall receive*" (D&C 29:6). In this way the leaders unlock the powers of Zion for their people. Joseph foresaw this work going forward on two fronts through the power and authority of the priesthood:
>
> "And whilst we are thus united in one common cause [on earth], to roll forth the kingdom of God, the heavenly Priesthood are not idle spectators, the spirit of God will be showered down from above and it will dwell in our midst" (*Teachings of the Prophet Joseph Smith*, 232).
>
> The establishment of Zion is a partnership between the Kingdom of God on the earth and that in Heaven.[195]

The prophet Micah's call to the church in his day continues to be the Lord's call to us today: "I will consecrate their gain unto the Lord, and their substance unto the Lord of the whole earth."[196]

Great blessings await those who live the higher law and bless the poor with the Lord's resources: "Blessed is he that considereth the poor."[197] The book of Proverbs promises happiness and financial security for such generosity: "He that hath mercy on the poor, happy is he."[198] Prosperity follows the man who digs deeply into his pocket to succor the poor: "He that maketh himself poor shall have great riches."[199]

Security is another blessing: "He that giveth unto the poor shall not lack."[200] The scriptures contain many evidences of righteous people who consecrated their all to save impoverished souls temporally, emotionally, or spiritually, and in the process experienced the Lord's security.

---
195   Thomas, *Light in the Wilderness*, 136–137.
196   Micah 4:13.
197   Psalm 41:1.
198   Proverbs 14:21.
199   Proverbs 13:7.
200   Proverbs 28:27.

One example is Elijah, who was fed by ravens and drank from a brook until the brook dried up. Then the Lord provided for him by sending him to a poor widow whose food had dwindled to "an handful of meal in a barrel, and a little oil in a cruse." At that point, Elijah applied the Lord's law of abundance to save the poor widow and her son. Acting in the name of the Lord, Elijah asked the widow to make him "a little cake." She was to first "bring it unto [Elijah] and after make for [herself] and for [her] son." In faith, the widow obeyed the law. When she consecrated what she had to the impoverished prophet, her security was assured. In return, Elijah, representing the Lord, gave her a blessing: "For thus saith the Lord God of Israel, The barrel of meal shall not waste, neither shall the cruse of oil fail, until the day [that] the Lord sendeth rain upon the earth." And the widow's blessings did not stop there. When her son fell ill and died, Elijah brought him back to life and restored him to his mother.[201] We can assume that the widow's faith and giving attitude saved her life and her son's life. Clearly, faith in the Lord's promises and providing for the needs of others results in security for our families.

Another example of blessings that flow to those who aid the needy is Zacchaeus, a rich man who loved the Lord and gave generously to the poor. When Jesus drew near to him, "Zacchaeus stood, and said unto the Lord; Behold, Lord, the half of my goods I give to the poor; and if I have taken anything from any man by false accusation, I restore him fourfold. And Jesus said unto him, This day is salvation come to this house."[202] The same could be announced to anyone who lives righteously and strives to bless the poor: "This day is salvation come to this house."

The Poor of the Lord's People Shall Trust in Zion

The scriptures are replete with hope for the poor who are among the people of Zion. For instance, the Lord promises to hear their cries for relief: "I have heard your prayers, and the poor have complained before me."[203] In fact, as a response to the cries of the poor, the Lord is motivated to establish Zion, a condition they can finally trust: "The Lord hath founded Zion, and the poor of his people shall trust in it."[204] Now Zion becomes their place of refuge.[205] In Zion, they will never again be treated badly. Zion is their rescue and their deliverance. The Lord "raiseth up the poor out of the dust."[206]

Because of their great relief, "the poor among men shall rejoice in the Holy One of Israel."[207] By whom does the Lord administer relief to his impoverished children? By the covenant people of Zion.[208] In Zion, the poor are comforted and raised up by their brothers and sisters who have consecrated their properties to care for them.[209] Consequently,

---

201 1 Kings 17:1–24.
202 Luke 19:8–9.
203 D&C 38:16.
204 Isaiah 14:32.
205 2 Nephi 14:6.
206 1 Samuel 2:7.
207 2 Nephi 27:30.
208 D&C 38:35.
209 D&C 42:30–31, 34, 39; 44:6; 51:5; 52:40; 72:12; 105:3.

in Zion there are no poor; Zion is like nowhere else on earth.[210] In Zion, the rich make themselves low so that the poor might be exalted.[211] No more will the poor mourn, for in Zion they receive equally from the Lord's and bishop's storehouses, which exist to protect and sustain them.[212] Moreover, the poor are extended relief by caring neighbors who give because they cannot stand poverty in any form. Therefore, through the organization of the priesthood and by means of the individual initiatives of caring neighbors, the poor are provided for in Zion and given ways to emerge from poverty.[213] The Lord has promised, "I will satisfy the poor with bread."[214] Bread is only the beginning of their blessings. In Zion, the poor will discover that the Lord has prepared a bounteous feast for them.[215]

Where does this all lead? Ultimately, the poor, now equal with their brothers and sisters, will be invited to the marriage of the Lamb.[216] After their long oppression, the poor shall inherit the earth.[217]

---

210 Moses 7:18.
211 D&C 104:16.
212 D&C 78:3; 82:11–12.
213 D&C 83:6.
214 Psalm 132:15.
215 D&C 56:8–11.
216 D&C 58:11.
217 D&C 88:17.

Chapter 6
Consequences of Seeking Wealth and Persecuting the Poor

Ironically, in attaining eternal salvation, poverty and persecution serve us better than wealth and acceptance. Brigham Young said, "When I see this people grow and spread and prosper, I feel that there is more danger than when they are in poverty. *Being driven from city to city or into the mountains is nothing compared to the danger of our becoming rich and being hailed by outsiders as a first-class community. I am afraid of only one thing. What is that? That we will not live our religion, and that we will partially slide a little from the path of rectitude, and go part of the way to meet our friends [the people of Babylon]*."[218]

Mormon, who is famous for adding insights to his narrative, offered this scathing rebuke of the Nephites who were once again saved and prospered by the Lord only to abandon their noble intentions for the pursuit of wealth:

> And thus we can behold how false, and also the unsteadiness of the hearts of the children of men; yea, we can see that the Lord in his great infinite goodness doth bless and prosper those who put their trust in him.
>
> Yea, and we may see at the very time when he doth prosper his people, yea, in the increase of their fields, their flocks and their herds, and in gold, and in silver, and in all manner of precious things of every kind and art; sparing their lives, and delivering them out of the hands of their enemies; softening the hearts of their enemies that they should not declare wars against them; yea, and in fine, doing all things for the welfare and happiness of his people; *yea, then is the time that they do harden their hearts, and do forget the Lord their God, and do trample under their feet the Holy One—yea, and this because of their ease, and their exceedingly great prosperity.*[219]

The list of consequences for such actions is sobering, as detailed below.

---
218 Young, *Discourses of Brigham Young*, 434; emphasis added.
219 Helaman 12:1–2; emphasis added.

Loss of the Providences of Heaven

Elder Joseph B. Wirthlin taught that if we perceive that our prayers are not being answered, we ought to ask ourselves if we are answering the cries of the poor, the sick, the hungry, and the afflicted within our influence.[220]

Brigham Young explained the consequences when we participate in wealth-seeking: "The Latter-day Saints who turn their attention to money-making soon become cold in their feelings toward the ordinances of the house of God. They neglect their prayers, become unwilling to pay any donations; the law of tithing gets too great a task for them; and they finally forsake their God, and the providences of heaven seem to be shut from them—all in consequence of this lust after the things of this world."[221]

Loss of Priesthood Power and Exaltation

Hugh Nibley said that Satan would "use the strongest, the most powerful pitch he could use, the most irresistible weapon in his arsenal, the one that is tried and true"[222]—lust for riches—to tempt us. President Young said that if a man attempts to "call around him property, be he a merchant, tradesman, or farmer, with his mind continually occupied with: 'How shall I get this or that; how rich can I get; or, how much can I get out of this brother or from that brother?' and dicker and work, and take advantage here and there—no such man ever can magnify the priesthood nor enter the celestial kingdom. Now, remember, they will not enter that kingdom."[223]

Loss of the Spirit

Joseph Smith spoke of the incompatibility of simultaneously seeking wealth and the Holy Ghost. We must be careful not to "grieve the Holy Spirit," he said. Rather, we must become "properly affected one toward another, and are careful by all means to remember, those who are in bondage, and in heaviness, and in deep affliction for your sakes." Then the caution: "And if there are any among you who aspire after their own aggrandizement, and seek their own opulence, while their brethren are groaning in poverty, and are under sore trials and temptations, they cannot be benefited by the intercession of the Holy Spirit."[224]

Loss of Revelation

Amulek taught that the heavens withdraw "if ye turn away the needy, and the naked, and visit not the sick and afflicted, and impart of your substance, if ye have, to those

---

220 Wirthlin, "The Law of the Fast," 73.
221 Young, *Discourses of Brigham Young*, 315.
222 Nibley, *Approaching Zion*, 332.
223 Young, *Journal of Discourses*, 11:297.
224 Smith, *Teachings of the Prophet Joseph Smith*, 141.

who stand in need." Then he pronounces the curse: "I say unto you, if ye do not any of these things, behold, your prayer is vain, and availeth you nothing, and ye are as hypocrites who do deny the faith."[225] Elder Joseph B. Wirthlin taught, "If you feel that Heavenly Father is not listening to your petitions, ask yourself if you are listening to the cries of the poor, the sick, the hungry, and the afflicted all around you."[226]

We live beneath our privileges, declared Brigham Young. "To get . . . revelation it is necessary that the people live so that their spirits are as pure and clean as a piece of blank paper . . . ready to receive any mark the writer may make upon it. When you see the Latter-day Saints greedy, and covetous of the things of this world, do you think their minds are in a fit condition to be written upon by the pen of revelation?"[227] Earlier, Joseph Smith taught the same principle: "God had often sealed up the heavens because of covetousness in the Church."[228]

We recall the parable of the sower. Jesus explained that the person who "received seed among the thorns is he that heareth the word,"[229] "and the cares of this world, and the deceitfulness of riches, and the lusts of other things entering in, choke the word and it becometh unfruitful."[230] That is, because of the deceitfulness of riches, the word of God can "bring no fruit to perfection."[231] Where there is no Spirit there is no life.

Loss of Happy Family Life and Spiritual Commitment

President Kimball added the risks of losing happy family life and spiritual decline to the dangers of pursuing wealth and withholding from the poor:

> It is hard to satisfy us. The more we have, the more we want. Why another farm, another herd of sheep, another bunch of cattle, another ranch? Why another hotel, another cafe, another store, another shop? Why another plant, another office, another service, another business? Why another of anything if one has that already which provides the necessities and reasonable luxuries? *Why continue to expand and increase holdings, especially when those increased responsibilities draw one's interests away from proper family and spiritual commitments, and from those things to which the Lord would have us give precedence in our lives?* Why must we always be expanding to the point where our interests are divided and our attentions and thoughts are upon the things of the world? *Certainly when one's temporal possessions become great, it is very difficult for one to give proper attention to the spiritual things.*[232]

---

225 Alma 34:28.
226 Joseph B. Wirthlin, "The Law of the Fast," 74.
227 Young, *Journal of Discourses*, 11:240–41.
228 Smith, *Teachings of the Prophet Joseph Smith*, 9.
229 Matthew 13:22.
230 Mark 4:19.
231 Luke 8:14.
232 Kimball, *The Teachings of Spencer W. Kimball*, 354.

Loss of the Lord's Help

"Whoso stoppeth his ears at the cry of the poor, he also shall cry himself, but shall not be heard."[233] Divine deafness is a terrible curse that the Lord imposes on the proud, the selfish, and the insensitive. When we stop listening to the poor, the Lord stops listening to us, and when he stops listening, he stops helping and prospering us—in fact, the things we attempt become stumbling blocks to us.

The Nephite king Limhi knew why his people had suffered severely without the Lord's rescue: "Therefore, who wondereth that they are in bondage, and that they are smitten with sore afflictions? For behold, the Lord hath said: I will not succor my people in the day of their transgression; *but I will hedge up their ways that they prosper not; and their doings shall be as a stumbling block before them.*"[234] When we stop our ears at the cries of the poor, we commit transgression. The Lord ceases to listen to us, and when he stops helping, our prosperity turns to poverty. Suddenly, we find ourselves in bondage with no relief and we wonder why.

Loss of True Worship

Brigham Young chastised the Saints for shifting their worship from the true God to the god of mammon: "Many professing to be Saints seem to have no knowledge, no light, to see anything beyond a dollar, or a pleasant time, a comfortable house, a fine farm, &c., &c. O fools, and slow of heart to understand the purposes of God and his handiwork among the people."[235]

And at another time: "Go to the child, and what does its joy consist in? Toys, we may call them, something that produces, as they think, pleasure; and so it is with our youth, our young boys and girls; they are thinking too much of this world; and the middle-aged are striving and struggling to obtain the good things of this life, and their hearts are too much upon them. So it is with the aged. Is not this the condition of the Latter-day Saints? It is. . . . *The Latter-day Saints are drifting as fast as they can into idolatry,* drifting into the spirit of the world and into pride and vanity."[236]

Failure in Our Mission

Our mission in life fails when we set our heart upon riches. Again, Brigham Young said, "If the Lord ever revealed anything to me, he has shown me that the Elders of Israel must let speculation alone and attend to the duties of their calling, otherwise they will have little or no power in their missions."[237] Elder Bruce R. McConkie explained it this way:

---

233   Proverbs 21:13.
234   Mosiah 7:28–29.
235   Young, *Journal of Discourses*, 8:63.
236   Young, *Journal of Discourses*, 18:239; emphasis added.
237   Young, *Discourses of Brigham Young*, 315.

Chapter 6 Consequences of Seeking Wealth and Persecuting the Poor

> The children of Zion fail in their great mission for two reasons: (1) Oftentimes they set their hearts upon temporal things and are more concerned with amassing the things that moth and rust corrupt, and that thieves break through and steal, than in laying up for themselves treasures in heaven. Hence the divine direction: "But the laborer in Zion shall labor for Zion; for if they labor for money they shall perish." (2 Nephi 26:31.) (2) Others fail to live by the high standards of belief and conduct imposed by the gospel. Of them the divine word says: "Your minds in times past have been darkened because of unbelief, and because you have treated lightly the things you have received—which vanity and unbelief have brought the whole church under condemnation. And this condemnation resteth upon the children of Zion, even all. And they shall remain under this condemnation until they repent and remember the new covenant, even the Book of Mormon and the former commandments which I have given them, not only to say, but to do according to that which I have written—that they may bring forth fruit meet for their Father's kingdom; otherwise there remaineth a scourge and judgment to be poured out upon the children of Zion." (D&C 84:54–58.)[238]

Loss of Peace

Peace is forfeited when we seek wealth over the things of God and when we turn a deaf ear to those in need. Brigham Young did not mince words on this subject:

> What is the matter with them? The god of this world has blinded their minds, they give way to selfishness, covetousness, and divers other kinds of wickedness, suffer the allurements of this world to decoy them from the paths of truth, forget their God, their religion, their covenants, and the blessings they have received, and become like beasts, made to be taken and destroyed at the will of the destroyer. This is the situation, not only of the great majority of the world, but of many of the inhabitants of these valleys; they have no correct idea of the day of destruction, the day of calamity; they have no realization of the day of sorrow and retribution. They put these things far away and do not wish to think about them, but say, "Let us eat, drink, and lay down and sleep, and that is all we desire"; then like the brutes they are happy. *It never enters the hearts of the mass of mankind that they are preparing for the day of calamity and slaughter.*[239]

The Doctrine and Covenants is filled with such warnings. Hugh Nibley offers the following list:

> Almost the first words spoken by the Lord himself to the boy Joseph in his first vision were, "Behold the world lieth in sin at this time and none doeth good no not

---

238 McConkie, *A New Witness for the Articles of Faith*, 580.
239 Young, *Journal of Discourses*, 3:273.

one, they have turned asside [sic] from the Gospel and keep not my commandments they draw near to me with their lips while their hearts are far from me and mine anger is kindling against the inhabitants of the earth to visit them acording [sic] to this ungodliness." The preface to the Doctrine and Covenants repeats this: "They seek not the Lord, . . . but every man walketh in his own way . . . in Babylon, even Babylon the great, which shall fall" (D&C 1:16). And so on down: "Behold, the world is ripening in iniquity" (D&C 18:6). "The hour is nigh and the day soon at hand when the earth is ripe; and all the proud and they that do wickedly shall be as stubble; . . . I will take vengeance upon the wicked, for they will not repent; for the cup of mine indignation is full" (D&C 29:9, 17). "All flesh is corrupted before me; and the powers of darkness prevail upon the earth, . . . and all eternity is pained, and the angels are waiting. . . . The enemy is combined" (D&C 38:11–12). (Do such words mean nothing to us?) "Behold, the day has come, when the cup of the wrath of mine indignation is full. . . . Wherefore, labor ye; . . . for the adversary spreadeth his dominions, and darkness reigneth; and the anger of God kindleth against the inhabitants of the earth; and none doeth good, for all have gone out of the way" (D&C 43:26, 28; 82:5–6). "Darkness covereth the earth, and gross darkness the minds of the people, and all flesh has become corrupt before my face. Behold, vengeance cometh speedily . . . upon all the face of the earth. . . . And upon my house shall it begin, . . . first among . . . you . . . who have professed to know my name and have not known me" (D&C 112:23–26).

So the word of the Lord is that Babylon is to remain in Babylon until the day of destruction. Things have not improved since Joseph Smith wrote of "the most damning hand of murder, tyranny, and oppressions, supported and urged on and upheld by the influence of that spirit which has so strongly riveted the creeds of the fathers, who have inherited lies, upon the hearts of the children, and filled the world with confusion, and has been growing stronger and stronger, and is now the very mainspring of all corruption, and the whole earth groans under the weight of its iniquity" (D&C 123:7). "Some may have cried peace," he wrote (and no man ever loved peace more than he), "but the Saints and the world will have little peace from henceforth." "*Destruction*, to the eye of the spiritual beholder, seems to be written by the finger of an invisible hand, in large capitals, upon almost every thing we behold." "There is a spirit that prompts the nations to prepare for war, desolation, and bloodshed—to waste each other away," said Brigham twenty years later. "Do they realize it? No. . . . Is it not a mystery?" "When the nations have for years turned much of their attention to manufacturing instruments of death, they have sooner or later used those instruments. . . . [They] will be used until the people are wasted away, and there is no help for it."[240]

---

240   Nibley, *Approaching Zion*, 44–45, quoting Smith, *Teachings of the Prophet Joseph Smith*, 160, 15; Young, *Journal of Discourses*, 8:174–75, 157.

What is the chief cause of this wickedness? As Nibley said, the Lord opened the Doctrine and Covenants with the answer: "They seek not the Lord to establish his righteousness, but every man walketh in his own way, and after the image of his own god, whose image is in the likeness of the world, and whose substance is that of an idol."[241] *Covetousness!*

The Lord will tolerate this condition only for so long. Brigham Young made the following prophetic statement: "You will see that the wisdom of the wise among the nations will perish and be taken from them. They will fall into difficulties, and they will not be able to tell the reason, nor point a way to avert them any more than they can now in this land. They can fight, quarrel, contend and destroy each other, but they do not know how to make peace. So it will be with the inhabitants of the earth."[242]

Loss of National Security

Commenting on the global implications of wealth-seeking, Joseph Fielding McConkie and Robert Millet offer this insight: "A civilization that wastes its strength in the pursuit of either wealth or glory will not stand. A nation that fosters or encourages selfishness, that allows greed and lust to go unchecked, will sink under its own weight. Babylon will fall because its citizenry will come in time to shun and hate and destroy all that oppose them. Zion will arise and shine forth as an ensign to the nations because its municipals seek the interest of their neighbors and do all things with an eye single to the glory of God (D&C 82:19)."[243]

The poor are the victims of individual and national selfishness. Hugh Nibley writes: "A community which can at tolerable expense eliminate human distress but refrains from doing so either must believe that it benefits from unemployment or poverty, or that the poor and unemployed are bad people, or that other more important values will be impaired by attempts to help the lower orders—or all of these statements." Quoting well-known economist Daniel Yergin, Nibley points out the poverty of the 1970s "could have been eliminated at a modest shift of $10–15 billion to the poor from the rest of the community. 15 billion is less than 1.5% of the GNP, about the size of one of the cheaper weapons systems."[244]

Imagine, now, the law of consecration as a solution for the world's poverty. How would life appear if love motivated the actions of governments and citizenries? We need not look beyond The Church of Jesus Christ of Latter-day Saints for an answer. Perhaps better than any other organization, the Saints voluntarily take care of each other by their consecrations, which are motivated by love. No wonder, then, that President George Q. Cannon called for a change of heart and for putting first things first: "We must serve God with all our hearts, our love and affections reaching after Him, and the things of this world must be looked upon by us as secondary considerations. They are good enough in their place; right enough to be attended to; but subordinate always to the love of God."[245]

---

241 D&C 1:16.
242 Young, *Journal of Discourses*, 10:315.
243 McConkie and Millet, *Doctrinal Commentary on the Book of Mormon*, 3:5.
244 Nibley, *Approaching Zion*, 515.
245 Cannon, *Journal of Discourses*, 22:288–89.

Chapter 7
Who Shall Enter?

The Savior's parable of the sheep and goats lays out the criteria for "everlasting punishment" and "eternal life." To the sheep, who represent the righteous, the Lord says: "Then shall the King say unto them on his right hand, Come, ye blessed of my Father, inherit the kingdom prepared for you from the foundation of the world: For I was an hungered, and ye gave me meat: I was thirsty, and ye gave me drink: I was a stranger, and ye took me in: Naked, and ye clothed me: I was sick, and ye visited me: I was in prison, and ye came unto me."

Then, to the goats, who represent the unrighteous: "Then shall he say also unto them on the left hand, Depart from me, ye cursed, into everlasting fire, prepared for the devil and his angels: For I was an hungered, and ye gave me no meat: I was thirsty, and ye gave me no drink: I was a stranger, and ye took me not in: naked, and ye clothed me not: sick, and in prison, and ye visited me not."[246]

Gospel writer Matthew B. Brown makes the following observation:

> How should Latter-day Saints prepare themselves to be counted among the sheep instead of the goats during the Final Judgment? The way is pointed out in simplicity within the text of the parable itself. According to the Son of God, true Saints who are prepared will (1) give food to the hungry and water to the thirsty, (2) provide shelter and clothing to the needy, and (3) minister to the sick and imprisoned.
>
> The Lord considers such charitable service for the benefit of His brethren as if it were being done for Him. As aptly stated in the Book of Mormon, those who are in the service of their fellow beings are considered to be in the service of God (see Mosiah 2:17). And the reward for engaging in freewill service is to be "blessed" by the Creator of heaven and earth with a blessing with eternal

---
246 Matthew 25:31–46.

What Doth It Profit?

Jesus' brother James had much to say about the attitude of the selfish rich, their wealth, and their treatment of the poor. He peppered his epistle with prophetic counsel that gives us cause for reflection. As an example, he wrote, "For the sun is no sooner risen with a burning heat, but it withereth the grass, and the flower thereof falleth, and the grace of the fashion of it perisheth: so also shall the rich man fade away in his ways."[248] That is, the rich man might prosper for a season, but his status is fleeting. As sure as the grass will wither in the heat of the sun or the petals of a flower will one day curl and fall, so will a rich man's affluence eventually fade.

James continued by stating that we often hold to an attitude that the Lord finds abhorrent: We favor the rich while oppressing the poor. "For if there come unto your assembly a man with a gold ring, in goodly apparel, and there come in also a poor man in vile raiment; and ye have respect to him that weareth the gay clothing, and say unto him, Sit thou here in a good place; and say to the poor, Stand thou there, or sit here under my footstool, Are ye not then partial in yourselves, and are become judges of evil thoughts?" The practice of partiality is an ugly one: "If ye have respect to persons, ye commit sin."[249]

"What doth it profit?" James asked. "If a brother or sister be naked, and destitute of daily food, and one of you say unto them, Depart in peace, be ye warmed and filled; notwithstanding ye give them not those things which are needful to the body; what doth it profit?"[250] In other words, when we see someone in need, do we pat them on the head and send them away with hollow words of comfort that will neither warm nor fill? When a coat is needed, words will not provide warmth; when food is needed, distant sympathy will not fill an empty belly. Zion people interpret encountering need as the Lord's bringing such situations to their attention. Having thus been *called*, they spring into action and supply the need until all are warmed and filled.

James was indignant with those who pray and ask God to add to their prosperity. Is there not hypocrisy in a prayer that solicits personal need when the underlying intent is to gain more for ourselves? Are we justified in asking God whether or not we should purchase things that accrue to our lusts? God turns a deaf ear to such prayers: "Ye ask, and receive not, because ye ask amiss, that ye may consume it upon your lusts."[251] This brand of hypocrisy incensed Brigham Young: "I have seen [men] who, when they had a chance

---

247 Brown, *Prophecies—Signs of the Times*, 129–30.
248 James 1:11.
249 James 2:2–4, 9.
250 James 2:15–16.
251 James 4:4.

to buy a widow's cow for ten cents on the dollar of her real value in cash, would make the purchase, and then thank the Lord that he has so blessed them."[252] James called such people enemies of God: "Know ye not that the friendship of the world is enmity with God? whosoever therefore will be a friend of the world is the enemy of God."

Are we really willing to act this way? This is not the gospel of Jesus Christ; this is not discipleship. James gave us the true definition: "Pure religion and undefiled before God and the Father is this, To visit the fatherless and widows in their affliction, and to keep himself unspotted from the world."[253] The essence of the gospel is to help the helpless and to remain separate from Babylon and her ways.

James pronounced woes upon the selfish rich: "Go to now, ye rich men, weep and howl for your miseries that shall come upon you. Your riches are corrupted, and your garments are moth-eaten. Your gold and silver is cankered; and the rust of them shall be a witness against you, and shall eat your flesh as it were fire. Ye have heaped treasure together for the last days." He condemned the businessman who oppresses the hirelings and enriches himself on their labor: "Behold, the hire of the labourers who have reaped down your fields, which is of you kept back by fraud, crieth: and the cries of them which have reaped are entered into the ears of the Lord of Sabaoth. Ye have lived in pleasure on the earth, and been wanton; ye have nourished your hearts, as in a day of slaughter."[254]

Throughout James's epistle, his question haunts us: *What doth it profit?* Jesus posed the same question to his disciples: "For what doth it profit a man if he gain the whole world . . . and he lose his own soul, and he himself be a castaway?"[255] And yet many persist.

The Voice of Seven Thunders

Brigham Young could not stand the ever-growing tendency toward covetousness among the Latter-day Saints, and he continually taught against it. In the last speech he gave, he cried:

> Now those that can see the spiritual atmosphere can see that many of the Saints are still glued to this earth and lusting and longing after the things of this world, in which there is no profit. . . . According to the present feelings of many of our brethren, they would arrogate to themselves this world and all that pertains to it, and cease not day or night to see that it was devoted to the building up of the kingdom of the devil, and if they had the power they would build a railroad to carry it to hell and establish themselves there. Where are the eyes and the hearts of this people? . . . All the angels in heaven are looking at this little handful of people, and stimulating them to the salvation of the human family. So also are the devils in hell looking at this people, too, and trying to overthrow us, *and the people are still shaking hands with the servants of the devil, instead of sanctifying themselves.*

---

252 Young, *Journal of Discourses*, 17:362.
253 James 1:27.
254 James 5:1–5.
255 JST, Luke 9:25.

Continuing, he asked us to imagine what wisdom our forefathers would impart to us: "What do you suppose the fathers would say if they could speak from the dead? . . . What would they whisper in our ears? Why, if they had the power the very thunders of heaven would be in our ears, if we could but realize the importance of the work we are engaged in. . . . *When I think upon this subject, I want the tongues of seven thunders to wake up the people.*"[256]

Choosing God over Mammon

The Lord gave us the law of consecration, in part, for our safety, security, and salvation. This law provides the *only* way to pass the mortal test of money and arrive in the celestial kingdom. That lofty goal requires us to be willing to choose consecration as a way of life over the way of Babylon. We must consider everything we are and have as belonging to God; we must view ourselves as stewards rather than owners; we must agree to be accountable to God for the things that he places in our safekeeping; and we must labor for the cause of Zion and not for selfish interests, including the accumulation of money. In other words, the law of consecration requires that we give to God our hearts and that we dedicate ourselves to his work and his children.

Our eventual placement in a kingdom of glory depends upon our adherence to the law of consecration and our living its principles out of love. According to John Tvedtnes, this law is illustrated in Doctrine and Covenants 76, the revelation that describes the various resurrections. He concludes, "Only those who obey the Lord's commandments out of love and a simple desire to do good will inherit the celestial kingdom. Those who obey out of fear of punishment or hope of reward, while good people, will inherit the terrestrial kingdom."[257] And we would add that telestial people are likely those who must be constrained to obey. These people are among those who have lived with scant desire to do good. They have rejected God and are only one degree above the worst group, the sons of perdition, who hated God and knowingly rebelled against him.

How, then, might we choose God over mammon, cease compromising, and stop trying to marry the two? We return to Jacob's formula for the answer: "Think of your brethren like unto yourselves, and be familiar with all and free with your substance, that they may be rich like unto you."[258] Clearly, we must start with love—love for God and his children: "Therefore all things whatsoever ye would that men should do to you, do ye even so to them."[259] If we truly love, we cannot stand to see suffering or lack of any kind. We attack every condition of lack and smother it with kindness and charity until lack ceases to exist among us. Because this love— charity, or "pure love of Christ,"[260] —expands with each charitable act, our ability to love approaches the quality of the Savior's love, which is infinite and "broad as eternity."[261] Then, when we encounter more suffer-

---
256 Young, *Journal of Discourses*, 18:305; emphasis added.
257 Tvedtnes, "They Have Their Reward," Feb. 21, 2007.
258 Jacob 2:18.
259 Matthew 7:12.
260 Moroni 7:47.
261 Moses 7:53.

ing, we are capable of feeling more empathy, which causes our capacity to love to grow. When that happens, we yearn for more resources so that we might alleviate more misery. That yearning conveys us to God, who is the source of all good things. To him we make our request for more resources and ability, for that is the eternal law: We must ask in order to receive. "And whatsoever ye shall ask the Father in my name, which is right, believing that ye shall receive, behold it shall be given unto you."[262]

At this point, we refer to the counsel of Jacob: "But before ye seek for riches, seek ye for the kingdom of God."[263] We make note here that the kingdom of God is founded upon the new and everlasting covenant, which gives us access to the Atonement. Jacob seems to be saying that the order of life for a covenant person is first to seek for all gospel covenants and ordinances and then live worthily of them.

But beyond ordering a life, there is another reason to put first things first. The new and everlasting covenant binds us to Christ in such a way that we become *partners* who share in the same work. When we, the junior partner, encounter need—the eradication of which is a purpose of the partnership—we are authorized by covenant to ask the senior partner for help and resources to supply the need. Because the sum of the assets of the two partners has been consecrated to the partnership, the junior partner may draw upon those assets by counseling with and by permission of the senior partner. Suddenly, the junior partner is in possession of incredible wealth because he has sought the kingdom of God first. Following this logic, there is no need that cannot be supplied if we are not of little faith and if we are true to the covenants and conditions of the partnership. Thus, when we seek for the kingdom of God first, the Lord makes available his riches for whatever we and he deem necessary. By covenant, we have both the right and the obligation to ask the Lord for his help and resources when we encounter those of his children who are in need.

Obtaining a Hope in Christ

We enhance our ability to ask for the Lord's help by taking the next step stated by Jacob: "Obtain a hope in Christ."[264] It is one thing to believe that Christ exists, but it is quite another to believe *who* he is. Therein lies our hope in Christ. When we understand that Jesus, like his Father, knows in detail our past, present, and future, that he possesses all power in heaven and on earth, that he is perfectly consistent, and that he loves us completely, then we have obtained a hope in him.

Jacob said if we obtain a hope in Christ, "ye shall obtain riches, if ye seek them; and ye will seek them for the intent to do good—to clothe the naked, and to feed the hungry, and to liberate the captive, and administer relief to the sick and the afflicted.'[265] It would be fair to say that to the degree we minister to the needy, we have received a hope in Christ. If we do not care for the Lord's children, we neither hope in him nor know him.

---

262 3 Nephi 18:20.
263 Jacob 2:18.
264 Jacob 2:19.
265 Jacob 2:19.

Freely Ye Have Received, Freely Give

And minister we must.

Jesus admonished the Seventy, "Freely ye have received, freely give."[266] Like us, the Seventy entered into the new and everlasting covenant by baptism and by ordination to the priesthood, and thus they embarked on the path leading to eternal life. Along the way, they freely received covenants and ordinances—*gifts*— "without price."[267] Because, the Seventy had been taught, the *only* way to arrive in the celestial kingdom is to "freely give" of what they had received to alleviate every form of oppression, they were to go forth distributing their gifts freely, so that they could bring as many people as possible to Christ, who would heal them. Forevermore, the Seventy would be called the "salt of the earth," the "light of the world,"[268] and "saviors on Mount Zion."[269] Their purpose would be to represent *the* Savior and do things as he would do. Thus, Jesus commanded them: "Heal the sick, cleanse the lepers, raise the dead, cast out devils."[270] In other words, attack misery wherever you encounter it; freely give of what you have received.

Representing Jesus is a weighty responsibility. In a remarkable manner, we become to Jesus what he is to his Father: "As my Father hath sent me, even so send I you."[271] Given this fact, can we justify ourselves in diverting our affections from the One who has entrusted and endowed us? Could we receive the Lord's goods then hoard them and ignore his children—the very ones he has sent us into the world to save? The Seventy knew better. They fulfilled their commission and returned rejoicing, absolutely astonished at the power of the gifts the Lord had given them: "And the seventy returned again with joy, saying, Lord, even the devils are subject unto us through thy name."[272]

Feeding the Lord's Lambs

To become Zion people and represent the Savior, we must become like him. That is the burden of baptism, according to Alma.[273] The Jews who desired to enter into the new and everlasting covenant and make such a transformation asked John the Baptist, "What shall we do then? He answereth and saith unto them, He that hath two coats, let him impart to him that hath none; and he that hath meat, let him do likewise."[274] Change begins with that simple formula: Quit being selfish; step outside of yourself, and find someone to help.

Peter took seriously his giving freely of what he had been given. When a lame man begged alms of him, he replied, "Silver and gold have I none; but such as I have give I thee: In the name of Jesus Christ of Nazareth rise up and walk."[275] Peter had previously

---

266 Matthew 10:8.
267 2 Nephi 9:50; 26:25; Alma 1:20; Isaiah 55:1.
268 Matthew 5:13–14.
269 Obadiah 1:21.
270 Matthew 10:8.
271 John 20:21.
272 Luke 10:17.
273 Mosiah 18:8–10.
274 Luke 3:10–11.
275 Acts 3:6.

given away all his silver and gold in the service of the Savior, but that did not stop him from continuing to minister. Such as he had, he gave freely. He had evidently learned this lesson on two special occasions when he had participated in feeding five thousand and, later, four thousand of the Lord's lambs.[276] In each giving experience, Jesus had commanded Peter and the Apostles to gather up the fragments, which, to their amazement, filled their baskets. Peter must have learned at least two lessons on these occasions: (1) My job is to feed the Lord's sheep; Jesus' job is to bless my meager offering so that it becomes enough to feed many. (2) When it is my turn to eat, I will always have enough; in fact, I will have more than I started with. Jesus is my perfect Partner.

By giving away our goods will we end up with less? No. As Peter learned, we are not really giving away our goods or money; we are planting them with the hope of an abundant harvest. Our offering is an act of faith in the Lord of the Harvest—faith that he will keep his promise and provide us untold blessings. This is Zion's celestial law of prosperity, the law that guarantees incredible returns, even "an hundredfold."[277] Our covenantal relationship with the Lord ensures our safety while we are giving. This is also called the manna principle, which supplies our daily bread,[278] that which is sufficient for our needs. But to obtain these blessings requires that we put first things first: "Seek ye first the kingdom of God, and his righteousness; and all these things shall be added unto you."[279] Then we can be assured that while we are feeding the Lord's lambs, he will take care of us. That is the promise of security enjoyed by generous Zion people.

Choosing God's Marvelous Work over Babylon's Charms

To live in this manner calls for a new way of thinking. While Babylon shouts, "Gather about you property for your security," Zion counters with "Man shall not live by bread alone, but by every word that proceedeth out of the mouth of God."[280] Our choice should be clear. When we took upon us the new and everlasting covenant and thereafter received the blessings of the priesthood, we agreed to come out of Babylon and choose God over mammon forevermore.

Choosing God over mammon also suggests that we choose to do his marvelous work as stated in Doctrine and Covenants 4: "Now behold, a marvelous work is about to come forth among the children of men. Therefore, O ye that embark in the service of God, see that ye serve him with all your heart, might, mind and strength, that ye may stand blameless before God at the last day." By taking upon us the new and everlasting covenant and receiving the priesthood, we signal our desire to choose and serve God over mammon, therefore we are "called to the work."

The work we have to do can seem as daunting as Peter's feeding of the five thousand with five loaves and two fishes: "For behold the field is white already to harvest."

---

276 Mark 6:35–44; 8:1–9.
277 Luke 8:8; Matthew 19:29.
278 Matthew 6:11.
279 Matthew 6:33.
280 Matthew 4:4.

Only the Lord of the Harvest can increase our meager efforts to reap such a harvest. Nevertheless, if we will courageously thrust in our sickle with our might, the Lord assures us of success and salvation to our souls.

While Babylon would qualify her servants with gold, silver, intellect, and flattering words, Zion would qualify her servants with "faith, hope, charity and love, with an eye single to the glory of God," and, additionally, "faith, virtue, knowledge, temperance, patience, brotherly kindness, godliness, charity, humility, diligence." Admittedly, Zion is a far cry from Babylon. But if we will embrace such a Zion-like lifestyle, the Lord promises us the key to his abundance: "Ask, and ye shall receive; knock, and it shall be opened unto you."[281]

It is interesting to note that the humble servants of Zion are often referred to as the "weak things,"[282] whom the Lord makes strong through his grace.[283] As long as the Lord is with us, we need not shrink from sacrificing to bless his children.

Invoking the Law of Asking to Receive

Feeding the Lord's lambs with scanty resources is a monumental act of faith. Only with love and driven by a determined desire to serve and trust in the Lord can we accomplish such a feat. The act of donating the widow's mite to help another person is a clear indication that we have chosen God over mammon. The Lord helps us with the "law of asking."

The law of asking is this: To receive anything from the Lord, we must first ask in faith. For example, the law of asking provides that upon request we may receive permission to draw upon the Lord's vast resources to feed his sheep. When we do so, we invoke another law—the law of abundance, or the hundredfold law. The promise of this law is that when we give as the Lord directs, we will always have enough for ourselves. The laws of asking and abundance were the laws that Jesus taught Peter and the Apostles when they fed the crowds of five and four thousand.[284]

One reason we must ask to receive is that asking builds faith. In fact, asking is an act of faith: We recognize the sovereignty of God; we acknowledge that he has infinite resources that he is willing to give us; and we concede that he has the power to make and keep promises and to do anything for or give anything to us. Additionally, by asking, we acknowledge that we share with him a *child-and-parent* relationship that has power to evoke a response from him. In other words, when we, his children, ask him, our Parent, for help, he will respond because he loves us. Moreover, the law of asking assumes a covenantal relationship that makes us *partners* with the Lord in his work. Therefore, we ask our senior Partner to access the resources of our partnership to do the defined work of the partnership, which includes caring for the senior Partner's children.

Asking to receive is an eternal principle. In fact, our eternal progression depends upon

---

281 D&C 4:1–7.
282 D&C 1:19; 35:13; 124:1; 133:59.
283 Ether 12:27.
284 Mark 6:35–44; 8:1–9.

the law of asking. Throughout eternity, we will surely go to God countless times to ask permission to draw upon the resources from his higher kingdom so that we might grow and manage the affairs of our emerging kingdoms. We will always be asking to receive.

In this life, we receive the highest blessings *after* we have asked. For example, we *receive* the Holy Ghost;[285] husbands and wives *receive* each other as gifts from God; worthy men *receive* the priesthood and thus *receive* the Lord;[286] and, ultimately, by continuing to ask to receive, we obtain the promise: "he that *receiveth* my Father *receiveth* my Father's kingdom; therefore all that my Father hath shall be given unto him."[287] To receive any good thing from God, we must first ask.

This is the doctrine of Zion that provides for the abundant life that Jesus promised.[288] This is a reward for those who choose God over mammon.

Conclusion

To answer the question, Who shall enter? the Lord gave us the parable of the sheep and the goats. On the Day of Judgment, our placement on the Lord's right or left hand will be determined by whether or not we exerted a sincere effort to bless the lives of others. That the Lord would single out this criterion above all others should cause us to reflect on our attitude toward money and the poor.

This theme is constant with prophets. James said: "For what doth it profit a man if he gain the whole world . . . and he lose his own soul, and he himself be a castaway?"[289] He warned the selfish rich that their attitude directly impacted their ability to retain their wealth. Eventually, he added, a rich man's affluence will fade. James also chastised the Saints for coveting their own property. Can we really claim discipleship when we turn away from the poor? Do we really believe that our prayers alone will provide shelter and nourishment? When a coat is needed, do we offer warm words? When food is needed, do we extend sympathy? As mentioned, James explained that true religion consists of visiting the fatherless and widows in their affliction and keeping one's self unspotted from the world."[290] James condemned the businessman who underpays a poor man or enriches himself on a poor man's labor. Such practices are inconsistent with Zion.

Brigham Young concurred and preached against such behavior throughout his life. Remember, in his last speech he mourned that the people were shaking hands with the servants of the devil, who are the merchants and speculators of Babylon, instead of sanctifying themselves. He cried, "When I think upon this subject, I want the tongues of seven thunders to wake up the people."[291]

To help us choose God over mammon, the Lord gave us the law of consecration. Only through this law can we acquire true safety, security, and salvation. Consecration

---

285 John 20:22.
286 D&C 84:35.
287 D&C 84:38; emphasis added.
288 John 10:10.
289 JST, Luke 9:25.
290 James 1:27.
291 Young, *Journal of Discourses*, 18 305.

requires a new way of thinking. We must consider everything that we are and have as belonging to God; we must view ourselves as stewards rather than owners; we must agree to be accountable to God for the things he places in our safekeeping; and we must labor for the cause of Zion and not for selfish interests, including the accumulation of money.

Jacob gave us an easy formula to accomplish this transformation of the heart: "Think of your brethren like unto yourselves, and be familiar with all and free with your substance, that they may be rich like unto you." And later, "But before ye seek for riches, seek ye for the kingdom of God."[292] This formula orders a consecrated life and also binds us to Jesus Christ in a covenantal partnership. Now we share in the same work, and the Lord makes available to us his riches for the purposes that he and we deem necessary. By covenant, we have both the right and the obligation to ask the Lord for his help and resources to carry out the work of the partnership, which includes caring for the Lord's needy children.

We enhance our ability to ask for the Lord's help by seeking first to "obtain a hope in Christ."[293] Again, our having received this hope is reflected by our attitude toward money and our treatment of his needy children. Hence, if our motivation is to care for the Lord's children, we both hope in him and know him; but if we do not care for the Lord's children, we neither hope in him nor know him. To those who have received a hope in Christ, the Lord admonishes, "Freely ye have received, freely give."[294] The only way to arrive in the celestial kingdom is to "freely give" of what we have received. Therefore, to save us by giving us opportunities to give, Jesus sends us out to find and succor his wanting children as the Father sent him.[295] Our challenge is to mirror his example.

A disciple's life is to be marked by feeding the Lord's lambs. The mighty change of heart is facilitated when we follow this course. Early on, we discover that our resources pale in comparison to the amount of want. But because we have a hope in Christ, we know that we can present our meager offering to the Lord, move forward doing our best, and that the Lord will bless the offering so that it becomes enough to feed many. A promise is associated with feeding the Lord's lambs: When it is our turn to eat, we will always have enough; in fact, we will have more than we started with. Peter learned this lesson: We are not really giving away our goods or money; we are planting them with the expectation of an abundant harvest. This is Zion's celestial law of prosperity, the law that guarantees incredible returns, "an hundredfold."[296] It means that while we are feeding the Lord's lambs he keeps us safe and secure. This is the manna principle that guarantees our daily bread[297] and sufficient for our needs. But to be effective, the hundredfold law requires that we put first things first: "Seek ye first the kingdom of God, and his righteousness; and all these things shall be added unto you."[298] Assuredly, as we feed the Lord's lambs, the Lord will take care of us.

---

292 Jacob 2:18.
293 Jacob 2:19.
294 Matthew 10:8.
295 John 20:21.
296 Luke 8:8; Matthew 19:29.
297 Matthew 6:11.
298 Matthew 6:33.

Chapter 7 Who Shall Enter?

A marvelous partnership forms when we make the decision to stand on the Lord's right hand. We are given the law of asking to receive. This law allows us access to our Partner's resources, which he consecrates to the partnership. The way we gain access to those resources is by asking for permission. Our earthly experiments with the law of asking set the stage for our eternal progression. We will build our kingdoms by asking to draw upon the resources of the higher kingdom. And we will do so then for the same reason that we do so now: to bless lives.

Chapter 8
Becoming the Pure in Heart

To abandon the ways of Babylon and embrace the ways of Zion requires a transformation of the heart beyond our mortal strength. To become pure in heart requires the Lord's grace.

What does "pure in heart" mean? First, we must define these terms:
- To "purify" something means to extract from it all contaminants and impurities;
- To "sanctify" something means to change its purpose or make it holy.

For example, on Sunday the priests take common bread and bless and sanctify it, whereupon the bread becomes holy. Its purpose has changed; now it is an emblem of the Atonement. Likewise, when common people step into the waters of baptism and submit to that ordinance, all sin is extracted from them and they become new creatures—sanctified and holy. To maintain that newness of life and follow the transformation to its perfection, they are given the gift of the Holy Ghost and commanded to *receive* it; that is, they are to receive every sanctifying effort the Holy Ghost offers in order to purify and sanctify their hearts. Now they are on a transformational path that will fit them for the kingdom of God.

A common metaphor for this process is the making of steel. When raw ore is placed in a crucible and heated in a furnace, the substance becomes molten and the properties separate. At that point, a skilled metallurgist can divide out the impurities from the pure, refined iron. An alloying process ensues whereby the metallurgist carefully combines select elements in perfect proportion with the pure iron. The result is steel. But the process is not yet complete. For steel to become strong it must be subjected to reheating in the furnace followed by pounding to align the molecules into their strongest position. The process of being thrust into the furnace and beaten is repeated multiple times until the steel is finally free from impurities and the molecules align so that the steel cannot be broken. At some point, the metallurgist pours the steel into a mold to change its purpose, and as a final step he polishes it. The finished product is incredibly strong and beautiful and will remain so indefinitely.

In a similar manner, we are immersed in the crucibles attendant to the mortal experience, those fiery trials that heat, pound, mold, and polish us so that we might be purified, sanctified, and conformed to the image of God.[299] The Holy Ghost has every right to direct this process. We agreed to it when we entered into the new and everlasting covenant at baptism. John Taylor wrote: "I heard the Prophet Joseph say, in speaking to the Twelve on one occasion: 'You will have all kinds of trials to pass through. And it is quite as necessary for you to be tried as it was for Abraham and other men of God, and (said he) God will feel after you, and He will take hold of you and wrench your very heart strings, and if you cannot stand it you will not be fit for an inheritance in the Celestial Kingdom of God.'"[300]

To become pure in heart and free from the bonds of self-interest, covetousness, enmity, and lack of empathy, we agree to submit to the purifying effects of the Holy Ghost. If we allow him to do his work, he will purify our hearts so that he can thereafter sanctify us and form us into the image of God, who is selfless, generous, charitable, and empathetic. The Apostle Paul said it this way: "Therefore if any man be in Christ, he is a new creature."[301] In other words, the Holy Ghost purifies us (removes impurities) so that he can sanctify us (change our purpose). Zion people are covenant people who submit to the purifying crucible and emerge sanctified as new creatures with a new purpose; they are saviors in the similitude of *the* Savior, dedicated to and capable of doing the work of redemption. When King Benjamin's people understood the possibilities of this transformation, they shouted what we might call the anthem of the pure in heart: "And they all cried with one voice, saying: Yea, we believe all the words which thou hast spoken unto us; and also, we know of their surety and truth, because of the Spirit of the Lord Omnipotent, which has wrought a mighty change in us, or in our hearts, that we have no more disposition to do evil, but to do good continually."[302]

Such people have a new attitude toward money and keenly feel an obligation to bless the Lord's needy children. President Spencer W. Kimball taught: "Zion can be built up only among those who are the pure in heart, not a people torn by covetousness or greed, but a pure and selfless people. Not a people who are pure in appearance, rather a people who are pure in heart. Zion is to be in the world and not of the world, not dulled by a sense of carnal security, nor paralyzed by materialism. No, Zion is not things of the lower, but of the higher order, things that exalt the mind and sanctify the heart."[303]

Burning Out Impurities

What impurities will we allow the Holy Ghost to burn from us so that we can become pure in heart? For the purposes of this book, let us mention two:

---

299 Romans 8:29.
300 Taylor, *Journal of Discourses*, 24:197.
301 2 Corinthians 5:17.
302 Mosiah 5:2.
303 Kimball, *The Teachings of Spencer W. Kimball*, 363.

Chapter 8   Becoming the Pure in Heart

Persecution of the poor

The word *poor* broadly means those who are financially, emotionally, physically, or spiritually in need. The Saints who were trying to establish Zion in Missouri were chastised by the Lord for failing to care for "the poor and afflicted among them."[304] In effect, they were persecuting the poor by ignoring or inadequately tending to the needs of their less fortunate brothers and sisters.

The selfish rich have always been condemned by the Lord: "But wo unto the rich, who are rich as to the things of the world. For because they are rich they despise the poor, and they persecute the meek, and their hearts are upon their treasures; wherefore, their treasure is their God. And behold, their treasure shall perish with them also."[305] The reasons for condemnation should be clear. A rich man makes at least three fatal decisions so that he might become and remain wealthy:

1. He uses his time, talents, and resources for the purpose of building his personal wealth.
2. He determines that the wealth belongs to him and is not a stewardship that is to be used to do the Lord's work.
3. He decides to keep his most of his wealth instead of giving it to the poor. By assuming this attitude, he despises the poor, persecutes the meek, and chooses Babylon over Zion.

Inequality

The Lord expects his covenant children to strive for equality.

> And you are to be equal, or in other words, you are to have equal claims on the properties, for the benefit of managing the concerns of your stewardships, every man according to his wants and his needs, inasmuch as his wants are just—
>
> And all this for the benefit of the church of the living God, that every man may improve upon his talent, that every man may gain other talents, yea, even an hundred fold, to be cast into the Lord's storehouse, to become the common property of the whole church—
>
> Every man seeking the interest of his neighbor, and doing all things with an eye single to the glory of God.[306]

Nephi said, "Behold, the Lord esteemeth all flesh in one; he that is righteous is favored of God."[307] That is, equality governs God's dealings with his children; and righteous Zion people, who also espouse equality, qualify for God's greatest blessings. What are the "favored of God" supposed to do with the blessings they receive? Clearly, they are supposed

---

304   D&C 105:3.
305   2 Nephi 9:30.
306   D&C 82:17–19.
307   1 Nephi 17:35.

to do that which qualified them to be called "righteous" in the first place: use that which God have given them to bless God's wanting children.

If we desire to become "righteous" Zion-like people and "the favored of God," we cannot treat God's children differently than he does. Nephi rhetorically asked, "Behold, hath the Lord commanded any that they should not partake of his goodness?" Then, answering, "Behold I say unto you, Nay; but all men are privileged the one like unto the other, and none are forbidden. . . . He inviteth them all to come unto him and partake of his goodness; and he denieth none that come unto him, black and white, bond and free, male and female."[308] Can we expect to be favored of God if we harbor an attitude of inequality?

The Lord treats his children equally, but the same is not always true of us. We are not excused. The law of consecration we have promised to obey stipulates that we are under covenant to lift and help others. It is simply anti-Zion to exalt ourselves while others languish in various forms of poverty. The Apostle Paul wrote, "Let no man seek his own, but every man another's good."[309] What is the result of seeking equality? "And the Lord called his people Zion, *because* they were of one heart and one mind, and dwelt in righteousness; and there was no poor among them."[310] Pay particular attention to the word *because* in this scripture. *Because* pure-hearted people strive to care for and level up their neighbors, and to esteem all of God's children as themselves, Zion flourishes. Thus, Zion is established *because* individuals make a choice to behave in a Zion-like manner.[311] President Gordon B. Hinckley said, "If we are to build that Zion of which the prophets have spoken and of which the Lord has given mighty promise, we must set aside our consuming selfishness. We must rise above our love for comfort and ease, and in the very process of effort and struggle, even in our extremity, we shall become better acquainted with our God."[312]

To become acquainted with our God, we must submit to the Holy Ghost as he works to purify and sanctify our hearts and transform us into a Zion person. Such a person will have no more disposition to do evil; he will cease from mammon-worshiping, selfishness, and turning aside from inequality and poverty. He will be "filled with the love of God" and "not content with blessing his family alone," but will range "through the whole world, anxious to bless the whole human race."[313]

What are the promises for the pure in heart? The scriptures speak of the glorious promises:
- Zion will spread and become glorious and great. (D&C 97:18)
- Zion will be honored by the nations of the earth. (D&C 97:19)
- The Lord will be Zion's salvation. (D&C 97:20)
- Zion will rejoice. (D&C 97:21)
- Zion will escape the Lord's vengeance. (D&C 97:22–25)

---

308 2 Nephi 26:28, 33.
309 JST, 1 Corinthians 10:24.
310 Moses 7:18; emphasis added.
311 McMullin, *"Come to Zion! Come to Zion!"* 94.
312 Hinckley, *Teachings of Gordon B. Hinckley,* 725.
313 Smith, *History of the Church,* 4:227.

What must we do to enjoy these blessings? "Zion shall escape if she observe to do all things whatsoever I have commanded her."[314] We know what we have been commanded to do; we simply must do it.

Charitable Service Propels Zion

The *selfishness* of Babylon must give way to the *selflessness* of Zion in order that Zion-like attributes might be established in a covenant person. The spirit of charitable service cannot be mandated; that spirit is a condition of the heart that motivates a person to care for and lift another. No wonder, then, that Zion is described as having no poverty of any kind.

Zion people can neither tolerate lack nor endure poverty among them. They attack misery wherever they find it. They abolish every form of scarcity, hurt, impairment, injustice, illness, and sorrow. They think of their brethren like unto themselves, and they are familiar with all and free with their substance, that others might be rich like unto themselves.[315] Therefore, they insist on having "all things common among them; therefore there [are] not rich and poor, bond and free, but they [are] all made free, and partakers of the heavenly gift." Consequently, there never could be a happier people.[316]

Zion people "love one another and serve one another." They "succor those that stand in need of [their] succor," and they "administer of [their] substance unto him that standeth in need." They "will not suffer that the beggar [put] up his petition to [them] in vain, and turn him out to perish."[317] Zion people "bear one another's burdens, that they may be light," and they "are willing to mourn with those that mourn; yea, and comfort those that stand in need of comfort."[318]

King Benjamin pointed out that some blessings can only flow from charitable service. For example, as we have mentioned, charitable service allows us to retain "a remission of [our] sins from day to day, that [we] may walk guiltless before God." Therefore, King Benjamin exhorted us, "I would that ye should impart of your substance to the poor, every man according to that which he hath, such as feeding the hungry, clothing the naked, visiting the sick and administering to their relief, both spiritually and temporally, according to their wants."[319] And of course, the poignant statement regarding service: "When ye are in the service of your fellow beings ye are only in the service of your God."[320]

In Doctrine and Covenants 42, the "law of the Church," we read the following verse: "For inasmuch as ye do it unto the least of these, ye do it unto me."[321] The implication is intriguing. Because God lacks for nothing and is in no need of our service to him,

---

314   D&C 97:25.
315   Jacob 2:17.
316   4 Nephi 1:3, 16.
317   Mosiah 4:15–16.
318   Mosiah 18:8–9.
319   Mosiah 4:26.
320   Mosiah 2:17.
321   D&C 42:38.

he passes on our desire to serve *him* to his children, who *do* need our help. As we transfer our service from him to his children, he does not forget our expression of love for him. He counts our service to his children as service to him, and he rewards us accordingly.

Now comes an interesting gospel phenomenon. God accepts our service as would a debtor, and, of course, God can be in debt to no one. Therefore, to arrest any hint of debt or imbalance in the checks and balances of heaven, God quickly erases any claim by immediately blessing us in excess of our service: "He doth immediately bless [us]; and therefore he hath paid [us]. And [we] are still indebted unto him, and are, and will be, forever and ever."[322] President Ezra Taft Benson taught, "Just as when one loses his life to God he really finds the abundant life; so also, when one sacrifices all to God, then God in return shares all that he has with him. Try as you may, you cannot put the Lord in your debt—for every time you try to do his will he simply pours out more blessings upon you. Sometimes the blessings may seem to you to be a little slow in coming; perhaps this tests your faith, but come they will and abundantly."[323]

On the subject of service alone, we live forever in the Lord's debt. We are always awarded more blessings than we expend in service, and for that reason we are gratefully "unprofitable servants."[324]

Grace *to* Grace by Grace *for* Grace

It is upon the principle of giving charitable service that we progress toward perfection. According to John the Baptist's testimony, Jesus progressed in this manner. John employed the word *grace* to explain this principle of progression: "And I, John, saw that he received not of the fulness at first, but received grace *for* grace. And he received not of the fulness at first, but continued from grace *to* grace, until he received a fulness."[325] In other words, Jesus grew in grace (light, truth, power, and perfection) by giving grace (service and blessings to others). Likewise, we progress from one grace to another by giving grace to others.

Progressing grace to grace by giving grace for grace!
Commenting, the Lord states: "For if you keep my commandments you shall receive of his fulness, and be glorified in me as I am in the Father; therefore, I say unto you, you shall receive grace *for* grace."[326]

Lacking for Nothing

The above definitions of grace are in addition to the common definition: the Lord's help, strength, or enabling power.[327] Jesus' grace is ever evident in the unequalled service he proffers. Here is a formula for receiving his help or grace: We come unto Christ in humility and

---

322 Mosiah 2:24.
323 Ezra Taft Benson, *BYU Speeches of the Year 1974* [1975], 311.
324 Mosiah 2:21.
325 D&C 93:12–13; emphasis added.
326 D&C 93:20; emphasis added.
327 Bible Dictionary, "Grace," 697.

Chapter 8   Becoming the Pure in Heart

faith, having done all we can do,[328] and then he makes up the difference. Consequently, we will never lack while we charitably serve the Lord's children. In this principle, we again hear overtones of Zion: *no lack* and *divine help* to accomplish the Lord's work.

Pertaining to the concept of *no lack*, we recall again the Lord's abundant grace to the wandering Israelites as recorded by the prophet Nehemiah:

> This is thy God that brought thee up out of Egypt, and had wrought great provocations;
>
> Yet thou in thy manifold mercies *forsookest them not* in the wilderness: the pillar of the *cloud departed not* from them by day, to lead them in the way; *neither the pillar of fire* by night, to shew them light, and the way wherein they should go.
>
> Thou gavest also thy good spirit to *instruct them,* and withheldest not thy *manna* from their mouth, and gavest them *water* for their thirst.
>
> *Yea, forty years didst thou sustain them* in the wilderness, [so that] they *lacked nothing*; their *clothes waxed not old, and their feet swelled not.*[329]

The Lord never forsook them. He was with them both day and night. He constantly instructed them. He provided manna and water to sustain them. For four decades of wandering, they lacked nothing! Amazingly, neither their clothing nor their shoes wore out. The Israelites experienced the Lord's grace.

We see these two elements of grace—no lack and divine help—in an incident in the Savior's life. Just before Jesus entered Gethsemane, he reminded his Apostles of their early missions when he had purposely placed them in a condition of lack by sending them out with neither purse nor scrip. He had expected them to give grace (charitable service) by means of his grace, that is, by relying completely on him and on nothing else. Now he asked them, "When I sent you without purse, and scrip, and shoes, lacked ye any thing? And they said, Nothing."[330]

They needed to internalize this lesson in order to continue giving service throughout their lives. From that experience of intentional privation, they had learned that what had initially appeared to be a condition of lack was not one after all; the Lord had provided his divine help (grace) to sustain them in proportion to the service (grace) they proffered to the people.

The situation had been carefully orchestrated by the Lord to teach them to trust him while they served. The Apostles needed to learn that the Lord could, through his grace, multiply the effects of their service and produce incredible blessings of sustenance for the people (think of feeding the five thousand and the four thousand), and they also needed to learn that by serving they would never lack. To accomplish their future missions, the Apostles needed firsthand experience to see if the Lord would be true to his promise. Without his grace, they could neither survive nor gain the necessary power to fulfill their callings.

---

328   2 Nephi 25:23: "for we know that it is by grace that we are saved [helped], after all we can do."
329   Nehemiah 9:18–21; emphasis added.
330   Luke 22:35.

Similarly, we need experience with the Lord and the principles that govern charitable service. For example, we need to internalize the fact that the Lord's way of resolving our lack is by our giving charitable service: as we give grace, we receive grace. That is the formula. When we experience a lack of something, we can go to the Lord and he will take care of us in proportion to how we take care of his children.

If Any of You Lack

James, the Lord's brother, offered a solution for those of us who lack anything: "If any of you lack wisdom, let him ask of God, that giveth to all men liberally, and upbraideth not, and it shall be given him."[331] Personalized, this scripture could read: "If I lack *anything*, I can ask of God, who will give to me *abundantly*, and he will never chastise me for having asked for his help. Instead, he will help me." This is the promise of grace!

Grace allows our lack to be swallowed up in Christ's abundance. We come unto him in humility and faith, we do all we can do, which must include offering charitable service, and then we have the assurance that he will make up the difference. By living this principle, we never need lack for anything. Our lack might include any physical, emotional, or spiritual deficit. Also, we might experience lack when we minister to the Lord's children. In any of these situations, when we experience lack and attempt to remedy the situation, we almost certainly will come up short; that is the condition of mortality. But because we have a covenant relationship with the Lord, we can "ask of God" to draw upon his resources and power, and he promises to give to us liberally. If we employ this principle and promise as we minister to his children, neither they nor we will ever lack.

On two remarkable occasions, the Apostles experienced the Lord's grace when they came up short in attempting to minister to people who lacked something. These occasions were when Jesus fed the five thousand and later the four thousand.[332] In each case, hungry people were in immediate need of help, and the Apostles could manage only scant resources. Jesus' response was identical in both cases: Bring all that you have or your best effort to me; I will bless it; and you will have enough to feed the people until they are filled. Then, when it is your turn to eat, you will also have enough. In fact, you will have more than you started with. Your responsibility is to feed my sheep, not to worry about having enough. Just go forth and minister, and I will multiply your efforts so that you never lack.

When we go to the Savior for his grace, we will not encounter someone who is lacking in grace. The Savior is *full* of grace.[333] We can also obtain a fullness of grace the same way the Savior did: by extending grace to others. We grow in our capacity to give grace by covenanting to consecrate all that we are and have, taking our best offering to the Lord for his blessing, then going forth in faith to feed the Lord's sheep. In return, he multiplies our efforts and resources, and thus provides us more grace to give away. It is a formula that applies to other gospel principles: "Blessed are the merciful: for they shall obtain mercy."[334] We could say, "Blessed are those who extend grace, for they shall obtain more grace."

---

331   James 1:5; emphasis added.
332   Mark 6:35–44; 1–9.
333   D&C 93:11.
334   Matthew 5:7.

Chapter 8   Becoming the Pure in Heart

For instance, if we were given a kernel of corn and ate it, the kernel would be gone forever. But if we were to plant the kernel and nourish it, the kernel would soon grow into a stalk with several ears and many kernels. Then, if we were to eat just a few of the kernels and plant the rest, the kernels would become a field of corn and a huge harvest. And it all began with a single kernel!

As we humbly seek and receive the Lord's grace, then extend that grace to others, the Lord will give us more grace, and the cycle of receiving and giving will continue until we are filled with grace. If we do not stop the cycle by hoarding the Lord's blessings, we will grow from grace to grace by giving grace for the grace until we are perfected by grace. Elder Boyd K. Packer said, "As you give what you have, there is a replacement, with increase!"[335] Of charitable service, President Gordon B. Hinckley promised that we cannot extend merciful blessings to God's children and not experience a harvest of merciful blessings in return.[336] We can readily see how giving and receiving grace provides for the condition of no poor among us.

---

[335]   Packer, "The Candle of the Lord," 54–55.
[336]   Hinckley, "Blessed Are the Merciful," 68.

Chapter 9
Charity—The Lifeblood of Zion

"Someone has wisely stated that hate is not the opposite of love. Apathy is."[337] President Joseph F. Smith taught, "It has been said by one, that 'we may give without loving, but we cannot love without giving.'"[338]

Only people who live the law of consecration can eradicate poverty from the earth. While improvements in the condition of man can be achieved by employing other methods, the law of consecration is and always has been the ultimate way by which the complete population of the poor is permanently rescued and elevated. How is this possible? Because, beyond all other considerations, the law or covenant of consecration is a law of love.

James the Lord's brother called love—the fuel that drives the engine of consecration—the royal law.[339] Jesus stated the law this way: "Thou shalt love the Lord thy God with all thy heart, and with all thy soul, and with all thy mind. This is the first and great commandment. And the second is like unto it, Thou shalt love thy neighbour as thyself." Thus, the royal law stands preeminent above all other laws; it is "the first and great commandment," and according to Jesus, upon this law "hang all the law and the prophets."[340] When all is said and done, we consecrate ourselves and all that we have and are because we love God and his children.

The quality of love that motivates us to sacrifice to lift and save others is called charity. "Charity *never* faileth," Moroni declared. If charity can never fail, Zion can never fail, because Zion is built upon charity, "the greatest of all," the celestial quality of love that "endureth forever."[341] Charity is the quintessential virtue, "the end of the commandment,"[342] the power that invigorates and propels the law of consecration and

---
337 Marvin J. Ashton, "Be a Quality Person," 64.
338 *Teachings of Presidents of the Church: Joseph F. Smith*, 192.
339 James 2:8.
340 Matthew 22:36–40.
341 Moroni 7:46–47; emphasis added.
342 1 Timothy 1:5.

makes way for the establishment of Zion. All things of this telestial world are programmed to fail. But when chaos abounds, men disappoint, health retreats, crime rots communities, employment disappears, finances plunge, bankruptcy threatens, relationships fold, and Babylon collapses under the weight of its own depravity, charity and all things built upon it stands firm and never fails!

Charity Defines Discipleship

Charity transforms a natural man into a sanctified Saint—a *Zion* person—someone who by nature seeks to comfort the downtrodden, redeem the oppressed, heal the sick and the afflicted, and console the brokenhearted.

Moroni calls charity "the pure love of Christ,"[343] the defining characteristic of Jesus Christ, and therefore the defining characteristic of his people. When people who are filled with charity encounter need, they confront it, as did their Master. They will not allow lack and suffering to exist in their presence. They are willing to consecrate all that they are and have to remedy the sufferings of the underprivileged. It is easy to see why the law of consecration, the foundational law of Zion, has little need to be legislated; consecration is built upon charity and is therefore a condition of the heart.

Keeping and Feeding—The Two Tests of Charity

Jesus gave us two tests of charity:
1. "If ye love me, *keep* my commandments."[344]
2. "If ye love me *feed* my sheep."[345]

Clearly, charity—pure, Christlike love—is defined by *action*. For example, to declare love to one's spouse is meaningless unless that declaration is backed by keeping one's vows and nourishing the relationship with acts of love and service: *keeping* and *feeding*. The spouse who professes love but is disloyal is a liar; the spouse who proclaims love but who is selfish and nonsacrificing is a hypocrite. There is no charity here.

Conversely, charity keeps its vows and seeks opportunities to nourish. Elder Marvin J. Ashton taught that the *keeping* element of charity centers on keeping the first and great commandment,[346] the royal law, which is a foundational law of Zion: "Thou shalt love the Lord thy God with all thy heart, and with all thy soul, and with all thy mind. . . . Thou shalt love thy neighbour as thyself."[347]

In keeping and feeding we stand proxy for the Savior and do as he would do if he were present. Therefore, to the extent that we keep the Lord's commandments, we show our love for him, and to the proportion that we feed the Lord's sheep, we keep the first and great commandment. This is the royal law of Zion.

---

343 Moroni 7:47.
344 John 14:15; emphasis added.
345 Paraphrased from John 21:16; emphasis added.
346 Ashton, "Love Takes Time," 108.
347 Matthew 22:36–40.

Charity—The Lifeblood of Zion

Most certainly, charity is love in action, and that action always involves sacrifice. Without the action of charitable sacrifice, Zion could not be established in the life of an individual, a marriage, a family, or in a priesthood society. It is by consecrated sacrifice that we keep the commandments and hold true to our covenants.[348] It is by sacrifice that we feed the Lord's sheep. Hence, it is by consecrated sacrifice that we truly love God and his children. Helping, giving, and loving always require selfless sacrifice. It is sacrifice, we sing, that "brings forth the blessings of heaven."[349]

Charitable service creates a positive imbalance that demands correcting. This is the *hundredfold* law,[350] which President Thomas S. Monson described this way: "It is an immutable law that the more you give away, the more you receive." Then, referencing a quote attributed to Winston Churchill, he said, "'You make a living by what you get, but you make a life by what you give.'"[351] The Lord always rewards us with more than we sacrifice.

This "immutable law"—the hundredfold law—drives Zion's cycle of abundance and makes Zion people exceedingly prosperous.[352] Of course, this law runs contrary to Babylon's practices of grabbing, competing, and hoarding. The hundredfold law, which flows from the law of consecration, stipulates that if we will give what we have and are, the Lord will reward us beyond our sacrifice: "an hundredfold."

As long as we do not stop the cycle abundance by keeping what we receive, we will become *vessels of help*. Through us the Lord will pour down blessings to his needy children, and in the process our prosperity will increase until it approaches the infinite abundance of the kingdom of heaven. This is why charity is the lifeblood of Zion, and consecrated sacrifice is the principle that propels Zion's prosperity.

When charity is planted in the hearts of a few, it acts as leaven "until the whole [of humanity is] leavened."[353] Others learn how to extend charity because we loved them first,[354] and soon Zion is anchored on the earth by charity. Joseph Smith said, "A man filled with the love of God is not content with blessing his family alone, but ranges through the whole world, anxious to bless the whole human race."[355]

Charity Is Defined by Service

President Hinckley called love "the lodestar of life." Citing the Savior's reference to the Final Judgment, President Hinckley reminded us that Jesus will say to those on his right hand that they shall inherit his kingdom because they effectively "fed, clothed, and visited Him" by blessing his children.

---

348 D&C 97:8.
349 Phelps, "Praise to the Man," *Hymns*, no. 27.
350 Genesis 26:12; 2 Samuel 24:3; Matthew 13:8–23; 19:29; Mark 10:30; Luke 8:8; D&C 98:25; 132:55.
351 Monson, "In Quest of the Abundant Life," 2.
352 4 Nephi 1:7.
353 Matthew 13:33; Luke 13:21.
354 1 John 4:19.
355 Smith, *History of the Church*, 4:227.

President Hinckley wrote: "One of the greatest challenges we face in our hurried, self-centered lives is to follow this counsel of the Master, to take the time and make the effort to care for others, to develop and exercise the one quality that would enable us to change the lives of others—what the scriptures call charity. . . . Best defined, charity is that pure love exemplified by Jesus Christ. It embraces kindness, a reaching out to lift and help, the sharing of one's bread, if need be."[356]

Zion people become angels to the poor and afflicted. We are taught that there are "angels round about [us], to bear [us] up."[357] As much as angels are instruments in the Lord's hands to sustain and help us to carry our heavy burdens, so we, by our charitable service, become angels to God's children and instruments in the Lord's hands to steady the weak and to heft their weighty load.[358] President Kimball said, "God does notice us, and he watches over us. But it is usually through another person that he meets our needs. Therefore, it is vital that we serve each other in the kingdom."[359]

Charitable Service Saves and Exalts

It is a gospel verity that charity saves the lives of both the giver and the receiver. Sometimes charity is a handout, but it is always a hand up. Either way, salvation comes to our souls when we lift another and give of ourselves and our means for the purest and highest of motivations—*love*.

We note with interest that it was only when the people of Limhi repented, unified, and began to practice a form of consecration to care for the widows and orphans that they were delivered from bondage.[360]

Charitable Service Protects the Giver

Cain first stated the motto of Babylon in the form of a question: "Am I my brother's keeper?"[361] That self-centered statement became the foundation of the anti-Christ doctrine advanced by others, including Korihor.[362] The entire anti-Christ philosophy is also anti-Zion. It is faithless, immoral, destructive, and selfish. In no way does it draw us to Christ, encourage us to depend on him, shelter us from the consequences of sin, provide for the poor, or make us our brother's keeper.

To Cain's selfish motto—"Am I my brother's keeper?"—the Lord countered with the doctrine of Zion that carries promises: "Blessed is he that considereth the poor: the Lord will deliver him in time of trouble. The Lord will preserve him, and keep him alive; and he shall be blessed upon the earth: and thou wilt not deliver him unto the will of his enemies. The Lord will strengthen him."[363]

---

356 Hinckley, *Standing for Something*, 6.
357 D&C 84:88.
358 Tanner, "All Things Shall Work Together for Your Good," 104.
359 Kimball, *The Teachings of Spencer W. Kimball*, 252.
360 Mosiah 21:16–18.
361 Genesis 4:9.
362 Alma 30:12–28.
363 Psalm 41:1–2.

Charity is the mantra of Zion. President Heber J. Grant said, "Make a motto in life: always try and assist someone else to carry his burden."[364] Charity is also the source of safety for Zion people. The prophet of Ecclesiastes stated that when we plant seeds of service to bless God's children, we also plant the seeds of salvation for our own souls. When evil attempts to overwhelm us, when terrifying storms gather above us, when temptations fell trees all about us, charity will protect us—"there [our safety] shall be." The prophet said we do not understand how God transforms our charitable acts into cloaks of safety; we only know that it happens. Therefore, we are to go about liberally planting the seeds of charitable service and enjoy the safety: "In the morning sow thy seed, and in the evening withhold not thine hand." We do not know which seeds of charity will take root or how they might prosper.[365] We only know that by sowing and nourishing charitable acts, many people will be blessed by our actions, and in the process we will be kept safe. Charity, then, is the source of safety and security for Zion people.

Charitable Service Prospers the Giver

The promise of charitable service is that of an abundant return. President Marion G. Romney taught the following truth: "You cannot give yourself poor in this work; you can only give yourself rich."[366] His statement is a confirmation of the ancient prophet's teaching: "Cast thy bread upon the waters: for thou shalt find it after many days."[367]

This principle suggests both a boomerang effect and a germination period. Bread that is cast upon the water will most certainly float back to land on the tide or a current; just so, our charitable actions will always return to bless us. Additionally, the seed that makes the bread that is cast upon the water will eventually find land, set down roots, sprout, and grow; similarly, charitable acts carry the potential of life within them. Charitable acts may take time to find ground and take root, but eventually those charitable acts will become a beautiful and fruitful tree. As President Romney promised, we cannot become impoverished by casting the seeds of charity upon the water, and we cannot consecrate ourselves poor.

Abundance flows to Zion people as they manifest charity. It is the *grace-for-grace* principle that we discussed. When they receive a blessing from the Lord, they look for ways to share that blessing with others. By so giving, they grow *from* grace (light, truth, power, and perfection) *to* grace (more light, truth, power, and perfection). Like Jesus, we progress incrementally toward a fullness of glory by keeping the commandments and giving charitable service.

Again we see the hundredfold principle in giving charitable acts.[368] Therefore, when we receive the seed of *grace* from God or from a charitable person, we should plant that seed, rather than hoard it, by giving the seed of charity to someone else. The replanting

---

364 Grant, *Teachings of Presidents of the Church: Heber J. Grant*, 139.
365 Ecclesiastes 11:2–6.
366 Romney, "Welfare Services: The Savior's Program," 92.
367 Ecclesiastes 11:1.
368 Matthew 19:29; Mark 10:30.

of the seed of charity will urge a plant to grow, which contains many seeds. Then if we will plant again, we will one day realize a marvelous harvest. Thus, ever repeating the cycle of planting and harvesting charity constitutes the mystery of Zion people's prosperity. It is the Zion principle of *giving then receiving* that results in abundant increase.[369]

Therefore, we need not worry about what will become of us if we consecrate our goods to bless others. Do we really believe that the Lord would allow us to end up with less? President Kimball refuted the idea and challenged our faith: "What are we to fear when the Lord is with us? Can we not take the Lord at his word and exercise a particle of faith in him? Our assignment is affirmative: to forsake the things of the world as ends in themselves; to leave off idolatry and press forward in faith; to carry the gospel to our enemies, that they might no longer be our enemies. We must leave off the worship of modern-day idols and a reliance on the 'arm of flesh,' for the Lord has said to all the world in our day, 'I will not spare any that remain in Babylon.'"[370]

Remember, prosperity, safety, and security can only found in extending charity. It is by consecrating our lives, property, time, and talents for the building up of God's kingdom that we prepare the way for the establishment of Zion.

Charity Is an Absolute

Few scriptural absolutes are as stunning as those describing charity:
- "If ye have not charity, ye are nothing."
- "Charity never faileth."
- "Charity . . . is the greatest of all."
- "Charity . . . endureth forever."[371]

In a world where everything fails, only those things that are built upon the foundation of charity will not fail. When we seek charity first, as exemplified by our seeking the kingdom of God and his righteousness first, we are promised that all else will fall into place and be added unto us.[372] Moreover, we are promised that because of charity, the blessings of the priesthood will flow to us forever without compulsory means.[373]

Charity Is a Gift—The Greatest Gift

Despite our best efforts, we never will obtain charity or know its power in our lives unless we seek charity in prayer. Charity is a spiritual gift that must be sought. Like the principle that states we are saved by grace only after all we can do,[374] we receive charity as a gift from the Holy Ghost only after we do all we can to obtain it. Therefore, because salvation is impossible without charity and because charity is delivered to us as a gift of the Holy Ghost, Mormon pleads with us to "pray unto the Father with all the energy of

---

369 Packer, "The Candle of the Lord," 54–55.
370 Kimball, *The Teachings of Spencer W. Kimball,* 417, quoting D&C 64:24.
371 Moroni 7:46–47.
372 3 Nephi 13:33.
373 D&C 121:46.
374 2 Nephi 25:23.

heart, that ye may be filled with this love, which he hath bestowed upon all who are true followers of his Son, Jesus Christ."

When charity finally enters our souls, Mormon continues, this love becomes the vehicle to make of us "sons of God." That is, charity has the power to make us "like him." Ultimately, it is only upon the principle of charity that we can become "as he is." This is our "hope, that we [through our charitable acts] may be purified even as he is pure."[375] This is the principal aim and the ultimate destination of the royal law, the celestial law of love upon which a Zion life is built.

Charity, as described in Matthew 22:37–39, is the quality of love that propels Zion's foundational law of consecration and fulfills the first and second commandments: "Thou shalt love the Lord thy God with all thy heart, and with all thy soul, and with all thy mind. This is the first and great commandment. And the second is like unto it, Thou shalt love thy neighbour as thyself." We consecrate because we love, and when charity motivates all we do, we become Zion and there are no poor among us.

---

[375] Moroni 7:48.

Chapter 10
Without Charity We Are Nothing

The truest form of love is reciprocal. The law of the Church (D&C 42) makes this statement: "Thou shalt live together in love."[376] Simply said, we must be willing to love God and his children, and in turn we must be willing to receive love from them. Love is the essence of the "the first and great commandment;"[377] it is the "royal law"[378] from which all other laws originate and from which power is derived. Without this love—*charity*—we are nothing.

If we were limited to use only one word to define Zion, that word would be *love*; likewise, if we were limited to use only one word to describe the power of Zion, it would be *love*. Significantly, of all the words the Apostle John could have used to portray God, he chose *love*.[379] President Gordon B. Hinckley wrote: "This principle of love is the basic essence of the gospel of Jesus Christ. Without love of God and love of neighbor there is little else to commend the gospel to us as a way of life."[380]

For the pure purpose of love we live the law of Zion, and that is done primarily by caring for the poor and the sick "with all tenderness."[381] Elder John A. Widtsoe taught: "The full and essential nature of love we may not understand. But there are tests by which it may be recognized. Love is always founded in truth. . . . Love is a positive active force. It helps the loved one. If there is need, love tries to supply it. If there is weakness, love supplants it with strength. . . . Love that does not help is a faked or transient love. Good as these tests are, there is a greater one. True love sacrifices for the loved one. . . . That is the final test. Christ gave of Himself, gave His life, for us, and thereby proclaimed the reality of his love for his mortal brethren and sisters."[382]

---

376 D&C 42:45.
377 Matthew 22:36–40.
378 James 2:8.
379 1 John 4:8.
380 Hinckley, *Faith: The Essence of True Religion*, 49.
381 D&C 42:43.
382 Widtsoe, *An Understandable Religion*, 72.

Charity—The Pure Love of Christ

Reciprocal love is the grand key of happiness and glory. Reciprocal love is true love, unconditional love, or *charity*. This quality of love encompasses the two laws upon which hang all the law and the prophets—(1) "Thou shalt love the Lord thy God with all thy heart, with all thy might, mind, and strength; and in the name of Jesus Christ thou shalt serve him," and (2) "Thou shalt love thy neighbor as thyself."[383]

Charity, then, not the outward rites of the law of Moses, is the driving force of Jesus' higher gospel law. Charity is the "new commandment"[384] Jesus attached to the higher law—*new* because it replaced the gospel motivation linked to the old law of rites and performances with the gospel motivation centered on the condition of the heart. Charity refers more to what we *do* than what we *feel*. There is a vast difference between being *loving* and feeling *in love*. Charity is saving love; charity lifts and rescues; charity forgives from enormous distances. As we experience the giving and receiving of charity, we eventually discover that we cannot escape its loving embrace: "charity endureth forever."[385]

Reciprocal love—freely given and freely received love—should be our primary focus if we desire to be disciples of Jesus Christ. Upon no other principle can the law of consecration be lived or Zion established. Loving God and loving our neighbor with the same attention and diligence that we show love to ourselves is the essence of the foundational law of the Church, which is the identical law that founds the celestial kingdom and Zion: the law of consecration.

We have two witnesses—Paul and Mormon—whose testimonies anchor the principles of Zion-like charity in our souls:

- Charity suffers long (endures hardship in faith or endures in faith with someone during his/her hardship)
- Charity is kind
- Charity does not envy
- Charity is not vaunted up (does not boast)
- Charity is not puffed up (is not proud)
- Charity does not behave unseemly (act inappropriately)
- Charity seeks not her own (is not selfish)
- Charity is not easily provoked (keeps anger under control)
- Charity thinks no evil (tries to focus on the good)
- Charity does not rejoice in iniquity but rejoices in the truth (does not enjoy the evil things of the fallen world but rather the true things of God)
- Charity bears all things (bears up under the weight of problems)
- Charity believes all things (recognizes and follows truth)
- Charity hopes all things (knows that ultimately God is in charge)
- Charity endures all things (is willing to make the necessary sacrifices in order to win the prize).[386]

---

383 Matthew 22:40.
384 John 13:34.
385 Moroni 7:47.
386 1 Corinthians 13:4–8; commentary added; see also Moroni 7:45.

Without charity, Paul said, we are nothing. Although we might accomplish many good works, speak with the tongue of angels, enjoy incredible spiritual gifts, bestow all our goods to feed the poor, and give our lives as martyrs, if we have not charity our good deeds profit us nothing.[387] In other words, we might go through the motions of Christian living, but without charity our actions are hollow, and Zion will remain a distant ideal.

The lesser law of Moses was constructed on the bedrock of rites and performances, but the higher law of Jesus Christ is built on the condition of the heart. We succor God's needy children because we are motivated by love. Consequently, Mormon noted, "charity never faileth." This "pure love of Christ" endures forever and transcends a world in which everything is programmed to fail. Therefore, charity stands above every other virtue and "is the greatest of all."[388] Without cultivating the highest virtue—charity—we can never expect to be able to live the highest of gospel laws—consecration. And if we cannot ascend to that level, we are nothing.

Charity Emerges from Faith and Hope

Having listed the characteristics of charity, Paul submitted a roadmap to achieve this quality of love: "And now abideth faith, hope, charity, these three; but the greatest of these is charity."[389] Faith, hope, charity—Christianity's quintessential virtues.

Mormon expanded our understanding by explaining how having hope helps us to attain these other virtues: "And again, my beloved brethren, I would speak unto you concerning hope. How is it that ye can attain unto faith, save ye shall have hope? . . . Wherefore, if a man have faith he must needs have hope."[390] The fact that Mormon listed hope twice is significant. Hoping that a principle is true leads us to experiment or act upon the principle. When we notice a desirable result from our action, hope increases. Combined, hope and faith lead to charity. By design, the action of faith is repentance, reconciliation with God, and a growing desire to serve him and his children.

Alma added *desire* to the process of developing charity. He said hearing the word of God starts the process. When we hear the word of God, we desire to know more; we desire to see if the principle will work in our lives; we begin to hunger and thirst to know more. Alma explained that the word of God is structured so that once it is planted in the soul, it will stir desire and hope: "And now my beloved brethren, as ye have *desired* to know of me what ye shall do."[391] That is, upon hearing the word, we begin to experience hunger pangs for light and truth—we are filled with desire. At some point, desire and hope motivate us to take a spiritual risk and to experiment with the word of God. By faith we summon courage to try an "experiment" with the word; we want to see if the desired result actually happens. The action of experimenting is not only an act of faith, but it is also a manifestation of our agency; it is the action of our hope. The moment that

---

387 1 Corinthians 13:1–3.
388 Moroni 7:46–47.
389 1 Corinthians 13:13.
390 Moroni 7:40, 42.
391 Alma 32:24; emphasis added.

action is applied to hope it becomes faith; and Alma made it clear that even a "particle of faith"—the smallest of actions—has power to take root in our souls.

At that point something marvelous begins to happen. Beyond our consciousness, a stirring occurs beneath the surface; roots start to extend from the hull of the seed and an independent life has begun. If we will hang on and tend the spot of ground where the seed has been planted, the new life will soon burst into open view. One day a tender plant will erupt through the soil; it will have changed from a seed of hope to a seedling of faith like a caterpillar transforms into a butterfly. As the seedling matures with measurable "swelling motions,"[392] we start to recognize that our experiment with the seed of faith was "good." Alma said, "It beginneth to enlarge my soul."

The evidence of growth leads us to hope more—hope is *confirmable expectation.* That is, we allow ourselves to imagine the bounteous harvest that will one day come from the seed; more importantly, we *expect* an abundant harvest. For our purposes, the product of the harvest is charity. Charity is always a product of hope and faith.

Alma explained that the trueness of the seed is confirmed by four tests:
1. We feel something positive stirring within us.
2. We feel invigorated, and we are motivated to become a better person.
3. The idea corresponds with, builds upon, and clarifies other ideas that we have had, and now it sparks new ideas.
4. The idea feels so good that we want to keep seeking after it to follow it to its perfect conclusion.

The "seed," or the word of God, is expansive, enlightening, and delicious. It increases faith; it is discernible; it is clearly good. If we do not neglect or reject it, the seed will grow into a tree that bears the beautiful fruit of charity, the love of God,[393] "which is most precious, which is sweet above all that is sweet, and which it white, yea, and pure above all that is pure."[394]

Charity Transforms the Heart

What does all this mean? Charity is a function of faith. We live in Babylon and see impoverished souls languishing in misery. We yearn to do something but lack information and faith. Then we hear the word of God telling us that if we sacrifice to reduce the misery, we will be blessed with abundance, safety, and security. The seed of hope burrows into our souls and takes root. We plant the seed by hope, and we nourish it by faith. Because the word, or seed, carries the genotype of divinity, it will transform its host into the image of God. With every swelling motion toward maturity, the word will change our heart until it resembles the heart of Jesus Christ. The more the seed of faith grows, the more we talk, act, serve, and love like the Savior. We are filled with charity, and, more importantly, we *become* charity, the "pure love of Christ."[395] As much as "God is love,"[396]

---

392 Alma 32:28.
393 1 Nephi 11:22.
394 Alma 32:26–43.
395 Moroni 7:47.
396 1 John 4:8.

so we become "this love."[397] Elder Dallin H. Oaks taught, "The reason charity never fails and the reason charity is greater than even the most significant acts of goodness [Paul] cited is that charity, 'the pure love of Christ' (Moro. 7:47), is not an act but a condition or state of being. Charity is attained through a succession of acts that result in a conversion. Charity is something one becomes."[398] Our experiment burns out all fear. Now we want to consecrate; now we desire to become Zion people in every way .

The glory of Zion is first to obtain charity and then to duplicate the process in others. Now we become those who plant the word of God; now we become God's servants, who help another hope-filled experimenter nourish his tender plant; now we become saviors in Zion who encourage, strengthen, and hold up the grower when the hot sun scorches his plant and when all seems lost; now we become God's friends, who finally share in his harvest. We *are* charity! We are those whose countenances reflect that of the Lord of the Harvest;[399] we are the ones who have loved with the pure love of Christ until we have brought our fellow beings into the full image of Christ.

This process never falls short or breaks down: "Charity *never* faileth!" If charity can never fail, Zion people can never fail, because Zion is built upon charity, "the greatest of all," the celestial quality of love that "endureth forever."[400] Charity is the quintessential virtue, "the end of the commandment,"[401] the power that invigorates and propels the law of consecration and the establishment of Zion.

Charity Promotes Equality, Unity and an Abundant Life

Charity is the principle upon which Zion people achieve equality and unity: "And above all things, clothe yourselves with the bond of charity, as with a mantle, which is the bond of perfectness and peace."[402] When Zion people give and receive charity, they cease to be afraid: "Perfect love casteth out all fear."[403] Therefore, in the life of a Zion person *all* things are to be done in charity.

According to Peter, we are to array ourselves in "fervent charity." Over time, this "pure love of Christ" becomes an integral part of our nature.[404] Elder McConkie taught: "Charity is more than love, far more; it is everlasting love, perfect love, the pure love of Christ which endureth forever. It is love so centered in righteousness that the possessor has no aim or desire except for the eternal welfare of his own soul and for the souls of those around him."[405]

When charity, the love exemplified by Zion people, is planted in the hearts of a few, it acts as leaven "until the whole [of humanity is] leavened."[406] Again we recall the words

---

397 Moroni 7:48.
398 Dallin H. Oaks, "The Challenge to Become," 32–34.
399 Alma 5:14.
400 Moroni 7:46–47.
401 1 Timothy 1:5.
402 D&C 88:125; see also Colossians 3:14.
403 Moroni 8:16.
404 1 Peter 4:8.
405 McConkie, *Mormon Doctrine*, 121, quoting 2 Nephi 26:30; Moroni 7:47; 8:25–26.
406 Matthew 13:33; Luke 13:21.

of Joseph Smith: "A man filled with the love of God is not content with blessing his family alone, but ranges through the whole world, anxious to bless the whole human race."[407] It is charity that infuses Zion people with power. According to Elder Ashton, charity is the crowning principle that makes possible eternal joy and progression.[408]

President Kimball gave other essential counsel concerning charitable service, which we will address in the next few pages (the emphasis in each of these quotes is mine):

Abundant life. "One has hardly proved his life abundant until he has built up a crumbling wall, paid off a heavy debt, enticed a disbeliever to his knees, filled an empty stomach, influenced a soul to wash in the blood of the lamb, turned fear and frustration into peace and sureness, led one to be 'born again.' One is measuring up to his opportunity potential when he has saved a crumbling marriage, transformed the weak into the strong, changed a civil to a proper temple marriage, brought enemies from the cesspool of hate to the garden of love, made a child trust and love him, changed a scoffer into a worshiper, melted a stony heart into one of flesh and muscle."[409]

To become like Christ, we must "give ourselves away." President Kimball said,

> Christ's life is the epitome of service. *Give yourselves away.* That's the life of the Savior of this world. He gave himself away when he personally went to the house of Peter and blessed his mother-in-law "who was sick of a fever." He gave himself away when he stood on the mount and preached for hours "the way of salvation" to the multitude. He gave himself away when he walked long, dusty, tortuous miles to Bethany to bring comfort and even life back to Lazarus, and to Mary and Martha, the sisters who were grieving. He gave himself away when he healed the sick and opened the blind eyes and cleared the stopped hearing and gave strength to the sick. He gave much of himself in every blessing. When the woman reached forth to touch the hem of his garment, he felt that power had gone out of him. He gave that power and part of himself willingly, and after three years of spectacular ministry, he voluntarily walked back into the trap set for him, announced his approaching fate, walked out of Gethsemane into the hands of mobsters and to the courts of politicians and to the cross and gave himself for all mankind.[410]

Perfect service by practicing service. "A striking personality and good character is achieved by practice, not merely by thinking it. Just as a pianist masters the intricacies of music through hours and weeks of practice, so mastery of life is achieved by the ceaseless practice of mechanics which make up the art of living. *Daily unselfish service to others is one of the rudimentary mechanics of the successful life.* 'For whosoever will save his life,' the Galilean said, 'shall lose it, and whosoever will lose his life for my sake shall find it.' (Matthew 16:25.) What a strange paradox this! And yet one needs only to analyze it to be convinced of its truth."[411]

---

407 Smith, *History of the Church*, 4:227.
408 Ashton, "Be a Quality Person," 64.
409 Kimball, *The Teachings of Spencer W. Kimball*, 249.
410 Kimball, *The Teachings of Spencer W. Kimball*, 250.
411 Kimball, *The Teachings of Spencer W. Kimball*, 250.

The divine paradox of service. "Only when you lift a burden, God will lift your burden. Divine paradox this! The man who staggers and falls because his burden is too great can lighten that burden by taking on the weight of another's burden. *You get by giving, but your part of giving must be given first.*"[412]

Glorious rewards from small charitable acts. "So often, our acts of service consist of simple encouragement or of giving mundane help with mundane tasks—*but what glorious consequences can flow from mundane acts and from small but deliberate deeds!*"[413]

Most essential quality. "[This is] perhaps the most essential godlike quality: *compassion and love*—compassion shown forth in service to others, unselfishness, that ultimate expression of concern for others we call love."[414]

Service is the next step in spiritual growth. "Let us not shrink from the next steps in our spiritual growth, brothers and sisters, by holding back, or sidestepping our *fresh opportunities for service* to our families and our fellowmen."[415]

Difficulties are opportunities for service. "Let us trust the Lord and take the next steps in our individual lives. . . . Sometimes the solution is not to change our circumstance, but to change our attitude about that circumstance; *difficulties are often opportunities for service.*"[416]

Service is a testimony. "The most vital thing we can do is to *express our testimonies through service*, which will, in turn, produce spiritual growth, greater commitment, and a greater capacity to keep the commandments."[417]

Service puts problems in perspective. "When we are engaged in the service of our fellowmen, not only do our deeds assist them, but we put our own problems in a fresher perspective. When we concern ourselves more with others, there is less time to be concerned with ourselves. In the midst of the miracle of serving, there is the promise of Jesus, that by losing ourselves, we find ourselves. Not only do we 'find' ourselves in terms of acknowledging guidance in our lives, but *the more we serve our fellowmen in appropriate ways, the more substance there is to our souls.*"[418]

Antidote for loneliness. "Perhaps you could take a loaf of bread or a covered dish to someone in need. Uncompensated service is one answer, one good answer to overcome loneliness."[419]

Charitable Service Saves and Exalts

Charity saves the lives of both the giver and the receiver. What the Lord said to missionaries could be said of anyone who is willing to enter the field of need and thrust in his sickle: "For behold the field is white already to harvest; and lo, he that thrusteth in

---

412 Kimball, *The Teachings of Spencer W. Kimball*, 251.
413 Kimball, *The Teachings of Spencer W. Kimball*, 252.
414 Kimball, *The Teachings of Spencer W. Kimball*, 253.
415 Kimball, *The Teachings of Spencer W. Kimball*, 253.
416 Kimball, *The Teachings of Spencer W. Kimball*, 254.
417 Kimball, *The Teachings of Spencer W. Kimball*, 254.
418 Kimball, *The Teachings of Spencer W. Kimball*, 254.
419 Kimball, *The Teachings of Spencer W. Kimball*, 256.

his sickle with his might, the same layeth up in store that he perisheth not, *but bringeth salvation to his soul.*"[420]

The world is filled with so much need, and the Lord has placed within our reach the power to supply that need. A joyful and bounteous harvest awaits those who give charitable service to the Lord's poor: "And if it so be that you should labor all your days in crying repentance unto this people, and bring, save it be one soul unto me, how great shall be your joy with him in the kingdom of my Father! And now, if your joy will be great with one soul that you have brought unto me into the kingdom of my Father, how great will be your joy if you should bring many souls unto me!"[421]

Moroni's Prayer for Latter-day Charity

Salvation, or the forfeiture of it, swings on the hinge of charity. Moroni looked into the future with the eyes of a seer and saw a woeful latter-day lack of charitable service. He mourned that our salvation would be at risk: "If the Gentiles [us] have not charity, because of our weakness, . . . thou wilt prove them, and take away their talent, yea, even that which they have received, and give unto them who shall have more abundantly." At that point, Moroni offered a prayer that we who live in the latter days might receive the gift of charity for our own salvation: "And it came to pass that I prayed unto the Lord that he would give unto the Gentiles grace, that they might have charity."[422]

Moroni's act of charity toward us precipitated Jesus' promise that he would provide the "Gentiles" of the last days his grace so that we might receive and exhibit charity, which virtue would open the door to our salvation: "I will show unto them that faith, hope and charity bringeth [souls] unto me." Moroni understood the foundational importance of charity, and he bore his testimony concerning it: "I remember that thou hast said that thou hast loved the world, even unto the laying down of thy life for the world, that thou mightest take it again to prepare a place for the children of men. And now I know that this love which thou hast had for the children of men is charity; wherefore, except men shall have charity they cannot inherit that place which thou hast prepared in the mansions of thy Father."[423] Our salvation is simply not possible without charity. This virtue is the prerequisite for our entering into the kingdom of heaven. Moroni concluded with these words: "Except ye have charity ye can in nowise be saved in the kingdom of God."[424]

As we have learned, when the Lord comes in his glory, he will divide out the sheep from the goats. To the sheep on his right hand he will say, "Come, ye blessed of my Father, inherit the kingdom prepared for you from the foundation of the world." The criteria for their salvation will be threefold: (1) They gave food and drink to those in need; (2) They used their time, talents, and resources for the poor; and (3) They ministered

---

420 D&C 4:4; emphasis added.
421 D&C 18:15–16.
422 Ether 12:35–36.
423 Ether 12:28–34.
424 Moroni 10:21.

to the sick and the imprisoned. In all their ministrations, they saw in each impoverished soul the image of Jesus Christ, whose child the impoverished, sick, or captive person was.[425] For what they did and who they became through the grace of Christ, they earned their exaltation.

Patience and Charity

President Heber J. Grant explained that charity is often characterized by patience: "The gospel of Christ is a gospel of love and peace, of patience and long suffering, of forbearance and forgiveness, of kindness and good deeds, of charity and brotherly love. Greed, avarice, base ambition, thirst for power, and unrighteous dominion over our fellow men, can have no place in the hearts of Latter-day Saints nor of God-fearing men everywhere."[426] People who are truly charitable suffer long with those to whom they minister.

Our leaders have offered insight into the relationship between patience and charity. Of the thirteen elements of charity listed by Mormon, four of them relate to patience:
1. charity suffereth long
2. is not easily provoked
3. beareth all things
4. endureth all things

We can neither achieve a Christlike character without charity nor patience.

Patience means to wait:
- "I will wait *for* you."
- "I will wait *with* you."
- "I will wait *upon* you." In other words, "I will serve you."

It is the virtue of patience that perfects the virtue of charity; moreover patience perfects all virtues. Patience moves us forward to completion and abundance: "But let patience have her perfect work, that ye may be perfect and entire, wanting nothing."[427] The need for patience is ever-present in our lives. We develop patience when we give and receive charity. Consecration requires patience, because the harvest of associated blessings lies in our future. In patience we suffer, or *allow*, adversity for a long time while waiting in faith for the Lord's deliverance. In patience we refrain from giving offense. In patience we forgive multiple times. In patience we show kindness when kindness is not returned. In patience we offer brotherly love over an extended period. Clearly, in patience we wait *for*, *with*, and *upon* the Lord and his children.

Charity and Virtue—Essential Elements of Priesthood Power

We know that we demonstrate our love for God by keeping his commandments and feeding his sheep. We know that showing love to others is requisite for the doctrine of the priesthood to distill upon our souls as the dews from heaven.[428] With confidence,

---
425 Matthew 25:34–40.
426 Grant, *Teachings of Presidents of the Church: Heber J. Grant*, 139.
427 James 1:4.
428 D&C 121:45.

then, we might point to charity as the preeminent virtue that transforms priesthood authority into priesthood power. Without charity, priesthood fails, and if priesthood fails, so do those who would called Zion.

Charity is the preeminent virtue that transforms those who are *called* into those who are *chosen*. Such people are the products of a new and purified heart. They operate "by persuasion, by long-suffering, by gentleness and meekness, and by love unfeigned . . . by kindness, and pure knowledge." Such people are filled with "charity towards all men, and to the household of faith," and virtue garnishes their thoughts unceasingly. Their charitable service and virtue summon the greatest of priesthood blessings: "Then shall thy confidence wax strong in the presence of God; and the doctrine of the priesthood shall distil upon thy soul as the dews from heaven. The Holy Ghost shall be thy constant companion, and thy scepter an unchanging scepter of righteousness and truth; and thy dominion shall be an everlasting dominion, and without compulsory means it shall flow unto thee forever and ever."[429] Clearly, priesthood power depends on a consecrated heart, virtue, and charitable service. When priesthood power is resident, it prepares the way for the establishment of Zion in a life, a marriage, a family, or a priesthood society.

Charity Draws the Lord Near

Things that are alike attract: "For intelligence cleaveth unto intelligence; wisdom receiveth wisdom; truth embraceth truth; virtue loveth virtue; light cleaveth unto light; mercy hath compassion on mercy and claimeth her own; justice continueth its course and claimeth its own; judgment goeth before the face of him who sitteth upon the throne and governeth and executeth all things."[430] The Charitable One draws near when we manifest charity.

Conversely, when we fail to exhibit charity, we sense distance between the Lord and ourselves. President Marion G. Romney suggested that we can close the gap by extending charity to others.[431] To demonstrate this point, he used the example of the law of the fast as explained in Isaiah 58:3–12. Often we wonder why it is that our fast seems to go unnoticed by the Lord. "Wherefore have we fasted . . . and thou seest not?" It is because we do not understand and keep the true law of the fast. We accomplish only two of the three criteria of that law (prayer and humility), but we neglect the third criterion: dealing our bread to the hungry, providing for the poor, and covering the naked. A fast that does not include extending charity to someone yields no more blessings than shedding a few extra pounds.

On the other hand, a true fast that includes charitable service caries these promises:
- "loose the bands of wickedness"
- "undo the heavy burdens"
- "let the oppressed go free"
- "break every yoke"

---

429 D&C 121:40–46.
430 D&C 88:40.
431 Romney, "The Royal Law of Love," 95.

Chapter 10 Without Charity We Are Nothing

If we desire these blessings, we must include giving charity to our fast: "Is not this the fast that I have chosen? . . . Is it not to deal thy bread to the hungry, and that thou bring the poor that are cast out to thy house? when thou seest the naked, that thou cover him."[432] Additionally, a true fast requires that we extend charity to the hurting members of our family: "And that thou hide not thyself from thine own flesh [family]?"[433]

The law of the fast serves as model for other laws of God. The principle of charity is woven into the fabric of each of them. If we would obtain the promised blessing for any obeyed law, we must extend charitable service to our family and to others of the children of God. Otherwise the desired blessings for living the law will be forfeited, and the distance between the Lord and us will remain unaltered.

But, if we will live the laws of God and give generous charitable service, the Lord will draw near: "Then shalt thou call, and the Lord shall answer; thou shalt cry, and he shall say, Here I am." The Lord always draws near to those who follow such a course, and when he comes, he always brings blessings with him:

> Then shall thy light break forth as the morning, and thine health shall spring forth speedily: and thy righteousness shall go before thee; the glory of the Lord shall be thy rereward [protector]. . . .
>
> And if thou draw out thy soul to the hungry, and satisfy the afflicted soul; then shall thy light rise in obscurity, and thy darkness be as the noonday:
>
> And the Lord shall guide thee continually, and satisfy thy soul in drought, and make fat thy bones: and thou shalt be like a watered garden, and like a spring of water, whose waters fail not.
>
> And they that shall be of thee [your posterity] shall build the old waste places: thou shalt raise up the foundations of many generations; and thou shalt be called, The repairer of the breach, The restorer of paths to dwell in.[434]

Such are the blessings of combining charity with the fast and all gospel laws!
- Answers to prayers
- Light bursting upon the soul, dispelling darkness
- Restoration of health
- Increase of righteousness and righteous influence.
- Divine protection and guidance
- Relief
- Deliverance
- Sustenance and abundance
- The constant flow of blessings
- Power
- Redemption
- Exaltation

---
432 Isaiah 58:6–7.
433 Isaiah 58:7.
434 Isaiah 58:8–12.

- The healing of our generations
- Multiplication of righteous posterity
- Becoming a savior to our family and to others

Charity Empowers All Gospel Laws

Extending charitable service to the needy is a fixed requirement for all gospel laws. For example, Amulek taught the people that the law of prayer, like the law of the fast, requires charitable giving to be effective: "After ye have done all these things, if ye turn away the needy, and the naked, and visit not the sick and afflicted, and impart of your substance, if ye have, to those who stand in need—I say unto you, if ye do not any of these things, behold, your prayer is vain, and availeth you nothing, and ye are as hypocrites who do deny the faith."[435]

This is the proper way to pray. If we pray and do not extend charitable service, we have not fulfilled the law that governs prayer, and, therefore, we cannot expect our prayers to be answered.

Neither fasting nor prayer nor substantially any other law of God becomes valid or a principle of power without charity. Neither can our testimony be a declaration of the truth unless our lives are filled with charity. Mormon said, "If a man be meek and lowly in heart, and confesses by the power of the Holy Ghost that Jesus is the Christ, he must needs have charity; for if he have not charity he is nothing; wherefore he must needs have charity."[436] Clearly, without charity, we are nothing.

---

435 Alma 34:28.
436 Moroni 7:44.

Chapter 11
The Hundredfold Law

Joseph Smith said, "We ought to have the building up of Zion as our greatest object."[437] Brigham Young laid the responsibility of Zion upon each of us, individually: "[Zion] commences in the heart of each person,"[438] and Elder Matthew Cowley stated unequivocally that individually, we are Zion.[439]

We cannot read these statements and the scriptures, especially latter-day scriptures, and avoid personal responsibility for becoming Zion people. Because Zion is built upon the foundational law of the celestial kingdom, which is consecration,[440] we must adopt a higher attitude toward our time, talents, possessions and the Lord's needy children. President Benson laid the obligation of becoming Zion people squarely on our shoulders. Zion, the priesthood society, he said, can only be brought about by Zion people. As more and more of us decide to embrace the principles of Zion, he said, the celestial order will finally exist among us; then we, individually and collectively, will be prepared to receive the Lord.[441]

Zion is the standard among celestial and celestial-seeking beings.[442] The celestial condition of Zion is the exact opposite of the telestial condition of Babylon;[443] therefore, we are constantly faced with choosing between the two. We cannot have it both ways. Let us examine the Zion way of obtaining safety and security.

---

437 Joseph Smith, *Teachings of the Prophet Joseph Smith*, 60.
438 Brigham Young, *Discourses of Brigham Young*, 118.
439 See Matthew Cowley, *Matthew Cowley Speaks*, 30.
440 D&C 105:4–5.
441 See Ezra Taft Benson, "Jesus Christ—Gifts and Expectations."
442 D&C 105:5.
443 See Hugh Nibley, *Approaching Zion*, 30.

The Law of Restoration

Zion's abundance flows from the plan, or law, of restoration.[444] If we would embrace this law, we would become sufficiently prosperous so that there would be no poor among us. The law of restoration becomes operational when we enter into the new and everlasting covenant at baptism and reaches its zenith in the Resurrection. Joseph Smith taught that to the degree we have sacrificed, suffered, or been opposed or denied, we shall be restored.[445] In fact, the Lord promised that we would be restored an hundredfold: "And every one that hath forsaken houses, or brethren, or sisters, or father, or mother, or wife, or children, or lands, for my name's sake, shall receive an hundredfold, and shall inherit everlasting life."[446]

The promise of hundredfold restoration is repeated so often in the scriptures that we are obligated to consider it as literal. The Apostle Paul wrote, "Eye hath not seen, nor ear heard, neither have entered into the heart of man, the things which God hath prepared for them that love him."[447] Here is how the law of restoration might work. Imagine sacrificing $10,000 to help a needy friend. Most of us would feel the acute sting of such a sacrifice. But suppose that the Lord were to restore to us $1,000,000. Suddenly, the $10,000 would become a nonissue. The law of restoration or the hundredfold law is a key to Zion's abundance.

Struggling with Zion and Babylon Principles

In a telestial world, especially one in which the philosophies of Babylon enjoy almost free reign, we struggle when we are confronted with celestial laws. Giving our way to prosperity is an example. We can point to nothing in our environment that suggests this law should work. In Babylon, we can no more make sense of *less is more* than we can of walking on water and not sinking. So how do we square with the idea that giving away our time, talents, and resources is the only way to achieve the unequalled prosperity of Zion and, ultimately, an inheritance in the celestial world? We must rely on the prophets to articulate celestial laws.

Following is how King Benjamin summed up the law of restoration:

> And behold, all that [God] requires of you is to keep his commandments; and he has promised you that if ye would keep his commandments ye should prosper in the land; and he never doth vary from that which he hath said; therefore, if ye do keep his commandments he doth bless you and prosper you.
>
> And now, in the first place, he hath created you, and granted unto you your lives, for which ye are indebted unto him.
>
> And secondly, he doth require that ye should do as he hath commanded you; for which if ye do, he doth immediately bless you; and therefore he hath paid you;

---

444 Alma 41:2.
445 Joseph Smith, *Teachings of the Prophet Joseph Smith*, 296.
446 Matthew 19:29.
447 1 Corinthians 2:9

and therefore he hath paid you. And ye are still indebted unto him, and are, and will be, forever and ever; therefore, of what have ye to boast?[448]

Here is how we might portray the celestial law of restoration as it applies to Zion's condition of abundance and prosperity:
- Our love of God motivates us to seek to serve him.
- Because God is not in need, he immediately asks us to transfer our service to his suffering or needy children.
- When we do what God asks of us, he accepts our sacrifice "unto the least of these" as if we had done it unto him.[449]
- Our sacrifice creates something akin to a credit in our favor, which credit demands payment.
- God gladly assumes this obligation, which is actually an opportunity to bless us. He rewards us for our service: first, because he loves us; second, because we have obeyed the law upon which the blessing is predicated,[450] and third, because our service has created an implied celestial deficit that needs correcting.
- Because God will not and cannot remain in a real or implied deficit position, "he doth immediately bless [us]; and therefore he hath paid [us]. And [we] are still indebted unto him, and are, and will be, forever and ever."
- What is the result? We live forever in the condition of divine debt—celestial debt—debt that is structured so that we can receive an abundance of blessings.

This is the hundredfold principle. We are always rewarded beyond our sacrifice. God overpays his obligations, and therefore we find ourselves eternally indebted to him and we always enjoy an abundance of blessings.[451]

New Math

In this telestial world, we cannot make sense of the law of restoration or the hundredfold law for an obvious reason: the math doesn't work. Let's take the law of tithing as an example. In our present environment, ten minus one equals nine; but in the celestial world, because we are dealing with a celestial law and celestial math, ten minus one can equal eleven or fifteen or fifty or "an hundredfold."[452] But never nine! Remember the kernel corn we talked about earlier?

Elder Boyd K. Packer said, "As you give what you have, there is a replacement, with increase!"[453] This in the hundredfold law: a most important principle of Zion that lends to safety, security and abundance.

---

448 Mosiah 2:22–24
449 See D&C 42:38
450 See D&C 130:21.
451 We are tempted to describe abundance in terms of finances, and it can certainly include such blessings; but abundance and prosperity more often refer to blessings that lend to safety, spiritual security, and an outpouring of divine favor.
452 See Gen 26:12; 2 Samuel 24:3; Matthew 13:8–23;19:29; Mark 10:30; Luke 8:8; D&C 98:25; 132:55.
453 Boyd K. Packer, "The Candle of the Lord."

What Doth It Profit to Cling to Our Property?

True safety and prosperity are found only in the sacrifice of all things through consecration and by following Christ. Jesus sounded a warning against our tendency to step into the snare of the love of money: "For what is a man profited if he shall gain the whole world and lose his own soul?"[454]

When a wealthy young man went away sorrowing after having received the Lord's answer regarding the price of becoming perfect, Jesus turned to his disciples and said, "A rich man shall *hardly* enter into the kingdom of heaven."[455] Imbedded in the Lord's explanation is an introduction to the law of consecration, which is founded on the law of restoration. This law is our safety net from the preoccupation of wealth, and it is a key to our becoming perfect.

To the rich young man, the Lord said, "If thou wilt be perfect, go and sell that thou hast, and give to the poor."[456] Although the rich man was clearly a good man who had lived the commandments, he could not bring himself to accept the law of consecration, which would have covered him in safety and security, and would have opened the door to perfection. Truly, it is *hard* for a rich man—or for that matter, a proud, selfish, power-hungry, recognition-seeking man—to lay aside the things of this world and still achieve heaven.

Safety and Perfection in Consecration

We learn several important principles of Zion from the incident of the Savior and the rich young man:

- Perfection hinges not on living the commandments alone but on living the law of consecration.
- The ultimate test of discipleship is the law of consecration.
- The law of consecration was instituted, in part, for our safety, because pursuing and hoarding wealth can result in the loss of exaltation.
- The law of consecration is hard to live, but it is harder for a rich man to live it.
- Only divine intervention can save the rich, those who have too much of what they do not need or deserve. But intervention is not necessarily guaranteed. Our choices concerning money can exalt us or damn us.
- Consecrating our excess to the poor tends to stockpile treasure in heaven, where treasure is needed.
- The law of consecration makes us truly safe and secure. The Lord invited the rich young man to "come and follow me," which implies true safety. If we are with the Lord, we are safe.
- Consecrated sacrifices earn an hundredfold return. If this is true, the rich young man would have received many more blessings than he sacrificed to bless the poor. In the process of giving, the Lord would have kept the young man safe, and the young man would have been on his way to perfection and eternal life.

---

454 Matthew 16:26.
455 Matthew 19:23; emphasis added.
456 Matthew 19:21.

Thus sang the psalmist: "Blessed is he that considereth the poor: the Lord will deliver him in time of trouble. The Lord will preserve him, and keep him alive; and he shall be blessed upon the earth: and thou wilt not deliver him unto the will of his enemies. The Lord will strengthen him upon the bed of languishing: thou wilt make all his bed in his sickness."[457] Deliverance, preservation, safety, blessings, protection, strength, and health—these are the blessings of consecration.

The Hundredfold Law

The incident of the rich young man disturbed the Apostles so much that they began to search their souls. Evidently, they wondered if they had fully complied with the laws of sacrifice and consecration so that they might achieve perfection and obtain eternal life. Jesus offered them an astonishing promise: "And every one that hath forsaken houses, or brethren, or sisters, or father, or mother, or wife, or children, or lands, for my name's sake, shall receive an hundredfold, and shall inherit everlasting life."[458]

Here the Lord makes two divine promises connected with consecration: (1) an hundredfold return, and (2) the promise of eternal life. Those who live this celestial law will be blessed beyond their sacrifice, and they will inherit exaltation![459] Whatever we give the Lord by way of consecrated sacrifice to his kingdom or his needy children will be restored to us an hundredfold. That is the celestial law upon which Zion is established.

As we have discussed, Jesus' Apostles had firsthand experience with the hundredfold law on at least two occasions; first, when Jesus fed the five thousand and second when he fed the four thousand.[460] Each time, Jesus required the Apostles to bring (consecrate) *all* that they could to the Lord. Then when Jesus blessed their offering, the resource multiplied and fed many. Of significance, in each instance Jesus instructed the Apostles to gather up the fragments and to take note of the resulting quantity. At a minimum, there are two lessons here:
1. The needs of the hungry took precedence over the Apostles' needs. Because the Apostles were servants to the people, they ate last.
2. When it was the Apostles turn to eat, they had enough and to spare. Amazingly, the five loaves and two fishes had not only fed thousands, the fragments now filled twelve baskets![461] *An hundredfold return!*

When we undertake to become a Zion person, we kneel at the altar and consecrate our all for the Lord's purposes. When we stand up from the altar, we are transformed. We are no longer owners, we are stewards; we are no longer overseers, we are servants. From that point forward, we place ourselves in a second position to the poor, whom we serve with the Lord's goods. We have nothing to risk by doing so. When it is our turn to eat,

---
457 Psalms 41:1–3.
458 Matthew 19:29.
459 See Matthew 19:16–30.
460 See Mark 6:35–44 and Mark 8:1–9.
461 See Mark 6:35–44.

the Lord guarantees that we will always have enough. In fact, we will have more than we gave away. Now we have sufficient to give again, and the cycle continues.

Freely Ye Have Received, Freely Give

The hundredfold law is synonymous with the law of restoration and part of the law of consecration, the foundational law of the celestial kingdom. We must learn to live this law by faith while we are in the telestial world. When we sacrifice and consecrate our time, talents, and resources to build the kingdom of God, to promote the cause of Zion, and to bless the lives of others, we invoke this celestial law of abundance. What the Lord said to his disciples, he repeats to us: "freely ye have received, freely give"[462]; "feed my lambs . . . feed my sheep."[463]

As the rich young man learned to his dismay, of the "many" who are called to eternal life, only a "few" will actually achieve it. When they do, it will be because they made a consecrated effort, allowing the law of restoration to engage, which triggered the powers of earth and heaven to work together to return an hundredfold reward and the promise of eternal life. This is the condition of former Zion peoples who achieved the condition of no poor among them.

---

462   Matthew 10:8.
463   John 21:15–16.

Chapter 12
Ultimate Abundance, Safety, and Security

In a day when treasures are slippery,[464] foundationless nations collapse under the weight of their pride,[465] enemies combine against righteousness,[466] and men's hearts begin to fail them,[467] we should "come to ourselves," as did the awakening prodigal,[468] come out from Babylon,[469] and "flee unto Zion for safety."[470] As prophesied, only Zion is a condition of abundance, safety, and security. "Surely Zion shall dwell in safety forever."[471] If we were not assured of safety, we would not have the faith to aim for no poor among us.

How does this safety come? By living the commandments, most specifically the law of consecration. Ultimate safety comes in no other way; neither do lasting abundance and security. Our attitude toward our money and the poor will determine our fate here and in eternity.

Wresting ourselves free from Babylon is not for the faint-hearted. From the moment that we declare our allegiance to Zion, Babylon will cry treason.[472] Then Babylon will withdraw its support and declare us enemies. The Lord's promises of protection for Zion people are comforting. What is said of Zion the society could be personalized and said of a Zion person, a Zion marriage, or a Zion family:

> [Zion is] a city [family] of refuge, a place [home] of safety for the saints of the Most High God;
> And the glory of the Lord shall be there, and the terror of the Lord also shall be there, insomuch that the wicked will not come unto it, and it shall be called Zion. . . .
> And it shall be said among the wicked: Let us not go up to battle against Zion, for the inhabitants of Zion are terrible; wherefore we cannot stand.[473]

---

464 Helaman 13:30–37.
465 1 Nephi 8:26.
466 D&C 38:12.
467 D&C 45:26; 88:91.
468 Luke 15:17.
469 D&C 133:7.
470 D&C 45:68.
471 Moses 7:20.
472 Nibley, *Approaching Zion*, p. 32–33.
473 D&C 45:66–67,70.

True Safety and Security

Clearly, God protects Zion people from the perils of the world. Other Zion scriptures that can be personalized:

> And all that fight against Zion [you and your family] shall be destroyed.[474]
>
> Verily, thus saith the Lord unto you—there is no weapon that is formed against you shall prosper; and if any man lift his voice against you he shall be confounded in mine own due time.[475]

The Lord has promised that the homes of latter-day Zion people will receive the same protection he extended to the ancient Israelites: "And the Lord will create upon every dwelling-place of mount Zion, and upon her assemblies, a cloud and smoke by day and the shining of a flaming fire by night; for upon all the glory of Zion shall be a defence."[476]

No false comfort of Babylon exceeds the safety of Zion provided by the power of God: "Therefore, let your hearts be comforted concerning Zion [you and your family]; for all flesh is in mine hands; be still and know that I am God."[477] The bounds of Zion's enemies "are set, they cannot pass . . . therefore, fear not what man can do, for God shall be with you forever and ever."[478]

Obtaining an Abundance in All Things

The condition of Zion is "that every man may improve upon his talent, that every man may gain other talents, yea, even an hundred fold."[479] Abundance, not poverty, describes Zion. But, as with other principles, abundance can be obtained in telestial, terrestrial, and celestial ways—and amounts!

Motivation lies at the heart of the issue. Whereas a telestial wealth is obtained through hoarding, personal genius, and self-service, celestial wealth is obtained by obedience to God's commandments, building up his kingdom, and improving the condition of his children.

Telestial and Celestial Wealth

The Babylon and Zion (Christ and Anti-Christ) motivations for obtaining wealth are set forth in the scriptures.[480] Nephi states the frightening situation of telestially-gotten wealth: "But wo unto the rich, who are rich as to the things of the world. For because they are rich they despise the poor, and they persecute the meek, and their hearts are

---

474 1 Nephi 22:14; see 2 Nephi 27:3; Moses 7:20.
475 D&C 71:9–11.
476 2 Nephi 14:5.
477 D&C 101:16.
478 D&C 122:9.
479 D&C 82:19.
480 Alma 30:12–18.

upon their treasures; wherefore, their treasure is their God. And behold, their treasure shall perish with them also."[431]

Early in his career, a telestially-minded rich man makes a conscious decision to suppress the divinely planted urge within him to take care of his neighbor. Otherwise, he could not become and remain telestially rich. Rather, such a man must learn to soothe his conscience by dealing out comfortable portions or nothing at all. Somehow he learns how to look himself in the mirror and declare that he has fulfilled his duty to God and his neighbors or that he has no such obligation. In the daily management of his affairs, he is ever vigilant to rationalize his seeking and hoarding wealth by quoting his responsibility to provide material things only for his family. While it's important to provide for our families as directed in 1 Timothy 5:8, it's important not to close our eyes to the needs of those outside our families. Remember, Joseph Smith said, "A man filled with the love of God, is not content with blessing his family alone, but ranges through the whole world, anxious to bless the whole human race."[482] In the eyes of God, at the moment a man sets his heart on building his personal treasure, that man begins to despise the poor and persecute the meek. Then, sadly, God is obliged to pronounce a "wo" upon him.

On the other hand, Jacob forwards the celestial or Zion law of wealth and its motivation:

> Think of your brethren like unto yourselves, and be familiar with all and free with your substance, that they may be rich like unto you.
> But before ye seek for riches, seek ye for the kingdom of God.
> And after ye have obtained a hope in Christ ye shall obtain riches, if ye seek them; and ye will seek them for the intent to do good—to clothe the naked, and to feed the hungry, and to liberate the captive, and administer relief to the sick and the afflicted.[483]

Clearly, celestially-gotten wealth follows those who "seek . . . first the kingdom of God, and his righteousness; and all these things shall be added unto you."[484]

Wealth-seeking is Strictly Forbidden

These scriptures point out an important distinction between the methods of Babylon and Zion for obtaining wealth. As we are told by virtually every prophet in the Book of Mormon, celestial wealth is obtained as a result of obedience to the commandments of God[485] and in becoming a conduit through which God can funnel relief to his needy children. Few other commandments are repeated as often as to not seek for riches but rather for the kingdom of God.

---
481 2 Nephi 9:30.
482 *History of the Church*, 4:227.
483 Jacob 2:17–19.
484 Matthew 6:33.
485 1 Nephi 4:14.

Some people rationalize their seeking for riches first because they claim to have the intent of eventually blessing the kingdom of God. But their motive is transparent; God has never authorized the sequence. The kingdom must be our first, entire, and eternal focus. We are under covenant *now* to use all our time, talents, and resources to do God's work, which is to save and elevate his children.[486] By doing so, God—not Babylon—will prosper us so that our capacity for blessing others increases; then we will progressively be able to give more. By following the correct celestial sequence that governs the obtaining of wealth we will learn to become like God, who is the most generous giver.

God or Mammon—The Ultimate Test

Developing this attitude toward wealth is a major step away from Babylon, which we must take in order to become Zion-like and Christlike. It is impossible to simultaneously serve God and mammon.[487] One master or the other will eventually claim our loyalty.

President Stephen L Richards said, "The accumulation and utilization of wealth confront the human family with some of its major challenges in determining the righteousness of goals and the correctness of behavior." Then, quoting Franklin D. Richards, he added, "'In many respects the real test of a man is his attitude toward his earthly possessions.' The prosperity that results from honest and intelligent work is not necessarily repugnant to the spiritual quality of life, but the Church consistently warns of the risks of selfishness and personal aggrandizement' that lurk in accumulating wealth. President Richards went on to say that Zion people believe that "everything rightly belongs to God (Mosiah 2:21–25) and comes to man 'in the form of trust property' to be used for God's purposes."[488]

When we lay claim to God's property as our own and use it contrary to its intended purpose (blessing God's children and building up of the kingdom of God for the establishment of Zion), we are like the employee who, without permission, pillages his employer's resources to personally profiteer. While it is true that he is entitled to a fair wage, he is not entitled to his employer's surplus.

Abundance and Personal Righteousness

Zion-like abundance and prosperity pivot on the principle of personal righteousness: "Inasmuch as ye shall keep the commandments of God ye shall prosper in the land."[489] In addition, President N. Eldon Tanner outlined five principles for personal economic affairs: "Pay an honest tithing, live on less than you earn, distinguish between needs and wants, develop and live within a budget, and be honest in all financial affairs."[490]

Consider the payment of tithes and offerings. Has anyone ever been impoverished

---

486   Moses 1:39.
487   Matthew 5:20; 6:24.
488   Richards, Conference Report, April 1923, 31,151.
489   Alma 36:30.
490   Tanner, "Constancy Amid Change," 81–82.

by paying them? It would be impossible. The true Paymaster invites us to prove, or test, him on this matter, and he is a God of truth who cannot lie.[491] Millions of tithe and offering payers can attest that the windows of heaven certainly spill out blessings that challenge their ability to receive.

Significantly, it is upon the principle of tithing that we initiate our retreat from Babylon and our return to Zion: "Wherein shall we return [to Zion]? . . . In tithes and offerings." Is it not interesting, according to Malachi, that tithing saves us from the devourer, ensures that the conditions of a telestial world will not destroy us, and makes of us a blessed and delightsome people?[492] Zion indeed! Only consecration, which is manifested through offerings, exceeds tithing in the blessings of plenty.

Exceedingly Prosperous

Zion is described as being exceedingly prosperous,[493] which includes material wealth. This leads us to believe that telestial prosperity, as much as we are awed by it, does not compare to the abundance enjoyed by Zion people.

Of course, the greatest wealth is not to be measured in terms of money: "Remember the worth of souls is great in the sight of God."[494] The Lord added, "And if a person gains more knowledge and intelligence in this life through his diligence and obedience than another, he will have so much the advantage in the world to come."[495] The Lord counseled, "Lay up for yourselves treasures in heaven."[496] And in our day, "Seek not for riches but for wisdom, and behold, the mysteries of God shall be unfolded unto you, and then shall you be made rich. Behold, he that hath eternal life is rich."[497]

Abundance, safety, security, friends, family, wisdom, and eternal life—these constitute true wealth. And this quality and quantity of wealth can only be accessed by living the law that provides it: the law of consecration. Thus, abundance, safety, and security are the conditions of Zion people. While we strive for no poor among us, the Lord prospers us and keeps us absolutely safe and secure.

Postlude

The laws that govern Babylon and Zion reside at opposite poles. One system of law persecutes the poor by way of selfish, wealth-seeking individuals, who, while neglecting the concerns of the kingdom of God, build to themselves personal "sanctuaries" with consecrated resources, covet their own property, withhold their time and talents, hoard their resources, and pursue self-serving interests;[498] the other system levels up God's children

---

491   N. B. Lundwall, comp., *A Compilation Containing the Lectures on Faith.*, (Salt Lake City: Bookcraft, n.d.),35–36.
492   Malachi 3:7–12.
493   4 Nephi 1:7.
494   D&C 18:10.
495   D&C 130:19.
496   Matthew 6:20.
497   D&C 6:7.
498   2 Nephi 28:13.

and saves them by way of individuals who consecrate all that they are and have for addressing the temporal, emotional, and spiritual needs of others. One system is founded on love of self, while the other is founded on love of God and his children. One system summons the Lord's rebuke—"But it is not given that one man should possess that which is above another, wherefore the world lieth in sin"[499]—while the other draws the Lord's blessing—"And surely there could not be a happier people among all the people who had been created by the hand of God."[500]

The laws of Babylon and Zion are stated so often and so well that we cannot plead ignorance. On the one hand, "Behold, the world at this time lieth in sin, and there is none that doeth good, *no not one*. And mine anger is kindling against the inhabitants of the earth to visit them according to this ungodliness."[501] On the other hand, "You are to be equal . . . every man according to his wants and his needs, inasmuch as his wants are just."[502] Latter-day scriptures point to the Lord's solution for the spiritual and temporal salvation of his people. Hugh Nibley wrote, "God has always commanded his people to give up that way of life [Babylon], come out of the world, and follow his special instructions. *The main purpose of the Doctrine and Covenants, you will find, is to implement the law of consecration.*"[503]

This idea is revolutionary, according to Joseph Smith; fully embraced it will change the world. This "revolution," said the Prophet, "will not be by sword or gun. . . [but by] the power of truth,"[504] which includes the revelation of celestial laws that must be learned and lived by covenant people in a telestial setting. Central to these laws is the last law that stands between us and celestial glory: the law of consecration.[505] Only this law has the power to eradicate poverty from families, communities, priesthood societies, and nations; only this law has the power to rescue and exalt both the receiver and the giver, and to purify the heart to the degree that it is fit to reside in the presence of God. We recall that the pure in heart are the "blessed" ones, who qualify to "see God."[506]

Mortal life has a narrow set of purposes compacted into one brief and intense test. Central to that test is our attitude toward money and the poor. How we pass the test will determine our eventual placement on the Lord's left or right hand, with eternal life or everlasting punishment in the balance. The first group will qualify for eternal life by their having denied themselves and extended charity to the poor. The Lord will say to them: "Come, ye blessed of my Father, inherit the kingdom prepared for you from the foundation of the world: For I was an hungered, and ye gave me meat: I was thirsty, and ye gave me drink: I was a stranger, and ye took me in: Naked, and ye clothed me: I was sick, and ye visited me: I was in prison, and ye came unto me." The second group will forfeit eternal blessings by their having lived a life of selfishness and apathy. The Lord will say to them: "Depart from me, ye cursed, into everlasting fire, prepared for the devil and his

---

499 D&C 49:20.
500 4 Nephi 1:16.
501 Dean C. Jessee, "The Early Accounts of Joseph Smith's First Vision," *BYU Studies*, 9 (Spring 1969): 280; emphasis added.
502 D&C 82:17; emphasis added.
503 Nibley, *Approaching Zion*, 174; emphasis added.
504 Smith, *Teachings of the Prophet Joseph Smith*, 366.
505 D&C 105:4–5.
506 Matthew 5:8.

angels: For I was an hungered, and ye gave me no meat: I was thirsty, and ye gave me no drink: I was a stranger, and ye took me not in: naked, and ye clothed me not: sick, and in prison, and ye visited me not."[507]

We can either sacrifice a life of selfishness for a life of holiness and receive everlasting enlargement or we can pursue wealth and cling to our time, talents, and resources and reap the Lord's condemnation. But we cannot have it both ways. Our choice will define our love and devotion to God and determine whether or not his children will languish in ongoing misery or achieve the state of former societies. May we choose wisely and achieve the reward of the Nephite faithful:

> There were no contentions and disputations among them, and every man did deal justly one with another.
> And they had all things common among them; therefore there were not rich and poor, bond and free, but they were all made free, and partakers of the heavenly gift. . . .
> And the Lord did prosper them exceedingly in the land. . . .
> And now, behold, it came to pass that the people of Nephi did wax strong, and did multiply exceedingly fast, and became an exceedingly fair and delightsome people.
> And they were married, and given in marriage, and were blessed according to the multitude of the promises which the Lord had made unto them. . . .
> And it came to pass that there was no contention among all the people in all the land; but there were mighty miracles wrought among the disciples of Jesus. . . .
> And it came to pass that there was no contention in the land, because of the love of God which did dwell in the hearts of the people.
> And there were no envyings, nor strifes, nor tumults, nor whoredoms, nor lyings, nor murders, nor any manner of lasciviousness; and surely there could not be a happier people among all the people who had been created by the hand of God.
> There were no robbers, nor murderers, neither were there Lamanites, nor any manner of -ites; but they were in one, the children of Christ, and heirs to the kingdom of God.
> And how blessed were they! For the Lord did bless them in all their doings.[508]

And so it can be in our day. Having no poor among us is but one decision away.

---

507 Matthew 25:31–46.
508 4 Nephi 1:2–18.

Bibliography

American Heritage Dictionary. Boston, MA: Houghton Mifflin, 2000.

Anderson, Dawn Hall, Susette Fletcher Green, and Dlora Hall Dalton, eds. *Clothed with Charity: Talks from the 1996 Women's Conference.* Salt Lake City, UT: Deseret Book, 1997.

Asay, Carlos E. "The Oath and Covenant of the Priesthood," *Ensign,* November 1985.

—*Family Pecan Trees: Planting a Legacy of Faith at Home.* Salt Lake City, UT: Deseret Book, 1992.

—*The Seven M's of Missionary Service: Proclaiming the Gospel as a Member or Full-time Missionary.* Salt Lake City, UT: Bookcraft, 1996.

Ashton, Marvin J. "Be a Quality Person," *Ensign,* February 1993.

—"Love Takes Time," *Ensign,* November 1975.

Bednar, David A. "Pray Always," *Ensign,* November 2008.

Benson, Ezra Taft. "A Vision and a Hope for the Youth of Zion," *Devotional Speeches of the Year.* Provo, UT: Brigham Young University Press, 1978.

—*A Witness and a Warning: A Modern-Day Prophet Testifies of the Book of Mormon.* Salt Lake City, UT: Deseret Book, 1988.

—"Beware of Pride," *Ensign,* May 1989.

—*Devotional Speeches of the Year.* Provo, UT: Brigham Young University Press, 1978.

—*God, Family, Country: Our Three Great Loyalties.* Salt Lake City, UT: Deseret Book, 1975.

—"In His Steps," *Ensign,* September 1988.

—"Jesus Christ—Gifts and Expectations," *New Era,* May 1975.

—*The Teachings of Ezra Taft Benson.* Salt Lake City, UT: Deseret Book, 1988.

—"What I Hope You Will Teach Your Children about the Temple," *Ensign,* August 1985;

Bible Dictionary. Salt Lake City, UT: The Church of Jesus Christ of Latter-day Saints, 1989;

Black, Susan Easton, et al. *Doctrines for Exaltation: The 1989 Sperry Symposium on the Doctrine and Covenants.* Salt Lake City, UT: Deseret Book, 1989.

—*The Iowa Mormon Trail: Legacy of Faith and Courage.* Orem, UT: Helix Publishing, 1997.

Bowen, Albert E. *The Church Welfare Plan.* Salt Lake City, UT: The Church of Jesus Christ of Latter-day Saints, 1946.

Brewster, Hoyt W. Jr. *Doctrine and Covenants Encyclopedia.* Salt Lake City, UT: Bookcraft, 1988.

Brown, Hugh B. *Continuing the Quest.* Salt Lake City, UT: Bookcraft, 1961.

Brown, Matthew B. *Prophecies: The Gate of Heaven.* American Fork, UT: Covenant Communications, 1999.

—*Signs of the Times, Second Coming, Millenium.* American Fork, UT: Covenant Communications, 2006.

Budge, Ernest A. Wallis. *Coptic Martyrdoms Discourse on Abbaton.* London: British Museum, 1914.

Burton, Alma P., ed. *Discourses of the Prophet Joseph Smith. Salt Lake City, UT: Deseret Book,* 1956.

Cannon, Donald Q. *Teachings of the Latter-day Prophets.* Salt Lake City, UT: Bookcraft, 1998.

Cannon, Elaine. "Agency and Accountability." Salt Lake City, *Ensign,* November 1983.

Cannon, George Q. "Beware Lest Ye Fall." Discourse delivered at the Morgan Utah Stake Conference, Sunday, February 16, 1896.
—*Gospel Truth: Discourses and Writings of President George Q. Cannon.* Salt Lake City, UT: Deseret Book, 1974.
Cannon, Joseph A. "Sanctification," *Mormon Times,* June 12, 2008, http://www.mormontimes.com.
Clark, E. Douglas. *The Blessings of Abraham—Becoming a Zion People.* American Fork, UT: Covenant Communications, 2005.
Clark, J. Reuben. *Church Welfare Plan: A Discussion.* Salt Lake, City, UT General Church Welfare Committee, 1939.
Clark, James R., comp., *Messages of the First Presidency of The Church of Jesus Christ of Latter-day Saints.* Salt Lake City: Bookcraft, 1965–75.
Clarke, Adam. *Clarke's Commentary on the Bible.* Grand Rapids, MI: Baker Book House, 1967.
Clarke, J. Richard. "Successful Welfare Stewardship," *Ensign,* November 1978.
Conference Report, 1897–2009, Salt Lake City, UT: The Church of Jesus Christ of Latter-day Saints.
Cook, Gene R. "Home and Family: A Divine Eternal Pattern," *Ensign,* May 1984.
—"The Seat Next to You," *New Era,* October 1983.
Cook, Lyndon. *Joseph Smith and the Law of Consecration.* Provo, UT: Keepsake Books, 1991.
Cowley, Matthew. *Matthew Cowley Speaks: Discourses of Elder Matthew Cowley of the Quorum of the Twelve of the Church of Jesus Christ of Latter-day Saints.* Salt Lake City, UT: Deseret Book Company, 1954.
Dalrymple, G. Brent. *The Age of the Earth.* Stanford, CA: Stanford University Press, 1991.
Dellenbach, Robert K. "Hour of Conversion," *New Era,* June 2002.
DeMille, Cecil B. *BYU Speeches of the Year.* Provo, UT: Brigham Young University Press, May 1957.
Durham, G. Homer, ed. *The Gospel Kingdom: Selections from the Writings and Discourses of John Taylor, Third President of The Church of Jesus Christ of Latter-day Saints.* Salt Lake City, UT: Bookcraft, 1943.
—*Gospel Ideals: Selections from the Discourses of David O. McKay.* Salt Lake City UT: Improvement Era, 1953.
Dibble, Philo. "Recollections of the Prophet Joseph Smith," *Juvenile Instructor,* June 1892.
Duffin, James G. "A Character Test," *Improvement Era,* February 1911.
Easton, M. G. *Illustrated Bible Dictionary.* Nashville: TN: Thomas Nelson, 1897.
"The Bondage of Sin," *Improvement Era,* February 1923.
Ehat, Andrew F. and Lyndon W. Cook. *The Words of Joseph Smith: The Contemporary Accounts of the Nauvoo Discourses of the Prophet Joseph.* Provo, UT: Religious Studies Center Brigham Young University, 1980.
Encarta World English Dictionary. New York, NY: St. Martins Press, 1999.
Eyring, Henry B. "Faith and the Oath and Covenant of the Priesthood," *Ensign,* May 2008.
Farley, S. Brent. "The Oath and Covenant of the Priesthood." *Sperry Symposium on the Doctrine and Covenants.* Salt Lake City: Deseret Book, 1989.

First Presidency, "What is the Doctrine of the Priesthood?" Salt Lake City, UT: *Improvement Era*, February 1961.
Faust, James E. "A Royal Priesthood," *Ensign*, May 2006.
—*In the Strength of the Lord: The Life and Teachings of James E. Faust*. Salt Lake City, UT: Deseret Book, 1999.
—"He Healeth the Broken Heart," *Ensign* July 2005.
—"Our Search for Happiness, *Ensign*, Oct. 2000.
—"Standing in Holy Places," *Ensign*, May 2005.
—"The Devil's Throat," *Ensign*, May 2003.
—"The Gift of the Holy Ghost—A Sure Compass," *Ensign*, April 1996.
—"The Shield of Faith," *Ensign*, May 2000.
"Galaxy Map." Washington D.C.: The National Geographic Society, June 1983.
Galbraith, David B., D. Kelly Ogden, and Andrew C. Skinner. *Jerusalem—The Eternal City*. Salt Lake City, UT: Deseret Book, 1996.
Gardner, R. Quinn. "Becoming a Zion Society," *Ensign*, February 1979.
—"I Have a Question," *Ensign*, March 1978.
Gibbons, Ted L. *Be Not Afraid*, Springville, UT: Cedar Fort, Inc., 2009.
Goddard, Wallace H. "Blessed by Angels." *MeridianMagazine.com*, July 27, 2009.
—*Drawing Heaven into Your Marriage*. Fairfax, VA: Meridian Publishing, 2007.
Grant, Heber J. *Teachings of Presidents of the Church*. Salt Lake City, UT: The Church of Jesus Christ of Latter-day Saints, 2002.
Guralnik, David B., ed. *Webster's New World Dictionary, 2nd College Edition*. New York City, NY: The New World Publishing Company, 1970.
Hafen, Bruce C. *The Broken Heart: Applying the Atonement to Life's Experiences*. Salt Lake City, UT: Deseret Book, 1989.
Haight, David B. "The Sacrament and the Sacrifice," *Ensign*, November 1989.
Hamilton, Edith. *Spokesman for God*. New York, NY: Norton and Company, 1977.
Hinckley, Gordon B. "Blessed Are the Merciful," *Ensign*, May 1990.
—*Faith: The Essence of True Religion*. Salt Lake City, UT: Deseret Book, 1989.
—"Our Mission of Saving," *Ensign*, November 1991.
—"Priesthood: The Power of Godliness," *Improvement Era*, December 1970.
—*Stand a Little Taller*. Salt Lake City, UT: Eagle Gate, 2000.
—*Standing for Something*. New York, NY: Three Rivers Press, 2000.
—*Teachings of Gordon B. Hinckley*. Salt Lake City, UT: Deseret Book, 2002.
—"The Dawning of a Brighter Day," *Ensign*, May 2004.
—"The Stone Cut Out of the Mountain," *Ensign*, 2007.
—"Till We Meet Again," *Ensign*, November 2001.
—"We Thank Thee for This Sacred Structure," *Church News*, 8 November 1997.
— "Your Greatest Challenge, Mother," *Ensign*, November 2000.
Holland, Jeffrey R. "Broken Things to Mend," *Ensign*, May 2006.
—"However Long and Hard the Road," *Ensign*, September 2002.
—*On Earth As It Is in Heaven*. Salt Lake City, UT: Deseret Book, 1989.

Holzapfel, Richard Neitzel and Thomas A. Wayment, eds., *The Life and Teachings of Jesus Christ: From the Transfiguration through the Triumphant Entry*. Salt Lake City, UT: Deseret Book, 2006.

Horton, George A. "Abraham's Act of Faith Reflects 'a Soul Like Unto Our Savior,'" *LDS Church News*, April 2, 1994.

"'Hymn of the Pearl': an Ancient Counterpart To 'O My Father.'" *BYU Studies*, vol. 36, 1996–97.

Hymns of the Church of Jesus Christ of Latter-day Saints. Salt Lake City, UT: The Church of Jesus Christ of Latter-day Saints, 1985.

Jackson, Kent P. and Robert L. Millet. eds. *Studies in Scripture*. Salt Lake City, UT: Deseret Book 1989.

Jensen, Marlin K. "Living after the Manner of Happiness," *Ensign*, December 2002.

Jenson, Andrew, *Historical Record: A Monthly Periodical*. Salt Lake City, UT: Deseret News, 1886—1890.

Jessee, Dean. "Joseph Knight's Recollection of Early Mormon History." Provo, UT: *BYU Studies*, vol. 17, no. 1, 1976.

Johnson, Clark V. *Doctrines for Exaltation: The 1989 Sperry Symposium on the Doctrine and Covenants*. Salt Lake City, UT: Deseret Book, 1989.

Josephus. *Complete Works*. William Whiston, trans., Grand Rapids, MI: Kregal Publications, 1960.

Kimball, Spencer W. "A Gift of Gratitude," *Tambuli*, December 1977.

—"Becoming the Pure in Heart," *Ensign*, May 1978.

—*Faith Precedes the Miracle: Based on Discourses of Spencer W. Kimball*. Salt Lake City, UT: Deseret Book, 1972.

—"The Fruit of Our Welfare Services Labors," *Ensign*, November 1978.

—"The Role of Righteous Women," *Ensign*, November 1979.

—*The Teachings of Spencer W. Kimball*. Salt Lake City, UT: Bookcraft, 1982.

—"Welfare Services: The Gospel in Action," *Ensign*, November 1977.

—"Young Women Fireside 1981—In Love and Power and without Fear," *New Era*, July 1981.

Kirchhoff, Frederick. "Reconstruction of Self in Wordsworth's 'Ode on Intimations of Immortality from Recollections of Early Childhood.'" *Narcissism and the Text*. New York, NY: New York University Press, 1986.

Kirtland Council Minute Book, eds. Fred Collier and William S. Hartwell, Salt Lake City, UT: Collier's Publishing, 1996.

Largey, Dennis L. *Book of Mormon Reference Companion*. Salt Lake City, UT: Deseret Book, 2003.

Larsen, Dean L. "A Royal Generation," *Ensign*, May 1983.

Larson, Stan "The King Follett Discourse: a Newly Amalgamated Text." Provo, UT: *BYU Studies*, Vol. 18, 1977–1978.

Layton, Lynne and Schapiro, Barbara A. *Narcissism and the Text: Studies in Literature and the Psychology of Self*. New York, NY: New York University Press, 1986.

Lee, Harold B. *Decisions for Successful Living*. Salt Lake City, UT: Deseret Book, 1973.

—"Stand Ye in Holy Places," *Ensign*, July 1973.
—*The Teachings of Harold B. Lee*. Salt Lake City, UT: Deseret Book, 1974.
Lightner, Mary. Address to Brigham Young University. *BYU Archives and Manuscripts, Writings of Early Latter-day Saints*, 1905.
Ludlow, Daniel H. *A Companion to Your Study of the Book of Mormon*. Salt Lake City, UT: Deseret Book, 1976.
—*Encyclopedia of Mormonism*. New York City, NY: Macmillan Publishing, 1992.
Lund, Gerald N. *Jesus Christ, Key to the Plan of Salvation*. Salt Lake City, UT: Deseret Book, 1991.
—"Old Testament Types and Symbols," *A Witness of Jesus Christ: The 1989 Sperry Symposium on the Old Testament*. ed. Richard D. Draper, Salt Lake City, UT: Deseret Book, 1990.
Lundquist, John M. and Stephen D. Ricks, eds. *By Study and Also by Faith: Essays in Honor of Hugh W. Nibley on the Occasion of His Eightieth Birthday*. Provo, UT: Maxwell Institute, 1992.
Lundwall, N. B. *Temples of the Most High*. Salt Lake City, UT: Bookcraft, 1965.
"Map: Old Testament Stories: Part Two," *Deseret News*. Jan. 8, 1994.
Maxwell, Cory H., ed. *The Neal A. Maxwell Quote Book*. Salt Lake City, UT: Bookcraft, 1997.
Maxwell, Neal A. *A Wonderful Flood of Light*. Salt Lake City, UT: Deseret Book, 1991.
—*But for a Small Moment*. Salt Lake City, UT: Bookcraft, 1987.
—"Consecrate Thy Performance." *Ensign*, May 2002.
—*Disposition of a Disciple*. Salt Lake City, UT: Deseret Book, 1976.
—"Enduring Well," *Ensign*, April 1997.
—*Even As I Am*. Salt Lake City, UT: Deseret Book, 1991.
—*If Thou Endure It Well*. Salt Lake City, UT: Bookcraft, 2002.
—*Lord, Increase Our Faith*. Salt Lake City, UT: Bookcraft, 1994.
—*Men and Women of Christ*. Salt Lake City, UT: Deseret Book, 1991.
—*Notwithstanding My Weakness*. Salt Lake City, UT: Deseret Book, 1981.
—*One More Strain of Praise*. Salt Lake City, UT: Deseret Book, 2003.
—"Patience," *Ensign*, October 1980.
—*That Ye May Believe*. Salt Lake City, UT: Bookcraft, 1994.
—*The Promise of Discipleship*. Salt Lake City, UT: Deseret Book, 2001.
—"These Are Your Days," *New Era*, January 1985.
McConkie, Bruce R. *A New Witness for the Articles of Faith*. Salt Lake City, UT: Deseret Book, 1985.
—*Doctrinal New Testament Commentary*. Salt Lake City, UT: Deseret Book, 1972.
—*Doctrines of Salvation: Sermons and Writings of Joseph Fielding Smith*, Salt Lake City, UT: Bookcraft, 1954–1956.
—*Mormon Doctrine*. Salt Lake City, UT: Bookcraft: 1966.
—"Obedience, Consecration, and Sacrifice," *Ensign*, May 1975.
—"The Doctrine of the Priesthood," *Ensign*, May 1982.
—*The Mortal Messiah: From Bethlehem to Calvary*. Salt Lake City, UT: Deseret Book, 1981.

Bibliography

—"*The Probationary Test of Mortality.*" Address delivered at the University of Utah Institute, January 10, 1982.

—*The Promised Messiah: The First Coming of Christ.* Salt Lake City, UT: Deseret Book, 1981.

—"The Ten Blessings of the Priesthood," *Ensign*, November 1977.

McConkie, Joseph Fielding and Robert L. Millet. *Doctrinal Commentary on the Book of Mormon.* Salt Lake City, UT: Deseret Book, 1987–1993.

—*Joseph Smith: The Choice Seer.* Salt Lake City, UT: Bookcraft, 1996.

—*Revelations of the Restoration.* Salt Lake City, UT: Deseret Book, 2000.

McKay, David O. *Gospel Ideals: Selections from the Discourses of David O. McKay.* Salt Lake City, UT: Deseret Book, 1993.

—*Pathways to Happiness.* Salt Lake City, UT: Bookcraft, 1957.

McMullin, Keith B. "Come to Zion! Come to Zion!" Salt Lake City, UT: *Ensign*, November 2002.

Merriam Webster's New World Dictionary, Third Edition. New York, NY: Simon and Schuster, 1998

Middlemiss, Clare. *Man May Know for Himself: Teachings of President David O. McKay.* Salt Lake City, UT: Deseret Book, 1967.

Millet, Robert L. "Quest for the City of God: The Doctrine Of Zion In Modern Revelation," *1989 Sperry Symposium on the Doctrine and Covenants.* Salt Lake City, UT: Deseret Book, 1989.

—*The Capstone of Our Religion: Insights into the Doctrine and Covenants.* Salt Lake City, UT: Deseret Book, 1989.

—*The Life Beyond.* Salt Lake City, UT: Deseret Book, 1986.

—*The Power of the Word: Saving Doctrines from the Book of Mormon.* Salt Lake City, UT: Deseret Book, 2000.

Monson, Thomas S. "In Quest of the Abundant Life." *Ensign*, March 1988.

Nelson, Russell M. "Personal Priesthood Responsibility," *Ensign*, October 2005.

—*The Power within Us.* Salt Lake City, UT: Deseret Book, 1989.

Nelson, William O. "Enoch and His Message for Latter Days," *Deseret News*, Feb. 5, 1994.

Neuenschwander, Dennis. "Ordinances and Covenants," *Ensign*, August 2001.

Nibley, Hugh. *Abraham in Egypt.* Salt Lake City, UT and Provo, UT: Deseret Book and FARMS, 2000.

—*An Approach to the Book of Mormon.* Salt Lake City, UT: Deseret Book, 1988.

—*Approaching Zion.* Salt Lake City, UT: Deseret Book, 1989.

—"Educating the Saints—A Brigham Young Mosaic." Provo, UT: *BYU Studies*, Vol 11, Autumn 1970.

—*Nibley on the Timely and the Timeless.* Provo, UT: Religious Studies Center, Brigham Young University, 2004.

—*Teachings of the Book of Mormon.* Provo, UT: Covenant Communications, 2004.

—*Temple and Cosmos: Beyond This Ignorant Present.* Salt Lake City, UT: Deseret Book, 1992.

Nibley, Preston. *Brigham Young: The Man and His Work,* 4th ed. Salt Lake City, UT: Deseret Book, 1960.

Nielsen, Donna B. *Beloved Bridegroom*. Salt Lake City, UT: Onyx Press, 1999.

Nyman, Monte S. and Charles D. Tate, Jr., eds. *Fourth Nephi through Moroni: From Zion to Destruction*. Salt Lake City, UT: Bookcraft, 1992.

—*The Capstone of Our Religion: Insights into the Doctrine and Covenants*. Salt Lake City, UT: Bookcraft, 1989.

Oaks, Dallin H. "Good, Better, Best," *Ensign*, November 2007.

—"He Heals the Heavy Laden," *Ensign*, November 2006

—"Preparation for the Second Coming," *Ensign*, November 2004.

—"Taking Upon Us the Name of Jesus Christ," *Ensign*, May 1985.

—"The Challenge to Become," *Ensign*, November 2000.

—"Timing," *Ensign*, October 2003.

Oaks, Robert C. "The Power of Patience," *Ensign*, November 2006.

Otten, L. G. and C. M. Caldwell. *Sacred Truths of the Doctrine and Covenants*. Salt Lake City, UT: Deseret Book, 1982–1983.

Pack, Frederick J. "Was the Earth Created in Six Days of Twenty-Four Hours Each?" *Improvement Era*, October 1930.

Packer, Boyd K. "Personal Revelation: The Gift, the Test, and the Promise," *Ensign*, November 1994.

—"Restoration," *First Worldwide Leadership Training Meeting*. Salt Lake City, UT: The Church of Jesus Christ of Latter-day Saints, January 2003.

—*That All May Be Edified*. Salt Lake City, UT: Bookcraft, 1982.

—"The Candle of the Lord," *Ensign*, January 1983.

—"The One Pure Defense (An Evening with President Boyd K. Packer)," Intellectual Reserve, 2004. Address to CES Religious Educators, 6 February 2004, Salt Lake Tabernacle.

Parry, Donald W., ed. *Temples of the Ancient World: Ritual and Symbolism*. Salt Lake City, UT and Provo, UT: Deseret and FARMS, 1994.

—*Understanding the Book of Revelation*. Salt Lake City, UT: Deseret Book, 1998.

Peterson, H. Burke. "Your Special Purpose," *New Era*, October 2001.

Pratt, Orson. *Times and Seasons*, vol. 6. no. 10, 1 June 1845.

Riddle, Chauncey C. "The New and Everlasting Covenant," 1989 *Sperry Symposium on the Doctrine and Covenants*. Salt Lake City: Deseret Book, 1989.

Roberts, B.H. *Comprehensive History of the Church of Jesus Christ of Latter-day Saints*. Salt Lake City, UT: Church of Jesus Christ of Latter-day Saints, 1930.

—*Seventy's Course of Theology*. Salt Lake City, UT: Deseret Book, 1931.

Romney, Marion G. "Church Welfare Services' Basic Principles," *Ensign*, May 1976.

—"Church Welfare—Temporal Service in a Spiritual Setting," *Ensign*, May 1980

—"Priesthood," *Ensign*, May 1982.

—"'In Mine Own Way,'" *Ensign*, November 1976.

—"The Celestial Nature of Self-reliance," *Ensign*, November 1982.

—"The Oath and Covenant Which Belongeth to the Priesthood," *Ensign*, November 1980.

—"The Purpose of Church Welfare Services," *Ensign*, May 1977.

—"The Royal Law of Love," *Ensign*, May 1978.
—"Unity," *Ensign*, May 1983.
—"Welfare Services: The Savior's Program," *Ensign*, October 1980.
Salt Lake School of the Prophets Minutes. Salt Lake City, UT: The Church of Jesus Christ of Latter-day Saints, 1899.
"Sermon Given to Different People," *LDS Church News*, Feb. 18, 1995.
Skidmore, Rex A. "What Part Should a Teenager Play in a Family?" *Improvement Era*, 1952.
Skinner, Andrew C. *Temple Worship: 20 Truths That Will Bless Your Life*. Salt Lake City, UT: Deseret Book, 2008.
—*The Old Testament and the Latter-Day Saints*. Salt Lake City, UT: Deseret Book, 2005.
Smith, Hyrum M. and Janne M. Sjodahl. *Doctrine and Covenants Commentary*. Salt Lake City, UT: Deseret Book, 1960.
Smith, Joseph. *Evening and Morning Star*, July, 1833.
—*History of The Church of Jesus Christ of Latter-day Saints*. Salt Lake City, UT: Deseret Book, 1980.
—*Lectures on Faith*. Salt Lake City, UT: Deseret Book, 1993.
Smith, Joseph F. *Gospel Doctrine: Selections from the Sermons and Writings of Joseph F. Smith*. Deseret News Press, 1919.
—*Teachings of Presidents of the Church*. Salt Lake City, UT: The Church of Jesus Christ of Latter-day Saints, 1998.
Smith, Joseph Fielding. *Church History and Modern Revelation*. Salt Lake City, UT: The Church of Jesus Christ of Latter-day Saints, 1946.
—"Our responsibility as Priesthood Holders," *Ensign*, June 1971.
—*Teachings of the Prophet Joseph Smith*. Salt Lake City, UT: Deseret Book, 1938.
—"The Duties of the Priesthood in Temple Work," *The Utah Genealogical and Historical Magazine*, vol. 30, no. 1, January 1939.
—*The Restoration of All Things*. Salt Lake City, UT: Deseret News Press, 1945.
Snow, Lorenzo. *The Teachings of Lorenzo Snow*, Salt Lake City, UT: Bookcraft, 1984.
Sorensen, A. D. "No Respector of Persons: Equality in the Kingdom," ed. Mary E. Stoval, *As Women of Faith: Talks Selected from the BYU Women's Conferences*. Salt Lake City, UT: Deseret Book, 1989, 55.
Stevenson, Edward. "Life and History of Elder Edward Stevenson." Provo, UT: Special Collections, Harold B. Lee Library, Brigham Young University, n.d.
Stuy, Brian H., comp., *Collected Discourses*. Burbank, CA: B.H.S. Publishing, 1983.
Summerhays, James T. "The Stripling Elect." *MeridianMagazine.com*, February 20, 2009.
Talmage, James E. *Articles of Faith*. Salt Lake City, UT: Deseret Book, 1984.
—*Jesus the Christ*. Salt Lake City: Deseret News Press, 1915.
—"The Eternity of Sex," *Young Woman's Journal*, October 1914.
—*The House of the Lord*. Salt Lake City, UT: Bookcraft, 1962.
Tanakh: A New Translation of the Holy Scriptures According to the Traditional Hebrew Text. Philadelphia, PA: Jewish Publication Society of America, November 1985.
Tanner, N. Eldon. "Constancy Amid Change," Ensign, November 1979.

Tanner, Susan W. "All Things Shall Work Together for Your Good," *Ensign*, May 2004.
—"My Soul Delighteth in the Things of the Lord," *Ensign*, 2008.
Taylor, John. *Teachings of the Latter-day Prophets*. Salt Lake City, UT: Bookcraft, 1998.
Times and Seasons, vol. 6. no. 10, 1 June 1845.
Thomas, M. Catherine. "Alma the Younger, Part 1," Provo, UT: Neal A. Maxwell Institute for Religious Scholarship, 1996.
—"Alma the Younger, Part 2," Provo, UT: Neal A. Maxwell Institute for Religious Scholarship, 1996.
—"Benjamin and the Mysteries of God," *King Benjamin's Speech*. Provo, UT: Foundation for Ancient Research and Mormon Studies, 1998.
Turner, Rodney. *Woman and the Priesthood*. Salt Lake City, UT: Deseret Book, 1972.
Tvedtnes, John A. *The Church of the Old Testament*. Salt Lake City, UT: Deseret Book, 1967.
—"They Have Their Reward," *MeridianMagazine.com*, February 21, 2007.
Van Orden, Bruce A. and Brent L. Top. *Doctrines of the Book of Mormon: The 1991 Sperry Symposium*, Provo, UT: Maxwell Institute, 1993.
Watt, George D., ed. *Journal of Discourses*. Liverpool, England: F.D. Richards, et al., 1854–1886.
Whitney, Newell K. in *Messenger and Advocate*, 3 September 1837.
Whitney, Orson F. *Gospel Themes*. Salt Lake City, UT: n.p., 1914.
—*Life of Heber C. Kimball*. Salt Lake City, UT: Bookcraft, 1975.
—*Saturday Night Thoughts*. Salt Lake City, UT: Deseret News, 1927.
Wickman, Lance B. "Today," *Ensign*, May 2008.
Widtsoe, John A. *An Understandable Religion*. Salt Lake City, UT: The Church of Jesus Christ of Latter-day Saints, 1944.
—*Priesthood and Church Government*. Salt Lake City, UT: Deseret Book, 1939.
—*Utah Genealogical and Historical Magazine*. Salt Lake City, UT: October 1934.
Williams, Clyde J. *The Teachings of Lorenzo Snow, Fifth President of the Church of Jesus Christ of Latter-day Saints*. Salt Lake City, UT: Bookcraft, 1984.
Wilson, Marvin. *Our Father Abraham*, Grand Rapids, MI: Eerdmans Publishing Co., 1989.
Winder, Barbara W. "Finding Joy in Life," *Ensign*, November 1987.
Wirthlin, Joseph B. "The Great Commandment," *Ensign*, November 2007.
—"The Law of the Fast," *Ensign*, May 2001.
Woodruff, Wilford. *The Discourses of Wilford Woodruff*. Salt Lake City, UT: Bookcraft, 1946.
Yarn, David H. *The Gospel: God, Man, and Truth*. Salt Lake City, UT: Deseret Book, 1965.
Yorgason, Blaine M. *I Need Thee Every Hour*. Salt Lake City, UT: Deseret Book, 2003.
—*Spiritual Progression in the Last Days*. Salt Lake City, UT: Deseret Book, 1994.
Young, Brigham in *Deseret News*, 10 October 1866.
—*Discourses of Brigham Young*. Salt Lake City, UT: Deseret Book, 1926.
—*Journal History*. 28 September 1846.
—*Millennial Star*, Vol. 16. Salt Lake City, UT: The Church of Jesus Christ of Latter-day Saints, 1840–1970.

Index and Concordance

This is a master index of the book series. The page number is specific to the book in which it is located. For example: 101:3 means page 101 in book 3. Marker "P" refers to Portrait of a Zion Person.

Aaronic Priesthood. *See* **Oath and Covenant of the Priesthood;** *See* **Patriarchal Order of the Priesthood;** *See* **Priesthood**
>40:2, 41:2, 12:3, 22:3, 23:3, 36:3, 39:3, 42:3, 59:3, 60:3, 76:3, 92:3, 93:3, 103:3, 104:3, 202:3, 204:3, 50:4, 131:5

abundance
>5:6, 8:6, 10:6, 13:6, 17:6, 18:6, 31:6, 41:6, 44:6, 46:6, 52:6, 70:6, 82:6, 87:6, 96:6, 101:6, 103:6, 106:6, 107:6, 110:6, 111:6, 112:6, 114:6, 115:6

Adam
>empowered to become a savior to his family
>>11:1

adultery. *See also* **immoral**
>Babylon distinguished by
>>50:2

adversary. *See also* **devil;** *See also* **hell;** *See also* **Lucifer;** *See also* **Satan**
>attacks Saints more viciously than others
>>44:1

adversity. *See also* **opposition;** *See also* **trial(s)**
>33:2, 51:2, 54:2, 56:2, 58:2, 61:2, 34:3, 66:3, 117:3, 132:3, 186:3, 178:4, 10:5, 27:5, 30:5, 76:5, 50:6, 101:6

affluence. *See also* **mammon;** *See also* **riches;** *See also* **wealth**
>85:1, 139:4, 103:5, 64:6, 71:6

agency
>a discussion of
>>62–68:4

Amulek
>52:1, 80:1, 51:2, 52:2, 55:3, 42:4, 59:4, 133:4, 180:4, 36:5, 71:5, 56:6, 104:6

angels
>involved in crucible experiences
>>26:5

anger. *See also* **contention**
>19:1, 57:1, 64:1, 75:1, 86:1, 87:1, 93:1, 96:1, 97:1, 98:1, 55:2, 23:3, 152:3, 169:3, 176:3, 5:4, 29:4, 34:4, 101:4, 111:4, 116:4, 121:4, 136:4, 165:4, 179:4, 180:4, 4:5, 15:5, 22:5, 41:5, 46:5, 79:5, 104:5, 107:5, 124:5, 17:6, 28:6, 34:6, 39:6, 60:6, 94:6, 116:6

anti-Christ
>17:P, 21:1, 49:1, 50:1, 51:1, 61:1, 79:1, 84:1, 85:1, 101:1, 54:2, 67:3, 87:4, 127:4, 175:4, 176:4, 33:5, 48:5, 7:6, 47:6, 88:6

apostasy
>27:1, 33:1, 34:1, 60:1, 68:1, 84:4, 108:5

apostle
>59:1, 17:2

Index & Concordance

Atonement
> 6:P, 14:P, 15:P, 24:P, 42:P, 11:1, 12:1, 22:1, 23:1, 42:1, 45:1, 47:1, 66:1, 7C:1, 1:2, 3:2, 6:2, 7:2, 9:2, 10:2, 16:2, 17:2, 18:2, 19:2, 20:2, 23:2, 24:2, 25:2, 26:2, 27:2, 28:2, 29:2, 30:2, 31:2, 32:2, 34:2, 35:2, 36:2, 37:2, 38:2, 39:2, 45:2, 55:2, 57:2, 66:2, 67:2, 72:2, 93:2, 98:2, 1:3, 10:3, 17:3, 20:3, 21:3, 35:3, 63:3, 70:3, 73:3, 76:3, 158:3, 180:3, 196:3, 211:3, 214:3, 1:4, 16:4, 18:4, 19:4, 20:4, 31:4, 41:4, 42:4, 56:4, 57:4, 59:4, 64:4, 99:4, 122:4, 162:4, 185:4, 1:5, 4:5, 29:5, 64:5, 84:5, 87:5, 91:5, 106:5, 107:5, 111:5, 113:5, 117:5, 129:5, 133:5, 137:5, 15:6, 42:6, 67:6, 75:6

Babel
> a counterfeit gate of God
>> 54:1
>
> Nimrod established kingdom in
>> 53:1

Babylon. *See also* **world**
> a discussion of
>> 49–105:1
>
> state of mind defined by excess, self-indulgence
>> 54:1

baptism
> 2:P, 18:P, 21:P, 25:P, 11:1, 19:1, 23:1, 9:2, 18:2, 19:2, 21:2, 28:2, 31:2, 33:2, 34:2, 35:2, 36:2, 37:2, 38:2, 40:2, 41:2, 44:2, 45:2, 49:2, 53:2, 60:2, 63:2, 64:2, 67:2, 68:2, 70:2, 73:2, 75:2, 81:2, 82:2, 91:2, 93:2, 98:2, 1:3, 2:3, 4:3, 5:3, 9:3, 10:3, 11:3, 17:3, 21:3, 23:3, 27:3, 39:3, 42:3, 66:3, 70:3, 71:3, 76:3, 80:3, 93:3, 99:3, 117:3, 143:3, 144:3, 153:3, 179:3, 187:3, 193:3, 200:3, 210:3, 214:3, 1:4, 14:4, 26:4, 39:4, 51:4, 52:4, 88:4, 142:4, 144:4, 145:4, 1:5, 17:5, 18:5, 60:5, 61:5, 62:5, 63:5, 82:5, 83:5, 106:5, 117:5, 133:5, 134:5, 135:5, 68:6, 75:6, 76:6, 106:6

Beatitudes *See also* **Sermon on the Mount**
> 16:P, 18:P, 28:P, 28:1, 49:3, 41:5, 82:5

believe. *See* **faith**
> in order to see
>> 68:5

Beloved Son. *See also* **Christ**; *See also* **Exemplar**; *See also* **Jehovah**; *See also* **Lamb**; *See also* **Savior**
> 47:1, 65:3, 111:3, 55:5, 56:5, 110:5, 115:5

Bible
> 39:1, 63:1, 83:1, 54:2, 7:3, 138:3, 203:3, 8:5

blasphemy
> 59:1, 82:3

bloodline
> men ordained to priesthood regardless of
>> 17:1

Book of Mormon
> 12:P, 19:P, 21:P, 30:P, 39:P, 42:P, 1:1, 2:1, 5:1, 12:1, 17:1, 31:1, 34:1, 37:1, 61:1, 64:1, 67:1, 70:1, 78:1, 103:1, 18:2, 51:2, 7:3, 17:3, 19:3, 45:3, 46:3, 69:3, 70:3, 92:3, 120:3, 123:3, 132:3, 141:3, 146:3, 153:3, 163:3, 171:3, 180:3, 5:4, 26:4, 40:4, 69:4, 85:4, 97:4, 99:4, 104:4, 108:4, 124:4, 135:4, 138:4, 139:4, 157:4, 161:4, 4:5, 8:5, 11:5, 23:5, 34:5, 59:5, 78:5, 96:5, 103:5, 109:5, 118:5, 127:5, 129:5, 11:6, 15:6, 20:6, 25:6, 44:6, 59:6, 61:6, 63:6, 113:6

Bridegroom *See also* **Christ, Jesus**
> 75:1, 85:1, 58:2, 71:2, 72:2, 73:2, 74:2, 75:2, 76:2, 77:2, 78:2, 79:2, 80:2, 81:2, 82:2, 83:2, 84:2, 85:2, 86:2, 87:2, 88:2, 89:2, 90:2, 91:2, 92:2, 93:2, 94:2, 95:2, 96:2, 97:2, 98:2, 111:3, 161:3, 173:3, 183:3, 98:4, 11:6

Brigham Young
> 14:P, 26:P, 39:P, 41:P, 3:1, 5:1, 6:1, 12:1, 39:1, 40:1, 44:1, 46:1, 90:1, 103:1, 1:2, 61:2, 1:3, 3:3, 19:3, 56:3, 96:3, 101:3, 102:3, 127:3, 128:3, 142:3, 164:3, 192:3, 193:3, 201:3, 214:3, 1:4, 10:4, 30:4, 47:4, 62:4, 75:4, 85:4, 87:4, 89:4, 97:4, 105:4, 106:4, 109:4, 113:4, 125:4, 131:4, 132:4, 133:4, 135:4, 137:4, 140:4, 141:4, 149:4, 150:4, 152:4, 1:5, 4:5, 11:5, 28:5, 41:5, 56:5, 73:5, 81:5, 84:5, 90:5, 91:5, 96:5, 97:5, 99:5, 101:5, 109:5, 127:5, 134:5, 136:5, 137:5, 11:6, 20:6, 21:6, 27:6, 30:6, 31:6, 45:6, 55:6, 56:6, 57:6, 58:6, 59:6, 61:6, 64:6, 65:6, 71:6, 105:6

brother of Jared
> 13:1, 74:1, 58:2, 184:3, 196:3, 209:3, 210:3, 8:5, 21:5, 29:5, 32:5, 34:5, 41:5, 43:5, 53:5, 58:5, 66:5, 68:5, 69:5, 70:5, 73:5, 86:5, 112:5, 119:5

Bruce R. McConkie
> 34:P, 36:P, 37:P, 11:1, 45:1, 85:2, 93:2, 2:3, 9:3, 11:3, 14:3, 21:3, 25:3, 33:3, 79:3, 214:3, 2:4, 8:4, 62:4, 68:4, 82:4, 135:4, 2:5, 7:5, 60:5, 64:5, 129:5, 58:6

business. *See* **mammon**

Cain
> 13:1, 51:1, 52:1, 53:1, 54:1, 61:1, 69:1, 72:1, 74:1, 77:1, 79:1, 90:1, 101:1, 109:3, 82:4, 127:4, 150:4, 175:4, 176:4, 47:6, 88:6

calling and election made sure
>> chronology of
>>> 83:3

carnal
> 20:P, 25:P, 41:P, 19:1, 23:1, 59:1, 62:1, 70:1, 89:1, 94:1, 101:1, 102:1, 8:2, 23:2, 25:2, 29:2, 33:2, 62:2, 23:3, 109:3, 172:3, 178:3, 64:4, 65:4, 100:4, 109:4, 149:4, 14:5, 44:5, 67:5, 93:5, 16:6, 26:6, 76:6

celestial kingdom
> 14:P, 16:P, 18:P, 22:P, 28:P, 34:P, 48:1, 14:2, 15:2, 16:2, 18:2, 21:2, 27:2, 37:2, 74:2, 2:3, 22:3, 23:3, 28:3, 34:3, 69:3, 71:3, 79:3, 103:3, 115:3, 121:3, 124:3, 125:3, 153:3, 168:3, 182:3, 186:3, 199:3, 2:4, 3:4, 4:4, 6:4, 8:4, 10:4, 15:4, 26:4, 29:4, 30:4, 38:4, 51:4, 52:4, 54:4, 63:4, 68:4, 73:4, 77:4, 79:4, 89:4, 90:4, 91:4, 95:4, 126:4, 132:4, 141:4, 144:4, 148:4, 150:4, 152:4, 185:4, 2:5, 11:5, 31:5, 50:5, 78:5, 120:5, 132:5, 134:5, 135:5, 3:6, 6:6, 9:6, 13:6, 31:6, 46:6, 56:6, 66:6, 68:6, 72:6, 94:6, 105:6, 110:6

charity
    a discussion of
        165–184:4
    characteristics of
        147–173:3

chaste
    5:2, 22:2, 66:2, 24:5, 57:5

Christ, Jesus. *See also* **Beloved Son;** *See also* **Exemplar;** *See also* **Jehovah;** *See also* **Lamb;** *See also* **Savior**
    a discussion of
        as Bridegroom
            72–98:2
        coming into his presence
            77:2
        taking name of, upon us
            59:2
    frees us from the powers of Babylon
        26:1

city of Enoch
    14:1, 16:1, 36:1, 5:3, 19:3, 23:5, 34:5, 72:5, 2:6

comforter *See also* **Holy Ghost**
    37:2, 86:2, 71:3

commerce *See also* **mammon**
    76:1, 79:1

compete, competition
    79:1, 88:1, 119:3, 132:3

consecrate, consecration
    a discussion of
        blessings of living
            33–50:4
        characteristics of the law of
            3–31:4
        guiding principles of
            62–91:4
    living law of, brings blessings of abundance
        18:1
    to set apart
        160:4

contention *See also* **anger**
    6:P, 12:P, 43:P, 19:1, 21:1, 24:1, 29:1, 64:1, 67:1, 79:1, 85:1, 88:1, 102:1, 8:3, 119:3, 128:3, 42:4, 48:4, 179:4, 180:4, 4:5, 43:5, 102:5, 103:5, 104:5, 107:5, 108:5, 2:6, 117:6

cooperate
  25:P, 6:2, 9:2, 100:5
corn
  kernel of, represents potential of grace freely given
    55:3
coronation
  1:2, 9:2, 98:2, 29:3, 30:3, 36:3, 184:3, 194:3, 195:3, 65:5, 73:5, 135:5
counterfeit
  Satan always has, to God's works
    61:1
covet
  36:P, 24:1, 70:1, 69:4, 86:4, 100:4, 102:4, 148:4, 16:6, 17:6, 18:6, 115:6
Creator. *See* **Christ, Jesus**
crown. *See* **coronation**
crucibles
  angels involved in
    26:5
  many, last fourteen years
    25:5
deceive. *See* **deception**
deception
  victims of, will not be condemned
    22:1
Deity. *See* **God**
deliverance
  20:P, 18:1, 25:1, 72:1, 8:2, 22:2, 35:2, 51:2, 52:2, 26:3, 121:3, 128:3, 140:3, 148:3, 44:4, 84:4, 125:4, 131:4, 161:4, 162:4, 163:4, 174:4, 178:4, 180:4, 185:4, 3:5, 16:5, 17:5, 19:5, 23:5, 26:5, 27:5, 29:5, 36:5, 38:5, 39:5, 40:5, 45:5, 48:5, 49:5, 50:5, 51:5, 52:5, 55:5, 57:5, 68:5, 69:5, 70:5, 71:5, 72:5, 73:5, 75:5, 76:5, 78:5, 45:6, 52:6, 101:6
descend
  we must, below all things to ascend above all
    39:1
devil. *See also* **adversary;** *See also* **hell;** *See also* **Lucifer;** *See also* **Satan**
  6:P, 35:P, 41:P, 21:1, 24:1, 44:1, 51:1, 52:1, 60:1, 61:1, 62:1, 63:1, 64:1, 68:1, 70:1, 72:1, 73:1, 84:1, 86:1, 90:1, 92:1, 100:1, 101:1, 102:1, 28:2, 32:2, 49:2, 89:2, 98:2, 97:3, 109:3, 131:3, 160:3, 163:3, 172:3, 188:3, 189:3, 19:4, 45:4, 63:4, 64:4, 65:4, 67:4, 70:4, 109:4, 113:4, 120:4, 138:4, 141:4, 149:4, 151:4, 152:4, 14:5, 18:5, 47:5, 55:5, 101:5, 104:5, 107:5, 120:5, 26:6, 27:6, 30:6, 38:6, 63:6, 65:6, 71:6, 117:6
disputations
  6:P, 17:P, 26:P, 30:1, 49:1, 57:1, 19:3, 42:4, 119:4, 107:5, 108:5, 109:5, 122:5, 2:6, 37:6, 117:6

Index & Concordance

elect
57:1, 63:1, 85:1, 101:1, 103:1, 43:2, 48:2, 92:2, 40:3, 63:3, 79:3, 80:3, 81:3, 82:3, 84:3, 85:3, 87:3, 105:3, 114:3, 140:3, 154:3, 203:3, 73:5, 74:5, 90:5, 96:5, 7:6

Elijah
23:P, 35:P, 31:1, 81:2, 12:3, 13:3, 14:3, 15:3, 16:3, 17:3, 65:3, 116:3, 121:3, 66:4, 130:4, 8:5, 51:5, 70:5, 92:5, 52:6

Eliza R. Snow
34:1

endow, endowment
Abraham administered, regardless of bloodline
17:1

Enoch
3:P, 12:P, 15:P, 33:P, 37:P, 39:P, 3:1, 4:1, 6:1, 7:1, 13:1, 14:1, 15:1, 16:1, 18:1, 32:1, 33:1, 36:1, 37:1, 55:1, 58:1, 74:1, 87:1, 88:1, 103:1, 11:2, 12:2, 5:3, 7:3, 9:3, 18:3, 19:3, 20:3, 24:3, 25:3, 27:3, 30:3, 46:3, 57:3, 72:3, 73:3, 89:3, 93:3, 116:3, 184:3, 198:3, 204:3, 207:3, 208:3, 209:3, 10:4, 11:4, 82:4, 86:4, 157:4, 23:5, 34:5, 37:5, 69:5, 72:5, 86:5, 89:5, 90:5, 94:5, 96:5, 100:5, 101:5, 112:5, 124:5, 125:5, 127:5, 132:5, 1:6, 2:6

equal
6:P, 7:P, 12:P, 33:P, 27:1, 41:1, 57:1, 65:1, 87:1, 13:2, 64:2, 4:3, 18:3, 40:3, 41:3, 50:3, 60:3, 90:3, 105:3, 106:3, 119:3, 132:3, 200:3, 9:4, 24:4, 26:4, 27:4, 30:4, 36:4, 37:4, 38:4, 39:4, 49:4, 58:4, 59:4, 61:4, 73:4, 74:4, 77:4, 90:4, 96:4, 125:4, 156:4, 183:4, 185:4, 4:5, 122:5, 123:5, 3:6, 10:6, 45:6, 53:6, 77:6, 107:6, 116:6

exalt
25:P, 1:2, 9:2, 32:2, 33:2, 45:2, 54:2, 57:2, 61:2, 28:3, 59:3, 132:3, 134:3, 142:3, 146:3, 4:4, 37:4, 52:4, 56:4, 109:4, 184:4, 93:5, 26:6, 76:6, 78:6, 108:6, 116:6

Exemplar. *See also* **Christ, Jesus;** *See also* **Jehovah;** *See also* **Lamb;** *See also* **Savior**
39:1, 65:3

Ezra Taft Benson
34:P, 8:1, 24:1, 41:1, 61:1, 67:1, 26:3, 109:3, 116:3, 205:3, 6:4, 15:4, 25:4, 26:4, 27:4, 28:4, 48:4, 59:4, 1:6, 80:6, 105:6

face-to-face
coming, with God is ultimate blessing and right of Zion people
97:3

family, families
3:P, 4:P, 23:P, 27:P, 29:P, 31:P, 32:P, 33:P, 34:P, 36:P, 37:P, 38:P, 42:P, 43:P, 6:1, 11:1, 12:1, 13:1, 14:1, 17:1, 18:1, 24:1, 26:1, 40:1, 42:1, 43:1, 45:1, 47:1, 54:1, 89:1, 93:1, 5:2, 23:2, 29:2, 32:2, 36:2, 37:2, 41:2, 50:2, 51:2, 52:2, 53:2, 62:2, 64:2, 68:2, 80:2, 83:2, 92:2, 5:3, 8:3, 12:3, 13:3, 14:3, 15:3, 16:3, 17:3, 20:3, 25:3, 26:3, 27:3, 28:3, 31:3, 32:3, 34:3, 65:3, 69:3, 70:3, 76:3, 78:3, 92:3, 100:3, 111:3, 113:3, 120:3, 136:3, 139:3, 146:3, 170:3, 178:3, 185:3, 186:3, 199:3, 200:3, 201:3, 204:3, 206:3, 207:3, 212:3, 4:4, 6:4, 8:4, 9:4, 23:4, 26:4, 27:4, 29:4, 30:4, 39:4, 41:4, 69:4, 72:4, 73:4,

74:4, 79:4, 82:4, 84:4, 86:4, 87:4, 133:4, 134:4, 141:4, 151:4, 157:4, 170:4, 171:4, 179:4, 180:4, 4:5, 21:5, 24:5, 42:5, 50:5, 51:5, 52:5, 62:5, 66:5, 71:5, 94:5, 95:5, 104:5, 107:5, 127:5, 133:5, 134:5, 5:6, 57:6, 65:6, 78:6, 87:6, 98:6, 102:6, 103:6, 104:6, 111:6, 112:6, 113:6, 114:6, 115:6

fathers
6:P, 18:1, 28:1, 35:1, 45:1, 63:1, 81:1, 91:1, 98:1, 32:2, 75:2, 13:3, 15:3, 17:3, 23:3, 27:3, 65:3, 77:3, 91:3, 104:3, 160:3, 161:3, 207:3, 118:4, 124:4, 128:4, 137:4, 141:4, 152:4, 67:5, 109:5, 124:5, 128:5, 136:5, 4:6, 37:6, 43:6, 48:6, 60:6, 66:6

fear
11:P, 26:P, 29:P, 42:P, 43:P, 23:1, 35:1, 37:1, 40:1, 53:1, 56:1, 64:1, 84:1, 85:1, 93:1, 94:1, 97:1, 59:2, 86:2, 39:3, 128:3, 130:3, 142:3, 149:3, 158:3, 169:3, 186:3, 196:3, 4:4, 22:4, 116:4, 141:4, 171:4, 172:4, 177:4, 27:5, 37:5, 57:5, 101:5, 133:5, 1:6, 35:6, 66:6, 90:6, 97:6, 98:6, 112:6

flatter
73:1, 96:1

forgive
10:P, 39:2, 40:2, 116:4, 178:4, 183:4, 35:6, 101:6

fornication
56:1, 57:1, 58:1, 59:1, 76:1, 80:1, 93:1, 50:2, 22:5

fourteen years
many crucibles last
25:5

fruit
ripe, falls from tree of life to rot on ground
96:1

fundamentalism
definition of
83:1

Gadianton robbers. *See also* **secret combinations**
97:1

Garden of Eden
13:1, 77:1, 108:4, 8:5, 28:5, 36:5, 72:5, 25:6

gathering
always associated with Zion
20:1

generosity. *See* **selflessness**

give yourself rich. *See also* **abundance**
8:P, 176:4, 89:6

God-like, godliness
become, by learning how to lift others
5:1

Index & Concordance 137

gold
    28:P, 38:P, 42:P, 27:1, 50:1, 52:1, 58:1, 59:1, 62:1, 76:1, 96:1, 22:2, 80:2, 94:2, 129:3, 151:3, 9:4, 40:4, 44:4, 82:4, 101:4, 103:4, 106:4, 109:4, 116:4, 118:4, 124:4, 132:4, 139:4, 140:4, 145:4, 146:4, 3:5, 21:5, 23:5, 24:5, 25:5, 26:5, 17:6, 19:6, 22:5, 27:6, 35:6, 36:6, 44:6, 55:6, 64:6, 65:6, 68:6, 69:6, 70:6

good
    definition of
        9:1

goods. *See* mammon

Gordon B. Hinckley
    6:P, 7:1, 28:2, 55:3, 172:3, 211:3, 37:4, 40:4, 41:4, 56:4, 59:4, 60:4, 164:4, 170:4, 87:5, 78:6, 83:6, 93:6

grace. *See also* mercy
    15:P, 19:P, 22:P, 4:1, 6:1, 10:1, 11:1, 28:1, 42:1, 4:2, 17:2, 18:2, 19:2, 20:2, 22:2, 23:2, 26:2, 29:2, 36:2, 38:2, 43:2, 45:2, 78:2, 16:3, 21:3, 24:3, 52:3, 53:3, 54:3, 55:3, 60:3, 64:3, 86:3, 104:3, 153:3, 198:3, 200:3, 57:4, 66:4, 79:4, 89:4, 92:4, 139:4, 146:4, 174:4, 175:4, 177:4, 181:4, 184:4, 7:5, 20:5, 31:5, 32:5, 45:5, 90:5, 124:5, 64:6, 70:6, 75:6, 80:6, 81:6, 82:6, 83:6, 89:6, 90:6, 100:6, 101:6

Harold B. Lee
    16:P, 28:P, 28:1, 82:1, 49:3, 130:3, 131:3, 204:3, 82:5, 147:5

heal
    21:P, 1:1, 2:1, 46:1, 135:3, 142:3, 152:3, 165:3, 171:3, 73:4, 77:4, 142:4, 144:4, 159:4, 160:4, 161:4, 184:4, 15:5, 113:5, 68:6, 86:6

healing
    we prepare for Zion by experiencing
        160:4

health
    23:P, 9:1, 76:1, 90:1, 100:1, 24:2, 29:2, 123:3, 18:4, 161:4, 180:4, 185:4, 15:5, 24:5, 25:5, 37:5, 57:5, 71:5, 72:5, 1:6, 86:6, 103:6, 109:6

heart
    a discussion of
        pure in
            77–108:5
    is altar of soul
        49:5
    must be changed to attain Zion
        12:1

Heber C. Kimball
    114:1, 83:3, 100:3, 101:3, 148:5

heir
    11:1, 53:1, 101:1, 29:3, 76:3, 195:3, 45:5

hell. *See also* **adversary;** *See also* **devil;** *See also* **Lucifer;** *See also* **Satan**
18:P, 41:P, 47:1, 63:1, 68:1, 70:1, 72:1, 73:1, 74:1, 101:1, 102:1, 26:2, 97:3, 109:3, 128:3, 131:3, 154:3, 160:3, 163:3, 188:3, 75:4, 109:4, 112:4, 113:4, 120:4, 126:4, 141:4, 149:4, 13:5, 14:5, 47:5, 56:5, 97:5, 5:6, 26:6, 29:6, 30:6, 39:6, 46:6, 65:6

Holy Ghost. *See also* **comforter**
presence of, signifies we are retaining remission of sins
38:2

homosexuality
56:1

Hugh Nibley
5:P, 26:P, 33:P, 5:1, 7:1, 8:1, 33:1, 34:1, 50:1, 51:1, 56:1, 57:1, 70:1, 71:1, 75:1, 77:1, 79:1, 80:1, 89:1, 92:1, 93:1, 47:3, 109:3, 110:3, 137:3, 6:4, 7:4, 16:4, 28:4, 50:4, 56:4, 85:4, 87:4, 93:4, 94:4, 98:4, 99:4, 105:4, 108:4, 110:4, 113:4, 127:4, 132:4, 136:4, 138:4, 150:4, 21:5, 22:5, 96:5, 7:6, 8:6, 12:6, 15:6, 21:6, 25:6, 27:6, 30:6, 47:6, 56:6, 59:6, 61:6, 105:6, 116:6

hundredfold
8:P, 25:2, 27:2, 29:2, 123:3, 126:3, 127:3, 141:3, 151:3, 36:4, 58:4, 67:4, 92:4, 145:4, 153:4, 170:4, 177:4, 184:4, 70:5, 118:5, 3:6, 6:6, 69:6, 70:6, 72:6, 87:6, 89:6, 106:6, 107:6, 108:6, 109:6, 110:6

husband. *See also* **marriage**
24:2, 66:2, 75:2, 76:2, 77:2, 78:2, 79:2, 80:2, 81:2, 83:2, 84:2, 85:2, 89:2, 90:2, 94:2, 97:2, 13:3, 15:3, 17:3, 23:3, 59:3, 64:3, 85:3, 110:3, 136:3, 179:3, 183:3, 198:3, 211:3, 41:4, 43:4, 98:4, 155:4, 156:4, 157:4, 42:5, 117:5, 11:6

hypocrisy
80:1, 41:2, 44:3, 47:3, 108:3, 110:3, 119:3, 159:3, 160:3, 165:3, 167:3, 140:4, 64:6

idleness
38:P, 27:1, 56:1, 119:3, 129:3, 20:4, 39:4, 83:4, 84:4, 85:4, 86:4, 101:4, 121:4, 157:4, 18:6, 41:6, 50:6

idolatrous
54:1, 88:1, 54:2, 171:3, 109:4, 117:4, 27:6, 35:6

immoral. *See also* **adultery**
58:1, 69:1, 76:1, 87:1, 171:3, 172:3, 176:4, 88:6

inequality
7:P, 86:1, 114:3, 124:3, 132:3, 139:3, 19:4, 29:4, 36:4, 39:4, 73:4, 85:4, 119:4, 124:4, 125:4, 150:4, 103:5, 38:6, 44:6, 45:6, 78:6

inherit, inheritance
a discussion of the chosen few
63–105:3

Israel
26:P, 18:1, 29:1, 32:1, 36:1, 42:1, 43:1, 45:1, 46:1, 65:1, 100:1, 14:2, 72:2, 81:2, 90:2, 91:2, 94:2, 14:3, 23:3, 31:3, 70:3, 76:3, 77:3, 111:3, 176:3, 180:3, 196:3, 18:4, 73:4, 100:4, 101:4, 104:4, 106:4, 126:4, 130:4, 131:4, 135:4, 150:4, 160:4, 35:5, 36:5, 41:5, 79:5, 110:5, 111:5, 112:5, 113:5, 114:5, 132:5, 4:6, 16:6, 17:6, 20:6, 21:6, 22:6, 46:6, 52:6, 58:6

Index & Concordance   **139**

James E. Faust
    8:P, 83:1, 93:3, 117:3, 43:4, 156:4, 162:4, 45:5, 91:5, 142:5

Jehovah. *See also* **Christ, Jesus;** *See also* **Exemplar;** *See also* **Lamb;** *See also* **Savior**
    18:1, 30:3, 66:4, 98:4, 100:4, 88:5, 98:5, 12:6, 16:6

Jerusalem. *See also* **Salem**
    14:P, 2:1, 9:1, 15:1, 16:1, 33:1, 36:1, 37:1, 47:1, 53:1, 55:1, 61:1, 75:1, 78:1 104:1, 1:2, 3:2, 51:2, 97:2, 1:3, 9:3, 18:3, 49:3, 100:3, 202:3, 1:4, 41:4, 1:5, 8:5, 20:5, 23:5, 63:5, 73:5, 87:5, 96:5, 97:5, 98:5, 113:5, 117:5, 118:5, 127:5, 128:5, 131:5, 134:5, 1:6

John A. Widtsoe
    8:1, 45:1, 61:1, 72:2, 164:4, 67:5, 93:6

Joseph Fielding Smith
    14:1, 81:1, 15:3, 21:3, 41:3, 56:3, 78:3, 102:3, 103:3, 190:3, 194:3, 208:3, 3:6

Joseph Smith
    4:P, 12:P, 18:P, 33:P, 39:P, 40:P, 41:P, 3:1, 5:1, 15:1, 26:1, 31:1, 32:1, 41:1, 44:1, 46:1, 48:1, 65:1, 67:1, 72:1, 90:1, 94:1, 103:1, 1:2, 3:2, 4:2, 6:2, 10:2, 15:2, 22:2, 23:2, 25:2, 26:2, 27:2, 28:2, 31:2, 42:2, 44:2, 45:2, 50:2, 58:2, 61:2, 62:2, 63:2, 87:2, 88:2, 90:2, 1:3, 5:3, 6:3, 7:3, 12:3, 13:3, 14:3, 15:3, 16:3, 17:3, 18:3, 20:3, 22:3, 25:3, 30:3, 31:3, 36:3, 43:3, 44:3, 57:3, 68:3, 69:3, 77:3, 81:3, 82:3, 83:3, 85:3, 86:3, 87:3, 88:3, 91:3, 93:3, 97:3, 98:3, 99:3, 100:3, 101:3, 104:3, 116:3, 120:3, 122:3, 125:3, 126:3, 140:3, 141:3, 160:3, 166:3, 177:3, 181:3, 182:3, 184:3, 188:3, 190:3, 191:3, 192:3, 193:3, 195:3, 196:3, 198:3, 200:3, 202:3, 203:3, 207:3, 208:3, 1:4, 4:4, 7:4, 10:4, 11:4, 12:4, 13:4, 28:4, 29:4, 30:4, 38:4, 39:4, 44:4, 45:4 46:4, 48:4, 57:4, 61:4, 65:4, 76:4, 77:4, 78:4, 100:4, 104:4, 107:4, 114:4, 133:4, 137:4, 142:4, 148:4, 157:4, 169:4, 171:4, 1:5, 4:5, 5:5, 8:5, 9:5, 14:5, 20:5, 24:5, 25:5, 27:5, 30:5, 31:5, 33:5, 34:5, 42:5, 45:5, 47:5, 54:5, 55:5, 56:5, 58:5, 64:5, 66:5, 68:5, 77:5, 81:5, 86:5, 88:5, 89:5, 93:5, 94:5, 95:5, 96:5, 97:5, 98:5, 99:5, 100:5, 108:5, 112:5, 118:5, 119:5, 123:5, 124:5, 126:5, 127:5, 129:5, 136:5, 1:6, 3:6, 5:6, 6:6, 16:6, 20:6, 22:6, 25:6, 31:6, 51:6, 56:6, 57:6, 60:6, 87:6, 98:6, 105:6, 106:6, 113:5, 116:6

journey
    a discussion of
        life's journey
            7–57:5

J. Reuben Clark
    44:1, 79:3, 21:4, 28:4

justice, justification
    discussion of
        6–17:2
    rewards those who are obedient to God's laws
        17:2

justified. *See* **justice, justification**

key(s)
    8:P, 23:P, 26:P, 2:1, 13:1, 18:1, 87:1, 101:1, 104:1, 28:2, 61:2, 22:3, 23:3, 24:3, 43:3, 44:3, 57:3, 60:3, 76:3, 83:3, 94:3, 95:3, 97:3, 98:3, 121:3, 122:3, 136:3, 141:3, 156:3,

157:3, 164:3, 176:3, 179:3, 181:3, 184:3, 190:3, 191:3, 192:3, 198:3, 9:4, 62:4, 66:4, 89:4, 106:4, 146:4, 153:4, 159:4, 164:4, 182:4, 26:5, 46:5, 47:5, 54:5, 64:5, 66:5, 87:5, 88:5, 108:5, 134:5, 22:6, 70:6, 94:6, 106:6, 108:6

King Benjamin

20:P, 19:1, 20:1, 21:1, 22:1, 23:1, 24:1, 25:1, 26:1, 8:2, 66:2, 7:3, 8:3, 9:3, 10:3, 11:3, 20:3, 51:3, 67:3, 152:3, 9:4, 35:4, 39:4, 78:4, 120:4, 121:4, 126:4, 127:4, 170:4, 36:5, 42:5, 59:5, 62:5, 63:5, 64:5, 66:5, 106:5, 108:5, 39:6, 46:6, 48:6, 76:6, 79:6, 106:6

king(s)

15:1, 16:1, 20:1, 21:1, 23:1, 25:1, 49:1, 85:2, 90:2, 92:2, 94:2, 95:2, 5:3, 7:3, 9:3, 10:3, 11:3, 29:3, 45:3, 111:3, 112:3, 113:3, 119:3, 139:3, 152:3, 198:3, 199:3, 20:4, 39:4, 76:4, 100:4, 108:4, 134:4, 8:5, 9:5, 39:5, 51:5, 54:5, 58:5, 60:5, 62:5, 63:5, 89:5, 1:6, 2:6, 16:6, 26:6, 46:6, 58:6

Korihor

50:1, 79:1, 127:4, 175:4, 47:6, 88:6

labor. *See also* **work**

35:P, 37:P, 38:P, 42:P, 20:1, 24:1, 27:1, 30:1, 42:1, 84:1, 39:2, 7:3, 19:3, 55:3, 146:3, 171:3, 17:4, 19:4, 39:4, 58:4, 62:4, 70:4, 71:4, 80:4, 82:4, 83:4, 84:4, 85:4, 86:4, 87:4, 88:4, 89:4, 90:4, 91:4, 92:4, 127:4, 135:4, 136:4, 140:4, 141:4, 151:4, 152:4, 156:4, 174:4, 176:4, 183:4, 185:4, 4:5, 26:5, 32:5, 33:5, 50:5, 92:5, 93:5, 95:5, 122:5, 137:5, 48:6, 59:6, 60:6, 65:6, 66:6, 71:6, 72:6, 100:6

lack. *See* **poor**

Laman

101:1, 20:5, 27:5

Lamb. *See also* **Christ, Jesus;** *See also* **Exemplar;** *See also* **Jehovah;** *See also* **Savior**

18:1, 172:4, 98:6

lawyers

86:1, 90:1, 119:4, 103:5, 37:6

Lehi

17:P, 27:P, 63:1, 64:1, 74:1, 94:1, 52:2, 58:2, 78:2, 195:3, 21:4, 42:4, 59:4, 3:5, 8:5, 9:5, 10:5, 17:5, 19:5, 21:5, 23:5, 26:5, 28:5, 31:5, 34:5, 41:5, 42:5, 51:5, 52:5, 58:5, 67:5, 73:5

lies

30:P, 9:1, 18:1, 22:1, 51:1, 63:1, 72:1, 19:2, 97:2, 9:3, 55:3, 60:3, 95:3, 97:3, 117:3, 139:3, 160:3, 181:3, 13:4, 41:4, 47:4, 65:4, 74:4, 137:4, 142:4, 156:4, 166:4, 7:5, 9:5, 19:5, 26:5, 87:5, 2:6, 60:6, 67:6, 101:6, 112:6

Lorenzo Snow

78:1, 6:4, 15:4, 17:4, 31:4, 47:4, 4:5, 94:5, 95:5, 100:5, 131:5, 136:5, 148:5

love. *See also* **charity;** *See also* **heart**

2:P, 7:P, 9:P, 10:P, 11:P, 12:P, 17:P, 20:P, 21:P, 22:P, 24:P, 27:P, 28:P, 34:P, 39:P, 43:P, 19:1, 22:1, 23:1, 24:1, 26:1, 29:1, 30:1, 33:1, 34:1, 42:1, 49:1, 64:1, 65:1, 70:1, 71:1, 76:1, 77:1, 79:1, 86:1, 87:1, 89:1, 91:1, 99:1, 3:2, 4:2, 5:2, 18:2, 19:2, 27:2, 38:2, 41:2, 44:2, 50:2, 54:2, 56:2, 57:2, 60:2, 61:2, 62:2, 66:2, 67:2, 69:2, 70:2,

Index & Concordance 141

72:2, 73:2, 74:2, 75:2, 76:2, 77:2, 78:2, 79:2, 80:2, 81:2, 82:2, 84:2, 86:2, 93:2, 95:2, 96:2, 97:2, 98:2, 99:2, 17:3, 30:3, 33:3, 44:3, 47:3, 48:3, 49:3, 50:3, 51:3, 52:3, 56:3, 57:3, 61:3, 68:3, 74:3, 75:3, 85:3, 86:3, 87:3, 90:3, 91:3, 92:3, 93:3, 95:3, 104:3, 108:3, 109:3, 111:3, 113:3, 114:3, 117:3, 118:3, 119:3, 122:3, 124:3, 125:3, 131:3, 132:3, 134:3, 138:3, 139:3, 140:3, 141:3, 142:3, 146:3, 147:3, 148:3, 153:3, 154:3, 155:3, 156:3, 157:3, 158:3, 159:3, 168:3, 169:3, 170:3, 171:3, 173:3, 178:3, 182:3, 185:3, 189:3, 203:3, 2:4, 19:4, 21:4, 23:4, 25:4, 26:4, 27:4, 33:4, 34:4, 35:4, 37:4, 38:4, 41:4, 42:4, 47:4, 50:4, 51:4, 52:4, 54:4, 55:4, 56:4, 57:4, 58:4, 60:4, 64:4, 70:4, 72:4, 73:4, 90:4, 91:4, 93:4, 95:4, 97:4, 98:4, 99:4, 100:4, 102:4, 107:4, 114:4, 116:4, 120:4, 121:4, 123:4, 138:4, 141:4, 142:4, 143:4, 146:4, 147:4, 148:4, 149:4, 152:4, 153:4, 155:4, 156:4, 157:4, 158:4, 163:4, 164:4, 165:4, 166:4, 167:4, 168:4, 169:4, 170:4, 171:4, 172:4, 173:4, 174:4, 175:4, 178:4, 179:4, 181:4, 182:4, 183:4, 184:4, 185:4, 186:4, 2:5, 16:5, 24:5, 30:5, 33:5, 42:5, 43:5, 52:5, 64:5, 66:5, 67:5, 69:5, 70:5, 71:5, 74:5, 77:5, 78:5, 79:5, 81:5, 85:5, 89:5, 92:5, 100:5, 106:5, 107:5, 108:5, 122:5, 124:5, 127:5, 133:5, 135:5, 137:5, 2:6, 5:6, 7:6, 8:6, 9:6, 11:6, 13:6, 15:6, 16:6, 18:6, 23:6, 31:6, 35:6, 38:6, 39:6, 43:6, 61:6, 66:6, 67:6, 70:6, 78:6, 79:6, 80:6, 85:6, 86:6, 87:6, 88:6, 91:6, 93:6, 94:6, 95:6, 96:6, 97:6, 98:6, 99:6, 100:6, 101:6, 102:6, 106:6, 107:6, 108:6, 113:6, 116:6, 117:6

low
    to make, is not demeaning
        34:4

Lucifer. *See also* **adversary**; *See also* **devil**; *See also* **hell**; *See also* **Satan**
    10:1

lukewarm
    being, is a one-way ticket to hell
        47:1

Mahan
    51:1, 52:1, 69:1, 79:1, 127:4, 151:4, 47:6

mammon. *See also* **materialism**; *See also* **money**; *See also* **riches**
    a discussion of
        choosing, over God
            99–137:4
        making friends with
            109:4

mansions
    37:P, 76:1, 73:2, 82:2, 86:2, 89:2, 93:2, 168:3, 203:3, 81:4, 175:4, 50:5, 100:6

marriage. *See also* **new and everlasting covenant**
    a discussion of
        how it's likened to new and everlasting covenant
            72–99:2

martyrdom
    34:1, 58:2

materialism. *See also* **mammon**
    25:P, 41:P, 62:1, 64:1, 68:1, 102:1, 109:4, 93:5, 26:6, 76:6

Matthew Cowley
    3:P, 4:P, 6:1, 46:1, 105:6

Melchizedek
    administered priesthood to Abraham/built temple in Salem
        16:1

Melchizedek Priesthood. *See also* **Aaronic Priesthood;** *See also* **oath and covenant of the priesthood;** *See also* **patriarchal order of the priesthood;** *See also* **priesthood**
    a discussion of
        4–209:3

merchandise. *See* **mammon;** *See* **money**

mercy. *See also* **grace**
    10:P, 17:P, 20:P, 21:P, 22:P, 23:P, 24:P, 23:1, 26:1, 30:1, 66:1, 100:1, 4:2, 6:2, 7:2, 8:2, 9:2, 10:2, 15:2, 16:2, 17:2, 18:2, 20:2, 23:2, 24:2, 26:2, 27:2, 28:2, 29:2, 30:2, 32:2, 34:2, 35:2, 36:2, 45:2, 57:2, 97:2, 54:3, 71:3, 156:3, 159:3, 165:3, 167:3, 98:4, 112:4, 122:4, 129:4, 130:4, 143:4, 148:4, 151:4, 179:4, 15:5, 16:5, 19:5, 44:5, 64:5, 77:5, 106:5, 113:5, 114:5, 124:5, 12:6, 29:6, 41:6, 49:6, 51:6, 82:6, 102:6

miracle
    17:P, 25:1, 30:1, 66:1, 64:2, 155:3, 9:4, 36:4, 51:4, 57:4, 60:4, 67:4, 70:4, 159:4, 160:4, 162:4, 163:4, 173:4, 25:5, 32:5, 39:5, 66:5, 101:5, 109:5, 99:6

miserable
    49:1, 50:1, 51:1, 60:1, 77:1, 78:1, 8:2, 16:2, 89:2, 132:3, 63:4, 13:5, 14:5, 16:5, 56:5, 30:6

money. *See also* **mammon;** *See also* **materialism;** *See also* **riches**
    love of, is root of all evil
        70:1

Moroni
    1:1, 31:1, 61:1, 90:1, 91:1, 92:1, 103:1, 12:3, 65:3, 68:3, 92:3, 166:3, 195:3, 209:3, 210:3, 5:4, 6:4, 107:4, 123:4, 124:4, 149:4, 165:4, 166:4, 174:4, 175:4, 178:4, 181:4, 182:4, 183:4, 31:5, 44:5, 53:5, 55:5, 70:5, 77:5, 109:5, 112:5, 118:5, 119:5, 22:6, 23:6, 43:6, 86:6, 100:6

mortality
    is testing ground for our genuine desires
        47:1

Moses
    4:P, 26:P, 18:1, 19:1, 28:1, 32:1, 34:1, 51:1, 74:1, 87:1, 88:1, 8:2, 22:2, 40:2, 81:2, 84:2, 14:3, 15:3, 16:3, 17:3, 18:3, 20:3, 23:3, 24:3, 40:3, 55:3, 63:3, 65:3, 66:3, 76:3, 77:3, 88:3, 89:3, 99:3, 104:3, 110:3, 175:3, 176:3, 177:3, 184:3, 195:3, 207:3, 208:3, 47:4, 50:4, 100:4, 101:4, 112:4, 118:4, 120:4, 126:4, 129:4, 151:4, 165:4, 166:4, 8:5, 9:5, 18:5, 23:5, 31:5, 32:5, 35:5, 41:5, 42:5, 54:5, 55:5, 67:5, 72:5, 74:5, 79:5, 86:5, 89:5, 112:5, 131:5, 16:6, 17:6, 29:6, 36:6, 38:6, 46:6, 49:6, 50:6, 94:6, 95:6

Index & Concordance

mother
46:1, 61:1, 62:1, 25:2, 51:2, 85:2, 59:3, 126:3, 158:3, 28:4, 110:4, 172:4, 21:5, 129:5, 27:6, 52:6, 98:6, 106:6, 109:6

murder
50:1, 53:1, 60:1, 62:1, 63:1, 69:1, 80:1, 90:1, 102:1, 96:2, 119:3, 146:3, 160:3, 53:4, 118:4, 137:4, 14:5, 108:5, 36:6, 60:6

murmur
22:2, 26:5

mysteries
26:P, 32:P, 39:P, 40:P, 18:1, 61:1, 44:2, 8:3, 10:3, 24:3, 30:3, 31:3, 43:3, 47:3, 49:3, 57:3, 72:3, 81:3, 87:3, 93:3, 95:3, 96:3, 97:3, 98:3, 176:3, 177:3, 181:3, 183:3, 187:3, 188:3, 189:3, 190:3, 191:3, 192:3, 46:4, 100:4, 108:4, 149:4, 59:5, 60:5, 66:5, 79:5, 85:5, 86:5, 87:5, 88:5, 116:5, 119:5, 16:6, 25:6, 115:6

natural man
25:P, 22:1, 78:1, 20:2, 21:2, 50:2, 178:3, 64:4, 95:4, 169:4, 182:4, 23:5, 25:5, 42:5, 43:5, 44:5, 45:5, 68:5, 76:5, 84:5, 91:5, 9:6, 86:6

Neal A. Maxwell
12:1, 40:1, 110:3, 113:3, 148:3, 15:4, 27:4, 57:4, 79:4, 148:5

needy. *See also* **poor**
3:1, 20:1, 24:1, 27:1, 56:1, 80:1, 91:1, 48:3, 114:3, 129:3, 7:4, 11:4, 14:4, 23:4, 24:4, 29:4, 33:4, 40:4, 54:4, 72:4, 75:4, 82:4, 90:4, 107:4, 117:4, 121:4, 122:4, 123:4, 124:4, 125:4, 126:4, 129:4, 130:4, 133:4, 139:4, 144:4, 149:4, 153:4, 158:4, 170:4, 179:4, 180:4, 71:5, 5:6, 8:6, 23:6, 36:6, 41:6, 43:6, 44:6, 45:6, 46:6, 50:5, 52:6, 56:6, 63:6, 67:6, 72:6, 76:6, 87:6, 95:6, 104:6, 105:6, 106:6, 107:6, 109:5, 113:6

Nehor
26:1, 84:1, 145:3

neighbor
7:P, 8:P, 9:P, 28:P, 30:P, 19:1, 29:1, 66:1, 18:3, 49:3, 96:3, 182:3, 21:4, 26:4, 33:4, 38:4, 56:4, 58:4, 77:4, 91:4, 100:4, 104:4, 118:4, 122:4, 158:4, 164:4, 165:4, 169:4, 184:4, 93:5, 94:5, 127:5, 16:6, 20:6, 36:6, 41:6, 77:6, 93:6, 94:6, 113:6

new and everlasting covenant. *See also* **marriage**
    a discussion of
        how it's likened to marriage
            72–99:2

Nimrod
51:1, 52:1, 53:1, 54:1, 55:1, 58:1, 61:1, 101:1

Noah
15:P, 14:1, 15:1, 16:1, 18:1, 36:1, 53:1, 55:1, 86:1, 87:1, 101:1, 102:1, 103:1, 7:3, 27:3, 207:3, 107:4, 32:5, 88:5, 101:5, 124:5, 125:5, 127:5, 22:6

oath and covenant of the priesthood. *See also* **priesthood**
1:P, 6:1, 32:1, 9:2, 34:2, 36:2, 47:2, 61:2, 98:2, 1:3, 2:3, 3:3, 4:3, 6:3, 21:3, 25:3, 30:3, 33:3, 35:3, 36:3, 39:3, 40:3, 41:3, 43:3, 47:3, 49:3, 53:3, 54:3, 55:3, 58:3, 59:3, 60:3, 61:3, 63:3,

64:3, 66:3, 68:3, 71:3, 72:3, 76:3, 77:3, 78:3, 80:3, 81:3, 82:3, 85:3, 87:3, 88:3, 90:3, 93:3, 94:3, 95:3, 97:3, 98:3, 102:3, 103:3, 104:3, 105:3, 106:3, 109:3, 115:3, 117:3, 126:3, 131:3, 135:3, 139:3, 140:3, 142:3, 143:3, 144:3, 159:3, 172:3, 173:3, 174:3, 175:3, 177:3, 179:3, 184:3, 189:3, 190:3, 193:3, 202:3, 208:3, 210:3, 211:3, 212:3, 213:3, 214:3, 1:4, 2:4, 14:4, 72:4, 90:4, 129:4, 142:4, 185:4, 1:5, 2:5, 59:5, 116:5, 134:5, 135:5, 136:5, 50:6

obedience
30:P, 32:P, 41:P, 17:1, 19:1, 21:1, 48:1, 3:2, 4:2, 6:2, 7:2, 10:2, 12:2, 13:2, 15:2, 17:2, 28:2, 29:2, 33:2, 34:2, 35:2, 37:2, 38:2, 39:2, 42:2, 51:2, 61:2, 31:3, 67:3, 68:3, 71:3, 75:3, 80:3, 94:3, 118:3, 121:3, 124:3, 126:3, 131:3, 134:3, 135:3, 146:3, 203:3, 208:3, 212:3, 16:4, 18:4, 26:4, 36:4, 41:4, 45:4, 50:4, 56:4, 60:4, 65:4, 67:4, 102:4, 156:4, 180:4, 7:5, 33:5, 35:5, 36:5, 45:5, 46:5, 47:5, 81:5, 84:5, 97:5, 135:5, 18:6, 112:6, 113:6, 115:6

offence
73:1

offering. *See* consecration; sacrifice; *See* offerings

offerings
those, ordered by Satan are always rejected by God
51:1

oneness. *See also* unity
6:P, 18:P, 19:P, 12:1, 49:1, 92:1, 23:2, 24:2, 25:2, 27:2, 28:2, 29:2, 48:2, 71:2, 79:2, 170:3, 5:4, 18:4, 31:4, 41:4, 42:4, 43:4, 44:4, 45:4, 47:4, 59:4, 65:5, 94:5, 115:5, 123:5

opposition. *See also* adversity
35:P, 33:1, 36:1, 54:1, 67:1, 70:1, 19:2, 26:2, 56:2, 117:3, 45:4, 62:4, 10:5, 18:5, 49:5

ordinance
6:1, 11:1, 31:1, 51:1, 28:2, 31:2, 34:2, 36:2, 37:2, 38:2, 45:2, 53:2, 56:2, 63:2, 64:2, 67:2, 69:2, 91:2, 4:3, 6:3, 9:3, 10:3, 14:3, 16:3, 20:3, 21:3, 28:3, 29:3, 77:3, 82:3, 84:3, 87:3, 99:3, 105:3, 194:3, 197:3, 205:3, 212:3, 28:4, 43:4, 159:4, 160:4, 161:4, 162:4, 163:4, 25:5, 46:5, 60:5, 91:5, 133:5, 75:6

parent
42:1, 46:1, 168:3, 53:4, 147:4, 153:4, 16:5, 62:5, 70:6

patience
23:1, 27:1, 73:1, 22:2, 76:2, 85:2, 86:2, 29:3, 97:3, 129:3, 148:3, 149:3, 150:3, 151:3, 155:3, 178:3, 181:3, 99:4, 146:4, 155:4, 178:4, 184:4, 85:5, 15:6, 70:6, 101:6

patriarchal order of the priesthood. *See also* Melchizedek Priesthood; *See also* oath and covenant of the priesthood

Paul
27:P, 39:P, 41:1, 57:1, 59:1, 70:1, 73:1, 88:1, 89:1, 91:1, 103:1, 27:2, 63:2, 64:2, 81:2, 85:2, 31:3, 40:3, 67:3, 90:3, 100:3, 149:3, 163:3, 171:3, 180:3, 189:3, 198:3, 37:4, 99:4, 117:4, 165:4, 166:4, 184:4, 13:5, 15:5, 29:5, 89:5, 119:5, 133:5, 15:6, 35:6, 76:6, 78:6, 94:6, 95:6, 97:6, 106:6

Paymaster
8:P, 17:1, 151:3, 70:4, 71:4, 88:4, 90:4, 183:4

Index & Concordance

peace
> 2:P, 5:P, 8:P, 12:P, 17:P, 20:P, 26:P, 27:P, 9:1, 15:1, 16:1, 23:1, 25:1, 27:1, 30:1, 46:1, 88:1, 8:2, 24:2, 39:2, 50:2, 51:2, 61:2, 95:2, 5:3, 6:3, 7:3, 8:3, 18:3, 28:3, 29:3, 46:3, 50:3, 66:3, 70:3, 83:3, 114:3, 119:3, 129:3, 140:3, 167:3, 172:3, 173:3, 199:3, 19:4, 22:4, 40:4, 44:4, 46:4, 115:4, 118:4, 119:4, 124:4, 125:4, 137:4, 140:4, 150:4, 151:4, 152:4, 162:4, 171:4, 172:4, 178:4, 27:5, 28:5, 38:5, 44:5, 46:5, 53:5, 55:5, 81:5, 83:5, 92:5, 94:5, 103:5, 104:5, 106:5, 107:5, 122:5, 128:5, 130:5, 132:5, 133:5, 1:6, 2:6, 13:6, 34:6, 37:6, 38:6, 45:6, 60:6, 61:6, 64:6, 97:6, 98:6, 101:6

persecute
> 27:P, 28:P, 30:P, 61:1, 67:1, 85:1, 91:1, 137:3, 152:3, 108:4, 122:4, 123:4, 124:4, 150:4, 42:5, 26:6, 41:6, 42:6, 44:6, 77:6, 112:6, 113:6

plague
> 82:1, 160:3, 124:4, 38:5, 44:6

poor. *See also* **needy**
> a discussion of
>> how we treat the,
>>> 120–137:4

popular
> 14:1, 66:1, 81:1, 83:1, 84:1, 87:1, 25:3, 132:3

possession. *See* **mammon**

praise. *See* **popular**

pray, prayer
> 80:1, 85:1, 98:1, 14:2, 20:2, 55:2, 86:2, 91:2, 92:2, 41:3, 70:3, 154:3, 158:3, 192:3, 197:3, 8:4, 9:4, 45:4, 46:4, 54:4, 60:4, 111:4, 112:4, 140:4, 162:4, 163:4, 181:4, 4:5, 19:5, 42:5, 51:5, 53:5, 67:5, 69:5, 77:5, 78:5, 87:5, 112:5, 114:5, 115:5, 116:5, 120:5, 121:5, 122:5, 123:5, 124:5, 28:6, 29:6, 64:6, 90:6, 104:6

premortal existence
> mature knowledge of gospel from, planted deep in our souls
>> 44:1

pride
> neither rich nor poor exempt from
>> 24:1

priest
> 17:1, 26:1, 84:1, 20:2, 41:2, 94:2, 95:2, 5:3, 6:3, 7:3, 9:3, 29:3, 42:3, 46:3, 65:3, 119:3, 152:3, 190:3, 198:3, 199:3, 88:4, 100:4, 40:5, 63:5, 89:5, 16:6

priestcraft
> 26:1, 51:1, 53:1, 61:1, 68:1, 84:1, 85:1, 145:3, 146:3

priesthood. *See also* **Aaronic Priesthood**; *See also* **Melchizedek Priesthood**; *See also* **oath and covenant of the priesthood**; *See also* **patriarchal order of the priesthood**
> a discussion of
>> Melchizedek
>>> 4–11:3, 182–192:3, 204–210:3

oath and covenant of the
39–60:3
restoration of the
12–16:3
priesthood society
1:P, 3:P, 4:P, 43:P, 3:1, 5:1, 6:1, 7:1, 12:1, 14:1, 46:1, 5:3, 6:3, 12:3, 21:3, 25:3, 28:3, 32:3, 35:3, 61:3, 85:3, 127:3, 206:3, 7:4, 14:4, 15:4, 22:4, 31:4, 74:4, 80:4, 90:5, 98:5, 99:5, 127:5, 87:6, 102:6, 105:6

princess. *See* **queen**

prison
88:1, 51:2, 52:2, 54:2, 88:2, 70:3, 100:3, 138:4, 139:4, 151:4, 152:4, 12:5, 29:5, 39:5, 75:5, 63:6, 116:6, 117:6

probation. *See* **mortality**

progress
perspective of our, compared to steps on an airplane
90:5

properties. *See* **property**

property
converting life into, is Satan's great secret
47:6

prophecies
93:1, 95:1, 97:1, 98:1, 109:3, 166:3, 4:5, 97:5, 103:5, 118:5, 119:5, 49:6

prosper. *See* **abundance**

publicans
80:1

pure in heart. *See also* **Zion**
2:P, 17:P, 25:P, 26:P, 38:P, 41:P, 43:P, 2:1, 3:1, 4:1, 6:1, 8:1, 12:1, 15:1, 19:1, 25:1, 33:1, 46:1, 48:1, 18:2, 47:3, 66:3, 71:3, 87:3, 161:3, 172:3, 178:3, 195:3, 207:3, 208:3, 2:4, 15:4, 16:4, 31:4, 73:4, 83:4, 95:4, 104:4, 109:4, 147:4, 1:5, 2:5, 3:5, 4:5, 18:5, 77:5, 78:5, 79:5, 80:5, 81:5, 82:5, 84:5, 87:5, 89:5, 90:5, 91:5, 93:5, 94:5, 95:5, 96:5, 101:5, 109:5, 114:5, 115:5, 116:5, 117:5, 118:5, 119:5, 120:5, 124:5, 125:5, 127:5, 130:5, 133:5, 134:5, 136:5, 9:6, 20:6, 26:6, 75:6, 76:6, 78:6, 116:6

purification
14:P, 18:2, 19:2, 20:2, 90:2, 91:2, 66:3, 137:3, 52:4, 162:4, 182:4, 3:5, 25:5, 26:5, 75:5, 79:5, 90:5, 115:5, 116:5, 120:5

queen(s)
93:1, 90:2, 93:2, 94:2, 199:3, 8:5

rainbow
sign of everlasting covenant
15:1

redeem, Redeemer, redemption
noble spirits in premortal life carried out work of
45:1

Index & Concordance

repent
> 20:P, 2:1, 10:1, 13:1, 16:1, 24:1, 70:1, 91:1, 98:1, 99:1, 5:2, 7:2, 16:2, 17:2, 19:2, 35:2, 36:2, 96:2, 5:3, 6:3, 19:3, 45:3, 46:3, 70:3, 103:3, 135:3, 153:3, 161:3, 188:3, 205:3, 37:4, 69:4, 84:4, 102:4, 111:4, 112:4, 117:4, 118:4, 121:4, 126:4, 135:4, 136:4, 148:4, 15:5, 46:5, 78:5, 82:5, 105:5, 106:5, 109:5, 2:6, 18:6, 28:6, 29:6, 35:6, 36:6, 39:6, 46:6, 47:6, 59:6, 60:6

resurrected
> 14:P, 13:1, 28:1, 64:1, 86:1, 95:1, 14:2, 26:2, 17:3, 91:3, 202:3, 203:3, 42:4, 13:5, 64:5, 105:5, 108:5, 121:5, 122:5, 132:5

revelation
> is key to magnifying callings and to learning
>> 95:3

riches. *See also* **mammon**; *See also* **materialism**; *See also* **money**; *See also* **wealth**
> 30:P, 32:P, 34:P, 38:P, 17:1, 27:1, 31:1, 33:1, 67:1, 71:1, 72:1, 76:1, 84:1, 86:1, 92:1, 93:1, 95:1, 96:1, 97:1, 99:1, 123:3, 125:3, 126:3, 128:3, 129:3, 130:3, 131:3, 133:3, 141:3, 142:3, 146:3, 167:3, 171:3, 193:3, 8:4, 9:4, 10:4, 26:4, 30:4, 38:4, 40:4, 69:4, 72:4, 83:4, 84:4, 85:4, 87:4, 88:4, 91:4, 93:4, 94:4, 99:4, 100:4, 101:4, 102:4, 103:4, 106:4, 108:4, 109:4, 110:4, 111:4, 113:4, 115:4, 116:4, 117:4, 118:4, 119:4, 120:4, 123:4, 124:4, 126:4, 127:4, 130:4, 132:4, 133:4, 135:4, 140:4, 142:4, 144:4, 148:4, 149:4, 150:4, 152:4, 158:4, 184:4, 44:5, 103:5, 104:5, 4:6, 7:6, 16:6, 17:6, 18:6, 19:6, 22:6, 25:6, 26:6, 28:6, 31:6, 33:6, 34:6, 36:6, 37:6, 38:6, 43:6, 44:6, 46:6, 47:6, 48:6, 51:6, 56:6, 57:6, 58:6, 65:6, 67:6, 72:6, 113:6, 114:6, 115:

Sabbath
> 42:P, 37:1, 38:2, 39:2, 40:2, 50:2, 51:2, 72:2, 99:4, 53:5, 15:6

sacrament
> 14:P, 23:P, 29:1, 14:2, 20:2, 36:2, 38:2, 39:2, 40:2, 41:2, 60:2, 67:2, 80:2, 81:2, 82:2, 89:2, 9:3, 11:3, 39:3, 42:3, 66:3, 75:3, 93:3, 165:3, 193:3, 210:3, 46:4, 17:5, 18:5, 60:5, 61:5, 62:5, 64:5, 117:5, 121:5

sacrifice. *See also* **consecration**; *See also* **offering**
> a discussion of
>> 3–31:4, 33–52:4, 61–92:4

Salem. *See also* **Jerusalem**
> 3:P, 9:1, 15:1, 16:1, 5:3, 27:3, 29:3, 45:3, 1:6, 2:6

salvation, plan of
> 50:1, 54:2, 25:3, 26:3, 31:3, 36:3, 68:3, 73:3, 12:5, 126:5, 130:5

sanctification
> 14:P, 18:P, 18:2, 20:2, 21:2, 90:2, 91:2, 9:3, 56:3, 66:3, 67:3, 68:3, 69:3, 70:3, 71:3, 74:3, 75:3, 77:3, 84:3, 104:3, 137:3, 210:3, 14:4, 18:4, 21:4, 31:4, 52:4, 132:4, 3:5, 27:5, 47:5, 75:5, 79:5, 90:5, 94:5, 99:5, 115:5, 116:5

sanctified body. *See* **sanctification**
sanctuaries. *See* **mammon**

Satan. *See also* **adversary;** *See also* **devil;** *See also* **hell;** *See also* **Lucifer**
>we must understand, in order to confront him
>>55:5

savior
>Adam empowered to become, to his family
>>11:1

Savior. *See* **Christ, Jesus;** *See* **Exemplar;** *See* **Jehovah;** *See* **Lamb**

saviors on Mount Zion
>43:1, 32:2, 40:2, 25:3, 35:3, 37:3, 43:3, 66:3, 69:3, 104:3, 156:3, 144:4, 184:4, 64:5, 116:5, 68:6

science
>57:1, 81:1, 83:1, 14:2, 163:3

seal
>26:1, 24:2, 76:2, 79:2, 93:2, 13:3, 16:3, 17:3, 81:3, 84:3, 99:3, 149:3, 168:3, 194:3, 199:3, 209:3, 52:4, 75:4, 108:4, 155:4, 162:4, 38:5, 58:5, 65:5, 67:5, 25:6

secret combinations. *See also* **Gadianton robbers**
>49:1, 60:1, 61:1, 91:1, 97:1, 99:1, 102:5, 103:5, 108:5

selfish
>9:P, 38:P, 58:1, 73:1, 89:1, 91:1, 96:1, 19:2, 32:2, 71:2, 21:3, 74:3, 88:3, 122:3, 124:3, 125:3, 131:3, 137:3, 153:3, 154:3, 157:3, 171:3, 27:4, 55:4, 82:4, 91:4, 97:4, 98:4, 112:4, 117:4, 134:4, 140:4, 141:4, 145:4, 149:4, 152:4, 156:4, 165:4, 169:4, 176:4, 94:5, 11:6, 18:6, 29:6, 30:6, 31:6, 35:6, 37:6, 45:6, 48:6, 58:6, 64:6, 65:6, 66:6, 68:6, 71:6, 72:6, 77:6, 86:6, 88:6, 94:6, 108:6, 115:6

selfless. *See also* **charity**
>1:P, 8:P, 10:P, 12:P, 23:P, 25:P, 31:P, 24:1, 29:1, 5:2, 32:2, 71:2, 21:3, 51:3, 171:3, 109:4, 170:4, 93:5, 100:5, 26:6, 76:6, 87:6

Sermon on the Mount. *See also* **Beatitudes**
>14:P, 16:P, 28:1, 18:2, 82:5, 118:5

servant
>37:P, 16:1, 27:1, 34:2, 61:2, 62:2, 69:2, 87:2, 88:2, 91:2, 92:2, 96:2, 6:3, 30:3, 41:3, 72:3, 82:3, 100:3, 101:3, 103:3, 115:3, 196:3, 211:3, 214:3, 12:4, 49:4, 50:4, 53:4, 74:4, 75:4, 78:4, 79:4, 81:4, 89:4, 183:4, 66:5, 97:5, 110:5

set apart. *See* **consecration**

sex
>57:1, 66:1, 76:1, 154:3, 97:4, 11:6

single women
>64:3

slippery treasures
>110:4, 27:6

snare
>70:1, 73:1, 109:3, 122:3, 124:3, 139:3, 99:4, 103:4, 113:4, 14:5, 15:6, 19:6, 30:6, 108:6

Index & Concordance 149

Sodom
    1:1, 54:1, 55:1, 56:1, 57:1, 86:1, 94:1, 101:1, 102:1, 103:1, 5:4, 121:4, 23:5, 41:6

sorrow. *See also* wailing
    21:P, 34:1, 35:1, 63:1, 93:1, 102:1, 88:2, 51:3, 151:3, 160:3, 19:4, 124:4, 127:4, 136:4, 10:5, 43:5, 44:5, 106:5, 44:6, 48:6, 59:6, 79:6

soul
    11:P, 16:P, 17:P, 23:P, 43:P, 20:1, 21:1, 22:1, 28:1, 60:1, 76:1, 8:2, 19:2, 26:2, 40:2, 41:2, 49:2, 55:2, 59:2, 61:2, 94:2, 7:3, 19:3, 44:3, 47:3, 67:3, 69:3, 83:3, 97:3, 100:3, 102:3, 108:3, 116:3, 119:3, 122:3, 144:3, 151:3, 156:3, 159:3, 165:3, 166:3, 172:3, 175:3, 182:3, 184:3, 189:3, 193:3, 213:3, 2:4, 9:4, 16:4, 20:4, 50:4, 54:4, 56:4, 60:4, 64:4, 65:4, 111:4, 114:4, 115:4, 118:4, 127:4, 140:4, 146:4, 152:4, 155:4, 160:4, 162:4, 164:4, 166:4, 167:4, 171:4, 172:4, 174:4, 175:4, 179:4, 180:4, 182:4, 183:4, 186:4, 2:5, 13:5, 15:5, 17:5, 44:5, 45:5, 49:5, 68:5, 71:5, 74:5, 80:5, 81:5, 84:5, 100:5, 108:5, 122:5, 5:6, 6:6, 29:6, 30:6, 32:6, 33:6, 37:6, 48:6, 50:6, 65:6, 71:6, 85:6, 86:6, 91:6, 95:6, 96:6, 97:6, 98:6, 100:6, 101:6, 102:6, 103:6, 108:6

Spencer W. Kimball
    8:P, 25:P, 33:P, 3:1, 7:1, 37:1, 55:1, 85:1, 21:3, 31:3, 35:3, 118:3, 140:3, 191:3, 7:4, 9:4, 15:4, 17:4, 23:4, 30:4, 31:4, 48:4, 59:4, 83:4, 86:4, 109:4, 134:4, 172:4, 173:4, 177:4, 37:5, 49:5, 92:5, 93:5, 98:5, 100:5, 26:6, 57:6, 76:6, 88:6, 90:6, 98:6, 99:6

stewardship(s)
    in heaven based on stewardships on earth
        50:5

storehouse
    7:P, 36:P, 17:1, 18:1, 64:2, 6:3, 38:4, 39:4, 48:4, 61:4, 71:4, 72:4, 74:4, 75:4, 77:4, 79:4, 83:4, 88:4, 91:4, 96:4, 131:4, 10:6, 51:6, 77:6

submission
    79:1, 118:3, 152:3, 31:5

surplus
    36:P, 18:1, 48:3, 12:4, 24:4, 69:4, 74:4, 75:4, 79:4, 90:4, 91:4, 94:4, 147:4, 9:6, 114:6

telestial
    3:P, 9:P, 10:P, 12:P, 25:P, 26:P, 30:P, 31:P, 32:P, 37:P, 38:P, 3:1, 6:1, 7:1, 8:1, 10:1, 17:1, 29:1, 39:1, 40:1, 47:1, 66:1, 80:1, 103:1, 14:2, 15:2, 23:2, 48:2, 60:2, 68:2, 69:2, 68:3, 80:3, 89:3, 114:3, 117:3, 124:3, 125:3, 140:3, 141:3, 144:3, 164:3, 211:3, 10:4, 15:4, 18:4, 25:4, 34:4, 35:4, 36:4, 64:4, 69:4, 73:4, 82:4, 83:4, 96:4, 101:4, 105:4, 141:4, 147:4, 148:4, 163:4, 185:4, 11:5, 12:5, 19:5, 31:5, 36:5, 70:5, 76:5, 84:5, 85:5, 91:5, 121:5, 126:5, 10:6, 17:6, 21:6, 66:6, 86:6, 105:6, 106:6, 107:6, 110:6, 112:6, 115:6, 116:6

temple
    covenants, necessary to establish Zion/is gathering place for Zion people
        31:1

temptation
    70:1, 133:3, 176:3, 43:4, 97:4, 99:4, 14:5, 120:5, 121:5, 11:6, 15:6

Ten Commandments
>15:2, 100:4, 148:4, 110:5, 16:6

ten virgins
>85:1, 103:1, 87:2, 90:2, 92:2

terrestrial
>testimony, bearing of, purifies heart; bearing of, is an act of love
>>56:3

tithes
>31:P, 34:P, 37:P, 42:P, 17:1, 37:1, 6:3, 8:4, 12:4, 13:4, 30:4, 81:4, 88:4, 89:4, 92:4, 96:4, 147:4, 118:5, 10:6, 12:6, 13:6, 51:6, 114:6, 115:6

tradition
>98:1, 72:2, 73:2, 75:2, 84:2, 7:3, 9:3

treasure. *See* **mammon**

trial(s). *See also* **adversity;** *See also* **opposition**
>29:P, 44:1, 56:2, 58:2, 83:3, 128:3, 148:3, 151:3, 124:4, 23:5, 27:5, 50:5, 58:5, 44:6, 50:6

unite, unity. *See also* **oneness**
>4:P, 6:P, 37:P, 3:1, 9:1, 14:1, 19:1, 68:1, 77:1, 78:1, 92:1, 23:2, 24:2, 25:2, 27:2, 69:2, 93:2, 74:3, 85:3, 114:3, 116:3, 140:3, 147:3, 170:3, 2:4, 19:4, 33:4, 41:4, 42:4, 43:4, 44:4, 45:4, 46:4, 47:4, 48:4, 49:4, 50:4, 51:4, 52:4, 54:4, 55:4, 58:4, 59:4, 60:4, 62:4, 82:4, 156:4, 171:4, 183:4, 185:4, 2:5, 50:5, 73:5, 100:5, 108:5, 97:6

universe
>composition of
>>89:3

vain
>22:P, 28:P, 64:1, 66:1, 69:1, 80:1, 86:1, 97:1, 98:1, 41:2, 45:3, 47:3, 51:3, 92:3, 107:3, 110:3, 114:3, 119:3, 135:3, 146:3, 153:3, 163:3, 164:3, 99:4, 110:4, 111:4, 115:4, 117:4, 118:4, 119:4, 122:4, 124:4, 126:4, 127:4, 133:4, 149:4, 175:4, 181:4, 57:5, 71:5, 95:5, 101:5, 102:5, 104:5, 4:6, 15:6, 28:6, 33:6, 36:6, 38:6, 41:6, 42:6, 44:6, 46:6, 57:6, 79:6, 104:6

veil
>40:1, 55:1, 80:2, 83:2, 84:2, 85:2, 95:2, 26:3, 91:3, 102:3, 178:3, 179:3, 180:3, 181:3, 183:3, 196:3, 209:3, 210:3, 54:4, 12:5, 67:5, 68:5, 79:5, 85:5, 89:5, 109:5, 131:5

violence
>14:1, 36:1, 87:1, 93:1, 95:1, 8:3, 121:3, 108:4, 26:6

wailing. *See also* **sorrow**
>94:1

war
>17:P, 26:P, 42:1, 44:1, 55:1, 62:1, 69:1, 78:1, 80:1, 85:1, 91:1, 102:1, 28:2, 83:3, 108:4, 137:4, 37:5, 102:5, 103:5, 108:5, 26:6, 60:6

warn
>95:1, 113:4, 124:4, 102:5, 103:5, 30:6, 44:6

Index & Concordance   **151**

wealth. *See also* **mammon;** *See also* **poor;** *See also* **riches**
    a discussion of
        proper use
            120–151:4
        seeking
            99–137:4

weapon
    29:P, 57:1, 71:1, 55:2, 99:4, 109:4, 132:4, 149:4, 16:6, 26:6, 56:6, 112:6

whore. *See* **Babylon**

wickedness
    today's level of, equals or exceeds times that of Noah's generation
        87:1

widow
    93:1, 7:4, 29:4, 104:4, 109:4, 130:4, 140:4, 146:4, 153:4, 51:5, 70:5, 20:6, 27:6, 52:6, 65:6, 70:6

wife. *See also* **marriage**
    45:P, 10:1, 33:1, 62:1, 24:2, 25:2, 58:2, 66:2, 74:2, 76:2, 77:2, 78:2, 79:2, 85:2, 92:2, 94:2, 95:2, 97:2, 13:3, 15:3, 17:3, 23:3, 31:3, 59:3, 82:3, 85:3, 110:3, 112:3, 126:3, 136:3, 183:3, 198:3, 199:3, 207:3, 211:3, 26:4, 41:4, 43:4, 45:4, 52:4, 98:4, 100:4, 156:4, 157:4, 10:5, 20:5, 24:5, 38:5, 42:5, 11:6, 16:6, 106:6, 109:6

wilderness. *See also* **Babylon**
    a discussion of
        our journey through the
            12–41:5

Wilford Woodruff
    40:1, 55:3, 131:3, 211:3, 148:5

wisdom
    21:P, 32:P, 23:1, 24:1, 26:1, 31:1, 33:1, 39:1, 59:1, 60:1, 64:1, 65:1, 78:1, 84:1, 98:1, 102:1, 45:2, 50:3, 54:3, 71:3, 93:3, 152:3, 161:3, 163:3, 164:3, 165:3, 166:3, 167:3, 168:3, 187:3, 201:3, 208:3, 6:4, 26:4, 27:4, 66:4, 77:4, 100:4, 105:4, 108:4, 109:4, 120:4, 122:4, 137:4, 141:4, 149:4, 152:4, 179:4, 65:5, 3:6, 16:6, 21:6, 25:6, 27:6, 38:6, 42:6, 61:6, 66:6, 82:6, 102:6, 115:6

work. *See also* **labor**
    Christ's, takes priority
        30:1

world, worldly. *See also* **Babylon**
    in, but not of
        74:1

yoke
    17:P, 23:P, 28:P, 62:1, 63:1, 101:1, 92:2, 160:3, 179:4, 68:5, 69:5, 71:5, 102:6

Zion
    an individual with a pure heart
        12:1
    begins in each person's heart
        1:1, 12:1, 13:1
    definition of, is perfection
        12:1
    is a return to the presence of God
        47:1
    is our ideal
        6:1
    principles of
        19:1
    we are
        46:1

Zion people
    characteristics of
        12:1
    temple gathering place for
        14:1

About the Author

Larry Barkdull is a longtime publisher and writer of books, music, art, and magazines. For nine years, he owned Sonos Music Resources and published the Tabernacle Choir Performance Library. He was also the owner and publisher of Keepsake Books. Over the past thirty years, he's published some six hundred products for numerous authors, composers, and artists. He's founded two nonprofit organizations: The Latter-day Foundation for the Arts, Education and Humanity (to promote LDS arts), and Gospel Ideals International (to promote the gospel of Jesus Christ on the Internet).

His books have sold in excess of 300,000 copies, and they have been translated into Japanese, Korean, Italian, and Hebrew. He is the recipient of the American Family Literary Award; the Benjamin Franklin Book Award; and *Foreword Magazine's* GOLD Book of the Year Award for best fiction. His most recent books are *Priesthood Power—Blessing the Sick and the Afflicted*; *Rescuing Wayward Children*; and *The Shepherd Song*.

He and his wife, Elizabeth, have ten children and a growing number of grandchildren. They live in Orem, Utah. Read more of his writings at Meridian Magazine.com.

www.ingramcontent.com/pod-product-compliance
Lightning Source LLC
Chambersburg PA
CBHW080441110426
42743CB00016B/3238